Impairment and Disability

Despite legislation intended to protect the interests of people with disabilities or impairments, discrimination persists. Discrimination that occurs at the beginning and end of human life is particularly noxious because it occurs at a time when people are especially vulnerable. This book examines how a rigorous ethico-legal analysis of the issues surrounding life-and-death decision-making in the context of disability might help prevent such discrimination. One of the key themes running through the text is how we might distinguish between justly differential treatment and unjust discrimination. It is argued that the capacity to maintain this distinction is central to efforts to create an ethico-legal environment in which the lives of people with impairments (disabilities) are not disvalued unnecessarily, and also to allow our decisions (and actions) at the beginning and end of life to resist the temptation to be ethically and legally simplistic.

Professor Sheila A.M. McLean has a worldwide reputation for her work in the study of medical ethics and law. She is the Director of the Institute of Law and Ethics in Medicine at the University of Glasgow.

Dr Laura Williamson is a Researcher at the Institute of Law and Ethics in Medicine, University of Glasgow.

Biomedical Law and Ethics Library
Series Editor: Sheila A.M. McLean

Scientific and clinical advances, social and political developments and the impact of healthcare on our lives raise profound ethical and legal questions. Medical law and ethics have become central to our understanding of these problems, and are important tools for the analysis and resolution of problems – real or imagined.

In this series, scholars at the forefront of biomedical law and ethics contribute to the debates in this area, with accessible, thought-provoking, and sometimes controversial ideas. Each book in the series develops an independent hypothesis and argues cogently for a particular position. One of the major contributions of this series is the extent to which both law and ethics are utilised in the content of the books, and the shape of the series itself.

The books in this series are analytical, with a key target audience of lawyers, doctors, nurses, and the intelligent lay public.

Forthcoming titles:

Horsey and Biggs, *Human Fertilisation and Embryology* (2007)
McLean and Williamson, *Impairment and Disability* (2007)
Gavaghan, *Defending the Genetic Supermarket* (2007)
Priaulx, *The Harm Paradox* (2007)
Downie and Macnaughton, *Bioethics and the Humanities* (2007)
McLean, *Assisted Dying* (2007)
Huxtable, *Euthanasia, Ethics and the Law* (2007)
Elliston, *Best Interests of the Child in Healthcare* (2007)

About the Series Editor

Professor Sheila Mclean is International Bar Association Professor of Law and Ethics in Medicine and Director of the Institute of Law and Ethics in Medicine at the University of Glasgow.

Impairment and Disability

Law and ethics at the beginning and
end of life

Sheila A.M. McLean and
Laura Williamson

Routledge·Cavendish
Taylor & Francis Group

First published 2007 by Cavendish Publishing

Transferred to digital printing 2007
by Routledge-Cavendish
2 Park Square, Milton Park, Abingdon, Oxon, OX14 4RN

Simultaneously published in the USA and Canada
by Routledge-Cavendish
270 Madison Avenue, New York, NY 10016

*Routledge-Cavendish is an imprint of the Taylor & Francis Group,
an informa business*

© 2007 Sheila A.M. McLean and Laura Williamson

Typeset in Times New Roman by
Newgen Imaging Systems (P) Ltd, Chennai, India

British Library Cataloguing in Publication Data
A catalogue record for this book is available from the British Library

Library of Congress Cataloging in Publication Data
McLean, Sheila.
    Impairment and disability : law and ethics at the beginning
and end of life / Sheila McLean and Laura Williamson.
        p. cm.
    Includes bibliographical references.
    1. Medical ethics. 2. Euthanasia – Moral and ethical aspects.
3. Terminal care – Moral and ethical aspects. I. Williamson, Laura.
II. Title.
    [DNLM: 1. Disabled Persons. 2. Ethics, Clinical. 3. Disabled
Persons – legislation & jurisprudence. 4. Human Rights. 5. Life.
6. Prejudice. WB 60 M478i 2007]

R726.1474 2007
179.7–dc22   2006025543

ISBN10: 1–84472–040–3 (pbk)
ISBN10: 1–84472–041–1 (hbk)

ISBN13: 978–1–84472–040–8 (pbk)
ISBN13: 978–1–84472–041–5 (hbk)

Contents

Chapter 1

Life, death, disability and impairment in context

Introduction

This book is concerned with way(s) in which some people – because of disability or impairment – are treated in the healthcare setting, specifically at the beginning and end of life. In particular, it addresses the extent to which ethical principles and/or legal rules can shape the way(s) in which impairment or disability is used to influence society's judgements about people; most particularly at the beginning and end of life. We are concerned with identifying how, and in what way(s), law and ethics in this area are coherent with the aims of living in a society which truly values the principle of non-discrimination. Moreover, we will evaluate the extent to which law and ethics may inform the debate about the treatment of people with impairment or disability, and/or be utilised to ensure that it is no longer valid to claim – as many do – that the prejudice of the 'abled' in respect of the 'dis-abled' results in discriminatory assumptions and practices which can have profoundly important consequences. In doing so, we will evaluate the models usually used to critique social and legal approaches to people who live with impairment or disability, and consider whether more is needed than simply resolving the apparent tensions between them. The healthcare setting is ripe for such an evaluation. Not only are the decisions made in that context of extreme importance, as they may predict life or death, but they also occur within a relationship that is already unequal.

Although healthcare professionals increasingly eschew the paternalism which once characterised the relationship between doctor and patient, there remains an inevitable inequality between them which permits of – even mandates – treatment which, at its best can be called beneficent and at its worst, paternalistic. While it is now both ethically and legally accepted that healthcare decisions are the primary responsibility (and right) of the legally competent, individual patient, nonetheless even now patients remain dependent on the quality and extent of information provided by the doctor or nurse.[1] However, medical decisions may

---

1 For further discussion, see McLean, S.A.M., *A Patient's Right to Know: Information Disclosure, the Doctor and the Law*, Aldershot, Dartmouth, 1989; Mason, J.K. and Laurie, G.T., *Mason and McCall Smith's Law and Medical Ethics* (7th Ed), Oxford, Oxford University Press, 2006.

be – at least in part – based on presumptions about people's ability to receive, retain or utilise information and on the authority often handed to clinicians to make decisions about legal competence or capacity.[2] For those with impairment or disability, it may be all too easy to make discriminatory judgements about their capacity, or – even more worryingly – about the quality of their lives, potentially leading to prejudicial treatment. As was said, for example, in the case of *Ms B*,[3] '...a seriously disabled person has the same rights as the fit person to respect for personal autonomy. *There is a serious danger, exemplified in this case, of a benevolent paternalism which does not embrace recognition of the personal autonomy of the severely disabled patient.*'[4] (emphasis added)

The law's traditional deference to medical judgements affects the rights of all patients,[5] but is likely – as we will see – to have a more significant effect on those with impairment or disability. Indeed, the presumption that life with impairment or disability is *inevitably* of lesser quality than one without them is probably common, and delimits the very foundations of our approach to people in those situations. The Disability Rights Commission (DRC) for example, has said:

> ...there is compelling evidence from research over a number of years up to the present day that discrimination in general health services exists. This qualitative research has recorded consistent testimony from disabled people and their families about the discriminatory attitudes they face from medical professionals, and the poorer services they receive in the NHS.[6]

Finally, the infantilisation that can characterise anyone's interaction with healthcare – however unintended by healthcare providers it may be – will arguably be more acutely experienced by those who often start on a far from level playing field – at least as far as others are concerned.

In this book we will examine claims that prejudicial attitudes towards impairment and disability result in discriminatory practices at the beginning and end of life. We will also argue that robust philosophical and legal resources are essential if such discrimination is to be removed from healthcare institutions and indeed from society itself. However, we will also argue that the resources currently offered by the law and applied ethics are not always sufficiently robust to prevent or correct discrimination when it is identified. This makes it difficult to evaluate what is discrimination and what is not, and poses profound difficulties in the assessment of treatment that is appropriate and that which is not. Yet it is important that we can do

---

2 See also the terms of the Adults with Incapacity (Scotland) Act 2001 and the Mental Capacity Act 2005.
3 This case will be discussed in more depth in Chapter 5.
4 *Re B (adult: refusal of treatment)* (2002) 65 BMLR 149 at p. 172.
5 For further discussion, see McLean, S.A.M., *Old Law, New Medicine*, London, Rivers Oram/Pandora Press, 1999.
6 Disability Rights Commission policy statement on voluntary euthanasia and assisted suicide, available at http://www.drc-gb.org (accessed on 9 July 2003).

this. Failure to do so leads to a 'one size fits all' approach to people without nuance or subtlety and can also lead to presuming homogeneity in a group of people who are every bit as disparate as those who do not appear to have an impairment. We say 'do not appear to have an impairment' because in reality, we all have characteristics (genetic, for example) which could be categorised as impairment, in that they deviate from some postulated norm. Viewed in this way, we could all be seen as impaired or disabled.[7] The assumption that there is an identifiable group of people who are 'disabled' therefore is in itself at odds with reality, and, even if it were not, it is surely society's role to minimise prejudicial presumptions that – in the healthcare setting in particular – can affect whether or not they are born and whether or not they should live. We do not deny that some impairments may well be relevant to the way in which healthcare professionals approach patients. For example, the patient in a permanent vegetative state will necessarily be treated differently from a competent, adult patient; a person with profound learning disabilities cannot be expected to meet the standards which are required to obtain a true consent to treatment. What is important, however, is the way(s) in which these differences are used, that is, whether they are unjustly discriminatory or relevant to the case in hand.

Disability: national and international responses

It can be said without equivocation that it is an important sign of a civilised society that it protects its vulnerable citizens. Recent history, however, has shown just how easy it is to deny fundamental social, legal and political rights to those who are disabled – or just different.[8] Unfortunately, it has been necessary to introduce legislation to try to require non-discrimination based on people's sex,[9] race[10] or – more recently – disability.[11] The capacity of the law to prevent discrimination against people with impairment or disability depends, we argue, on its foundation in ethically sound and appropriate principles as well as on social and cultural change. The limitations of the law have been noted by Johnstone, who says:

> The law plays both an important symbolic and practical role in forming the ideological systems that legitimise specific sets of values and assumptions in society. It is, therefore, fundamental in forming the framework within which both groups and individuals interpret their participation in society. However, the traditional assumptions that the law does not discriminate have

---

7 The notion that disability is a universal phenomenon will be examined in Chapter 2.
8 For further discussion, see McLean, S.A.M., 'The Right to Reproduce', in Campbell, T., Goldberg, D., McLean, S. and Mullen, T. (eds), *Human Rights: From Rhetoric to Reality*, Oxford, Basil Blackwell, 1986, 99–122.
9 Sex Discrimination Act 1975.
10 Race Relations Act 1976.
11 The Disability Discrimination Act 1995; The Disability Discrimination Act 1995 (Amendment) Regulations 2003; The Disability Discrimination Act 2005.

to be questioned. Although appearing impartial and neutral, the officers of the law and the judiciary are subject to the same prejudices as those from whom it is meant to stand apart.[12]

The law, as well as the personnel involved in its implementation, therefore, need both to establish appropriate goals and put in place the mechanisms to ensure their implementation.

In recent years, there has been a plethora of national and international pronouncements on the philosophies and aims underpinning the appropriate response to people with impairments or disabilities. For example, The Madrid Declaration, heralding 2003 as the Year of People with Disabilities (YPD) says:

> The Madrid Declaration takes as a starting point the analysis of the current situation of people with disabilities in the European Union.... It proposes a general vision, in which disabled people are not objects of charity and patients, but independent citizens fully integrated in society.[13]

The values which were promoted throughout the year were briefly described as follows:

- nothing about disabled people without disabled people;
- disabled citizens are entitled to the same rights as other citizens;
- disabled people want equal opportunities, not charity;
- creating a society for all;
- empowerment and emancipation;
- full equality and participation in all sectors of life;
- disabled people as active citizens;
- making the environment accessible;
- independent living;
- respect for diversity.

The announcement of the YPD followed a series of other declarations, promulgations and regulations emphasising the need to obtain equal rights for disabled people. For example, in 1971, the United Nations promulgated the Declaration on the Rights of Mentally Retarded Persons,[14] Art 1 of which states:

> The mentally retarded person has, to the maximum degree of feasibility, the same rights as other human beings.

---

12 Johnstone, D., *An Introduction to Disability Studies* (2nd Ed), London, David Fulton Publishers, 2001, p. 42.
13 http://www.madriddeclaration.org (accessed 16 June 2003 and 9 September 2003).
14 Proclaimed by General Assembly resolution 2856 (XXVI) of 20 December 1971 at http://daccess-ods.un.org/TMP/9814504.html (accessed on 30 June 2006).

The Declaration on the Rights of Disabled People was promulgated in 1975 and asserted that:[15]

> Disabled persons have the inherent right to respect for their human dignity. Disabled persons, whatever the origin, nature and seriousness of their handicaps and disabilities, have the same fundamental rights as their fellow-citizens of the same age, which implies first and foremost the right to enjoy a decent life, as normal and full as possible.[16]

In 1995, the European Parliament[17] called:

> ...on the Commission and the Member States, in their revision of the Treaties at the Intergovernmental Conference, to build in a clause forbidding discrimination on the grounds of disability; ...

In 1996, the 'Resolution on the rights of disabled people' was promulgated by the European Parliament,[18] and called:

> ...on Member States to include a non-discrimination clause on grounds of disability in the revised treaty on European Union, to enact a new legal basis for social programmes, and to introduce non-discrimination measures at Member State level, and to treat disability rights as a civil rights issue; ...

In 1996, the European Parliament affirmed the following:

> The European Parliament
>
> 1. Repudiates forcefully the thesis that disabled persons, patients in a persistent vegetative state and new-born children have no unrestricted right to life;
> 2. Reaffirms its unshakeable conviction that the right to life must be recognised in respect of every human being independently of his or her state of health, gender, race or age; ...
> 4. Calls on parliaments, governments and associations within and without the European Union decisively to counteract attacks on the right to life of disabled persons and new-born children...[19]

---

15 Proclaimed by General Assembly resolution 3447 (XXX) of 9 December 1975 at http://daccess-ods.un.org/TMP/1495738.html (accessed on 30 June 2006).
16 Art 3.
17 The European Parliament 'Rights of Disabled People', Minutes of 14 December 1995 at http://www3.europarl.eu.int (accessed on 16 June 2003).
18 The European Parliament, Minutes of 13 December 1996 at http://www3.europarl.eu.int (accessed on 16 June 2003).
19 European Parliament, Minutes of 23 May 1996 at http://www3.europarl.eu.int (accessed on 16 June 2003).

On 28 January 2003, it was announced that:

> The Council of Europe Parliamentary Assembly will adopt tomorrow the report 'Towards full social inclusion of persons with disabilities'. Among other important measures, the report recommends the inclusion of explicit reference to discrimination on the grounds of disability in the main Council of Europe legal instruments.[20]

On 12 March 2003:

> A proposal for a European Union law which for the first time prohibits discrimination against disabled people in housing, education, transport and in all its other forms, will be unveiled at the European Parliament in Strasbourg . . .[21]

Within the European Union (EU), the needs and interests of disabled people are also identified and protected by the European Disability Forum (EDF), which describes itself as:

> . . . . a European umbrella organisation representing more than 50 million disabled people in Europe. Its mission is to ensure disabled citizens' full access to fundamental and human rights through their active involvement in policy development and implementation in the European Union.[22]

The Council of Europe's Convention on Human Rights and Biomedicine[23] explicitly requires that decisions taken on behalf of those who are not otherwise competent should be taken only in their best interests, and declares that '[t]he interests and welfare of the human being shall prevail over the sole interest of society or science.'[24]

National legislation in the United Kingdom includes the Disability Discrimination Act 1995, the Disability Discrimination Act 1995 (Amendment) Regulations 2003, The Disability Discrimination Act 2005, the Special Educational Needs and Disability Act 2001 and the Disability Rights Act 1999, which established the DRC. This body has the statutory responsibility to:

- work towards the elimination of discrimination against disabled persons;
- promote the equalisation of opportunities for disabled persons;

20 Brussels, 28 January 2003 at http://www.edf-feph.org (accessed on 16 June 2003).
21 http://www.edf-feph.org (accessed on 16 June 2003).
22 http://www.edf-feph.org (accessed on 13 May 2005).
23 *Convention for the Protection of Human Rights and Dignity of the Human being with Regard to the Application of Biology and Medicine*, Oviedo, 4.IV.1997.
24 Art 2.

- take such steps as it considers appropriate with a view to encouraging good practice in the treatment of disabled persons; and
- keep under review the working of the Disability Discrimination Act 1995.[25]

As the law's response is of considerable importance in what follows, it is worth pausing briefly to outline its statutory provisions. First, legislation defines what is disability. The 1995 Act declared that 'a person has a disability for the purposes of this Act if he has a physical or mental impairment which has a substantial and long-term adverse effect on his ability to carry out normal day-to-day activities'.[26] Discrimination is defined in the 2003 regulations in this way:

(1) For the purposes of this Part, a person discriminates against a disabled person if –

   (a) for a reason which relates to the disabled person's disability, he treats him less favourably than he treats or would treat others to whom that reason does not or would not apply, and
   (b) he cannot show that the treatment in question is justified.

(5) A person directly discriminates against a disabled person if, on the ground of the disabled person's disability, he treats the disabled person less favourably than he treats or would treat a person not having that particular disability whose relevant circumstances, including his abilities, are the same as, or not materially different from, those of the disabled person.[27]

Moreover, the 2003 regulations introduced a new, and essentially subjective, offence of harassment which is described in this way:

(1) For the purposes of this Part, a person subjects a disabled person to harassment where, for a reason which relates to the disabled person's disability he engages in unwanted conduct which has the purpose or effect of –

   (a) violating the disabled person's dignity, or
   (b) creating an intimidating, hostile, degrading, humiliating or offensive environment for him.

(2) Conduct shall be regarded as having the effect referred to in paragraph (a) or (b) of subsection (1) only if, having regard to all the circumstances, including in particular the perception of the disabled person, it should reasonably be considered as having that effect.[28]

25 s 2 (1).
26 s 1(1).
27 3A.
28 3B.

The 2005 Act expanded the definition of disability to include 'a person who has cancer, HIV infection or multiple sclerosis'.[29]

Superimposed on the national legislation and the common law is Art 14 of the European Convention on Human Rights, which was directly incorporated into UK law by the Human Rights Act 1998. This Article prohibits discrimination on the grounds of 'sex, race, colour, language, religion, political or other opinion, national or social origin, association with a national minority, birth or other status'. Although disability is not mentioned specifically, it is implausible that it would not be included under 'other status'. However, it should also be noted that by and large Art 14 is not an independent right; therefore, the anti-discrimination provision can only be used when one of the other rights guaranteed by the Convention is engaged. Its protection, therefore, is by no means absolute.

This brief, and by no means comprehensive, account of some of the national and international initiatives in this area serves to demonstrate the extent to which law has striven towards eradication of discrimination against people with impairment or disability. However, even legal acknowledgement of the importance of non-discrimination has proved to be inadequate to eradicate prejudice and – as we see later – in situations involving healthcare at the beginning and end of life, it is the common law rather than statutory law which has dominated decision making. Thus, the limitations of legislation are evident; we must also look to ethical principles to guide decision makers, and to provide a yardstick against which we can measure their decisions. Despite the promulgations briefly referred to above, then, there remain concerns that disabled people *are* discriminated against in many aspects of life. The EDF, for example, says:

> ... disabled people are still on a daily basis being discriminated against in various sectors, for example: employment, education, transport and free movement, access to goods and services etc, and as long as these discriminatory barriers exist, disabled people can not exercise their rights and freedoms. To be treated equally and to not be discriminated against is a human rights issue and it can not be considered as being within a human rights approach to tolerate any kind of discrimination. People with disabilities are demanding equal opportunities and access to all societal resources.[30]

Evidence about the fact of disability discrimination abounds. Light, for example, notes that of the incidences of abuse of disabled people's human rights: '141 of the reports – affecting at least 423,427 disabled people – recorded in the

29 5 18(3).
30 http://www.edf-feph.org/en/policy/nondisc/nond_pol.htm (accessed on 13 May 2005).

[Disability Awareness in Action Human Rights] database – concern breach of Article 3: the right to *life, liberty and personal security*.'[31] (original emphasis)
Light further provides a breakdown of the people most at risk of discrimination:

> 63% of *cases* recorded on the Database involve the abuse of people with physical impairments, 44% involve people with learning impairments and 26% people with mental illnesses. However, the review of cases fails to reveal that, in fact, when *victim* numbers are calculated, people with mental illness and learning difficulties are at highest risk (55% and 38% more likely to be victims, respectively); those at greatest risk are people with multiple impairments.[32]

The DRC also claims that '[d]iscrimination against disabled people is still rife in Britain today . . . '.[33] Moreover, the Learning Disability Task Force 'believes that people with learning disabilities are still being excluded and discriminated against by services and society. This means that people with learning disabilities are still getting treated unfairly and missing out on the things that other people get'.[34]

Conclusion

In this book, we seek to achieve a number of things. First, by bringing the scrutiny of ethics and law to this area we hope to offer a relevant account of the treatment of people with disability or impairment within the context of healthcare decision making, particularly at the beginning and end of life. Second, we attempt to explore the ethical and legal constructs within which decisions are made and set these within the context of concepts of disability. Third, as we have said, we will focus this analysis on the critical times at the beginning and the end of life. It is essential before proceeding to specific consideration of decisions at the beginning and end of life that we analyse two critical issues: thus, the next chapter will consider the different ways in which disability is conceptualised and the impact these different concepts can have on clinical decision making. Chapter 3 will then explore a range of ethical principles and concepts which enable us to articulate the characteristics which give value to human life and which should, therefore, be protected by the various participants in life-and-death decision-making in the context of disability.

---

31 Light, R., 'A Real Horror Story: The Abuse of Disabled People's Human Rights', *Disability Awareness in Action Human Rights Database*, Disability Awareness in Action, 2002 at p. 19.
32 *Ibid.*, p. 20.
33 Disability Rights Commission, The DRC 2003 Attitudes and Awareness Survey, preamble available at http://www.drc-gb.org (accessed on 29 June 2006).
34 *Rights, Independence, Choice and Inclusion*, January 2004, p. 13.

Chapters 4, 5 and 6 will then address specific incidences of decision making at the beginning and end of life, leading us to conclude on the role actually or preferably played by ethics and law in this important area. We approach this subject then from the perspective of ethics and law, not as disability theorists. However, it is important that the mainstream theoretical positions of people with impairment or disability are examined, and this will be undertaken in Chapter 2.

Chapter 2

Conceptualising disability

Introduction

Two distinct ways of conceptualising 'disability' have tended to dominate literature on this topic, namely, the 'medical' and the 'social' models of disability. The medical model is associated with the conviction that disability is a direct consequence of physical or mental pathology. Exponents of the social model, on the other hand, hold that disability is a consequence of the failure of society to accommodate the needs of people with physical and mental differences (impairments). It is important to begin our ethico-legal examination of life-and-death decision-making by evaluating these disparate approaches to disability. This is necessary because the way disability is understood influences the issues that must be addressed in respect of disabled lives and the way(s) in which it is thought most appropriate to resolve them.

Initially in this chapter we will outline the claims associated with the medical model and then review criticisms that have been made of this approach. The social model will then be outlined and evaluated in the same manner. Based on these assessments we will consider how these different understandings of disability contribute to efforts to make sound ethical decisions concerning life-and-death issues. We will argue that neither of these approaches on its own permits a full appreciation of the complexities that many life-and-death decisions raise, nor, taken alone, can they resolve them. With this concern in mind we will end this chapter by critically appraising an approach to disability that aims to incorporate the best of both the social and medical approaches to disability.

The medical model

The term medical model is primarily used by those who are critical of a tendency – which they associate with biomedical science – to see disability as being exclusively the result of physical and mental impairment. That is, within the medical model impairments themselves are seen as disabling. As the World Health Organisation (WHO) has explained:

> The medical model views disability as a problem of the person, directly caused by disease, trauma or other health condition, which requires medical care provided in the form of individual treatment by professionals. Management of the disability is aimed at cure or the individual's adjustment and behaviour change. Medical care is viewed as the main issue, and at the political level the principal response is that of modifying or reforming health care policy.[1]

The causal link made within biomedicine between impairment and disability is based on a particular understanding of health and the goals of medicine, namely, that health is to be equated with being free from disease, and medicine with curing disease and impairment, or with securing what Sabin and Daniels have referred to in their discussion of medical necessity as 'normal species functioning'.[2] Sabin and Daniels summarise the aims of this approach by stating:

> According to the normal function model, the central purpose of health care is to maintain, restore, or compensate for the restricted opportunity and loss of function caused by disease and disability. Successful health care restores people to the range of capabilities they would have had without the pathological condition or prevents further deterioration.[3]

Boorse supports the idea that the fundamental aim of healthcare is to restore 'normal functioning' and also stresses that this 'medical conception of health as absence of disease is a value-free theoretical notion. Its main elements are biological function and statistical normality'.[4] This is an argument with which Daniels concurs:

> Disease and disability, both physical and mental, are construed as adverse departures from or impairments of species-typical normal functioning organization, or 'normal functioning' for short. The line between disease and disability and normal functioning is drawn in the relatively objective and nonevaluative context provided by the biomedical sciences ... [5]

---

1 World Health Organisation (WHO), *ICF: Introduction*, Geneva, WHO, 2001 at p. 20.
2 Sabin, J.E. and Daniels, N., 'Determining "Medical Necessity" in Mental Health Practice', *Hastings Center Report*, 24, 6, 1994, 5–13 at p. 10.
3 *Id.*
4 Boorse, C., 'Health as a Theoretical Concept', *Philosophy of Science*, 44, 1977, 542–573 at p. 542.
5 Daniels, N., 'Justice, Health, and Healthcare', *American Journal of Bioethics*, 1, 2, 2001, 2–16 at p. 3 note 1.

The reputed objectivity of the medical approach to health and disability has led to assumptions that decisions made drawing upon the medical model must have a high degree of reliability. Hence, it is perhaps not surprising that the medical model acts as the foundation of many legal judgements in the area of healthcare. The impact of the medical model on legal decisions at the beginning and end of life will be assessed in later chapters. Here it is only necessary to note that the definition of disability contained in the UK's Disability Discrimination Act 1995 is one that is identified closely with the medical model. The Act states:

> ... a person has a disability for the purposes of this Act if he has a physical or mental impairment which has a substantial and long-term adverse effect on his ability to carry out normal day-to-day activities.[6]

Moreover, the dominance of the medical model pervades the recent amendments to this Act, which – although contextualising disability to some extent by placing emphasis on the experience of disabled people[7] – adds, as we have seen, to the legal definition of disability those who are, for example, suffering from cancer and HIV/AIDS.[8] Thus, the understanding of disability in the Act is still one which sees a causal relationship between physical and mental impairment and disability. Later in the chapter we consider the ramifications of this understanding of disability for life-and-death decision-making. However, to ensure that this is based on adequate information we will now examine some of the criticisms which have been made in relation to this model of disability.

Medical model: normality critique

Disability theorists have criticised the claim that the goal of medicine is to restore 'normal' functioning to those with impairments because it implies that disabled people are 'abnormal'. As Swain et al. have said:

> The normality-abnormality construct is an inherent feature of the medical model of disability where disability is perceived as an aberration which needs to be removed, corrected or hidden.[9]

Johnstone highlights the implications of the normal–abnormal dichotomy by suggesting that it implies that while able-bodied people are 'normal, good, clean, fit, able, independent', disabled people are 'abnormal, bad, unclean, unfit, unable

---

6 Disability Discrimination Act 1995, Part I Disability s 1(1).

7 *Ibid.*, s 4.

8 *Ibid.*, s 18(3)(1).

9 Swain, J., French, S. and Cameron, C., *Controversial Issues in a Disabling Society*, Buckingham, Open University Press, 2003 at p. 81f.

and dependent'.[10] This approach, he claims 'categorises the able-bodied as somehow "better" than or superior to people with disabilities'.[11] While Silvers explains that the limitations:

> ...imposed on people because of their physical, sensory, and cognitive impairments contain biased theoretical components that distort the impact of impairment. Such discriminatory theorizing takes impairment to be inescapably negative, so that whoever is impaired must thereby be in deficit, incompetent, and suffering and needy.[12]

Thus, the normal–abnormal dichotomy at the heart of the medical model has the potential to disvalue the lives of people who are, or are likely to become, impaired, those who are not medically speaking 'normal'. Furthermore, Barnes and Mercer emphasise that the association between disability and abnormality, and 'able-bodiedness' and normality, are socially pervasive and not restricted to the judgements of professionals. They argue that:

> ...a marked divide between 'abled-bodied' and 'disabled' people has been established at the cultural level. 'Able-bodied normalcy' is embedded in everyday thinking and behaviour as a privileged or desirable state of being.[13]

In addition to concerns over the desirability of measuring disabled lives against some criterion of 'normality', there are also fundamental difficulties with determining how to identify what counts as 'normal functioning' within the diverse human species. In this respect, Cohon is critical of a number of the ways in which abnormality is defined and equated with disability.[14] She dismisses the idea that it is sound to adopt a statistically based account of what is 'normal'. To support her argument she explains that a global nuclear accident that left the majority of humanity with radiation sickness would not make such impairment normal.[15] Cohon also rejects the suggestion that it is possible to identify what is normal or abnormal for human beings by merely observing how different aspects of the human body function. This is because in using this

10 Johnstone, D., *An Introduction to Disability Studies* (2nd Ed), London, David Fulton Publishers, 2001 at p. 17.
11 *Ibid.*, p. 16.
12 Silvers, A., 'Formal Justice', *Disability, Difference, Discrimination: Perspectives on Justice in Bioethics and Public Policy*; Silvers, A., Wasserman, D. and Mahowald, M.B., 13–145, New York and London, Rowman & Littlefield Publishers, 1998 at p. 85.
13 Barnes, C. and Mercer, G., *Disability*, Oxford, Polity, 2003 at p. 21f.
14 Cohon, R., 'Disability', in Post, S.G. (ed), *Encyclopedia of Bioethics*, 655–668, New York, MacMillian, 2004, at p. 656f.
15 *Ibid.*, p. 656.

method one would witness (observe) both 'normal' and 'abnormal' species functioning and yet possess no resources to determine which type of functioning is species typical or which most desirable.[16] In light of these concerns Cohon contends:

> ...a state of a human being is an abnormality of the type relevant to impairment only if the state is such that if all human beings had had it from the beginning of human prehistory and otherwise were as they in fact are today, the human species would have been unlikely to survive. If the state (1) is of that kind, (2) is not a diversity-requiring trait, and (3) is not a trait that is characteristic of and limited to certain stages of human development, it is abnormal.[17]

That is, if a condition is likely to have made humans less likely to survive as a species and is not related to diversity (for example, gender) or human development (for example, the weakness of infants and the elderly) then it can be classed as an abnormality. However, despite the difficulties that surround efforts to identify what is normal for humans, Cohon retains the conviction that some physiological and mental impairments compromise the ability of humans to flourish. In this way, despite her concerns about how we determine what is 'normal', Cohon concurs with the claim of the medical model that impairment can disable individuals and in some sense make lives worse off.

Like Cohon, Harris warns against defining disability by appealing to ideas of normalcy. He explains that this is because:

> Normal species functioning cannot form part of the definition of disability because people might be normal and still disabled. Suppose due to further depletions in the ozone layer, all white skinned people were very vulnerable to skin cancers ... but brown or black skinned people were immune. We might regard whites as suffering from substantial disabilities relative to their darker skinned fellows ... even though their functioning was quite species typical or normal.[18]

Harris identifies disability as a '... condition that someone has a strong rational preference not to be in and one that is in some sense a harmed condition',[19] and explains that he understands a 'harmed condition' as a state that clinicians in an accident and emergency department would endeavour to correct. Indeed the 'staff would be negligent if they failed to reverse or remove it'.[20]

---

16 *Ibid.*, p. 656f.
17 *Ibid.*, p. 657.
18 Harris, J., 'One Principle and Three Fallacies of Disability Studies', *Journal of Medical Ethics*, 27, 2001, 383–387 at p. 384.
19 *Id.*
20 Harris, J., 'One Principle and Three Fallacies of Disability Studies', *Journal of Medical Ethics*, 27, 2001, 383–387 at p. 384.

Thus, like Cohon and the medical model Harris understands disability to be based on physical or mental impairment and not only on social limitations.

This discussion suggests that the quest to find criteria to allow us accurately to identify what should be seen as 'normal' and 'abnormal' in respect of human functioning is misguided. We have also seen that undesirable connotations can be associated with the terms 'normal' and 'abnormal' and that in the context of disability these negative assumptions can serve to disvalue the lives of people with impairments. Despite these concerns we concur with Cohon, Harris and certain disability theorists that some human lives are marked by physical and mental characteristics (impairments) that it would be preferable not to have. This is because impairments can make life more difficult and undermine its quality. That said, this does not mean that the lives of all individuals with impairments lack value and impaired individuals should certainly not be subjected to derogatory attitudes and poor decisions that undermine their abilities and preferences. However, in the case of impairments which are truly severe, decisions may have to be taken about whether such lives lack so many basic features – which cannot be corrected – that life is and will remain of limited or no value for the individual in question. As we will examine in the following sections, efforts to make decisions at the beginning and end of life concerning which lives are too compromised to be regarded as valuable are also problematised by the fact that judgements in the area are not value-neutral – despite what exponents of the medical model contend – and the power of the medical profession risks obscuring the opinions of disabled people.

Medical model: professionalisation and medicalisation critiques

As the WHO has emphasised, the medical model places considerable authority in the hands of medical professionals. This situation has led Johnstone to comment that:

> What has come to be described as the 'medical' model, emerged from the tendency of most of us to see medical practice as the epitome of a powerful professional group. Doctors carry with them an aura of God-life responsibility over life and death.[21]

The influence and power of medical professionals manifests itself in a number of ways in the context of disability (impairment) which must be identified. For example, the juxtapositioning of potentially vulnerable patients with authoritative decision makers has the potential to result in disregarding the

21 Johnstone, *op. cit.*, p. 17.

interests and decisions of the former. At the root of this resides the dynamics of
the doctor–patient relationship. Historically, it is not only 'disabled people' who
have had their treatment and interests autocratically determined by doctors, but
patients from all social groups. The British Medical Association (BMA) has, for
example, recently explained the developments that have taken place in the
relationship between doctors and patients. Whereas at the beginning of the
nineteenth century the aim of doctors was:

> ...to sort out what would be best for patients without necessarily involving
> them in the choices. From today's perspective, such guidance can be seen as
> embodying the best and worst aspects of paternalism in that doctors were
> expected to be thoughtful and caring of their patients but without engaging
> with them as equals ...From the 1950s, this interpretation became
> increasingly discredited and by the 1980s such paternalism was seen as
> completely outmoded. Although paternalistic attitudes often had a
> benevolent goal and were motivated by a perceived need to protect the
> vulnerabilities of sick people, they infantilised patients and removed their
> choices.[22]

This highlights that there has been a move away from seeing patients as the
objects of medical interventions – a shift that has created an environment in
which patients are generally viewed as the self-determining *subjects* of medical
treatment. However, it is debatable whether the same change of attitude has
taken place in situations which involve 'disabled' patients. Disability
organisations continue to identify cases which suggest that the opinions of
disabled patients can be denigrated in healthcare institutions.[23] Furthermore, it
appears that some of the problems and assumptions we have examined in respect
of the medical model may impede a move towards seeing disabled patients as
powerful moral agents. For example, the distinction we have identified at the
heart of the medical model between 'normal' and 'abnormal' human functioning
could have a detrimental impact on how the medical profession perceives the
capacities of disabled (impaired) patients. As the medical model implicitly
presents impairment as a 'tragedy' or 'misfortune' it may inadvertently result in
individuals with impairments being denied the right to be involved in decisions
concerning their lives and underestimate or disregard positive features of
disabled (impaired) lives. Indeed it has been suggested that the impact of the

22 British Medical Association, *Medical Ethics Today: The BMA's Handbook of Ethics and Law*
    (2nd Ed), London, BMA & BMJ Books, 2004 at p. 25f.
23 See, for example, www.Notdeadyet.org; http://www.drc-gb.org/the_law/ drc formal_investigations/
    equal_treatment_investigation.aspx and the material on bioethics and disability listed by
    Disabled Peoples' International at http://v1.dpi.org/lang-en/resources/ topics_list?topic=2 (all
    sites accessed on 1 June 2006).

medical model is so detrimental that it has led to the assumption '. . . that physical death is better than the social death of disability'.[24]

Another way in which the power of healthcare professionals can have a detrimental impact on disabled people has been identified by Finkelstein. He claims that disabled people have often been disempowered by what he terms the 'professionalisation' of disability. He explains:

> Since the turn of this century the number of workers, professional and lay, in industrial societies who work in the field of disability has increased enormously. Almost every aspect of the life of a person who is disabled has its counterpart in a 'profession' or voluntary organisation. Potential and real control over the life of a disabled individual is a modern fact.[25]

This tendency to subject all areas of disabled lives to the care (control) of professionals forms part of a more general drive to 'medicalise' life. That is, as Irvine Zola and others have argued, modern society increasingly allows medicine to define the nature of illness and allows the extension of medicine into areas of life which do not require medical intervention.[26] One ramification of this is that medical professionals become the gatekeepers of what is 'normal' and what is 'pathological'. As Illich argues:

> Society has transferred to physicians the exclusive right to determine what constitutes sickness, who is or might become sick, and what shall be done to such people.[27]

The ability of medical professionals to control not just individual relationships with patients but also to define what counts as illness and normality directs and restricts discussions of disability to the medical sphere and can have serious implications for disabled people who come into contact with healthcare facilities. As Hughes states:

> The definition of disability as a corporeal problem has meant that, for the most part, throughout modernity, disabled people have come under the

24 Swain, J. and French, S. 'Towards an Affirmative Model of Disability', *Disability and Society*, 15, 4, 2000, 569–582 at p. 572.
25 Finkelstein, V., *Attitudes and Disabled People*, New York, World Rehabilitation Fund, 1980.
26 Zola, I., 'Medicine as an Institution of Social Control', *Sociological Review*, 20, 4, 1972, 487–504 at p. 504; Illich, I., *Limits to Medicine-Medical Nemesis: The Expropriation of Health*, London and New York, Marion Boyars, 1995. *Medical Nemesis* originally published 1975.
27 Illich, I., *Limits to Medicine-Medical Nemesis: The Expropriation of Health*, London and New York, Marion Boyars, 1995. *Medical Nemesis* originally published 1975.

jurisdiction, control and surveillance of (bio)medicine. This process of locating disability within the disciplinary scope of medicine has influenced profoundly the state of knowledge about it. Disability has been understood as sickness, and disabled people have been understood as invalids.[28]

The use of the term invalid – or similar derogatory epithets – to describe people with impairments (disabled people) illustrates in a particularly acute manner that such individuals are often seen as sub-optimal and so inevitably compromises the social status of individuals with impairments. In the context of our discussion of life-and-death decision-making, this predicament raises questions regarding whether such negative attitudes impact on the type and quality of treatment they receive within healthcare environments and the importance which is given to the wishes of competent disabled patients. Moreover, it may affect the extent to which the voice of people with disabilities is given authority or weight, disvaluing their experiences, their opinions and in many cases their lives

Medical model: neutrality critique

At the beginning of this chapter we saw that those who hold that the primary aim of medicine is to restore 'normal species functioning' think that accomplishing this goal entails what is largely a value-free enterprise.[29] That is, the decisions that medical professionals make about what counts as 'normal functioning' and human well-being are presented as objective, unbiased judgements. It has, however, long been recognised that scientific claims are not value-neutral.[30] In the context of medicine, Downie and Calman highlight how the technical decision making associated with medicine feigns an objectivity which ' conceals from healthcare practitioners and the general public the pervasive nature of moral and value judgements inevitably made in the diagnosis and treatment of patients or clients ... [31]

In respect of disability and impairment, Marks has noted that:

Medicine's drive to make normal that which it considers to be pathological and dysfunctional claims to be value neutral. Yet in practice, medicine

28 Hughes, B., 'Disability and the Body', in Barnes, C., Oliver, M. and Barton, L. (eds), *Disability Studies Today*, Oxford, Polity, 2002, 58–76 at p. 58.
29 Boorse, C., 'Health as a Theoretical Concept', *Philosophy of Science*, 44, 1977, 542–573 at p. 542; Daniels, N., 'Justice, Health, and Healthcare', *American Journal of Bioethics*, 1, 2, 2001, 2–16 at p. 3, note 1.
30 See, for example, Thomas Kuhn's seminal work in the philosophy of science Kuhn, T., *The Structure of Scientific Revolutions*, Chicago, University of Chicago Press, 1970.
31 Downie, R.S. and Calman, K.C., *Healthy Respect: Ethics in Health Care* (2nd Ed), Oxford, Oxford University Press, 1994 at p. 24.

contains a series of latent normative assumptions about value, beauty and function which influence its practices.[32]

The normal–abnormal dichotomy at the heart of the medical model is not therefore a value-free diagnostic device that allows us to identify unambiguously the features that are required to make life worthwhile and those which make it too burdensome, nor to decide who will and will not be treated or saved. Rather, 'normality' and 'abnormality' are evaluative terms that signal what we approve or disapprove: a valuable life to one may well be unbearable to another. Swain *et al.* have claimed that:

> The normal–abnormal construct is not neutral but is permeated with moral judgement and evaluation, with 'normality' being equated with virtuousness, and abnormality with shame and scorn.[33]

This is substantiated by Barnes and Mercer, who say:

> The notion of 'able-bodied' assumes normative or universal standards by which all other 'bodies' are judged. The disabled population is set apart, as 'Other', or as deviant in specific ways.[34]

The latent value-laden nature of clinical decision making is particularly problematic in the context of disability because of the negative attitudes which can underpin our approach to impairment. That is, because the aim of medicine is to salve impairment it follows that any person with an impairment will be viewed as in some way flawed and in need of 'correction'. In addition, we have seen that a host of other assumptions or prejudices about the disabled can accompany the conviction that impairment needs to be treated. While the medical approach to disability asserts that it is impairment that disables, in this context it is possible that the value judgements that are made concerning the actual or potential ramifications of impairment are themselves disabling. This concern is exacerbated by the authority that is often attributed to clinical decision makers by the medical model of disability.

Despite these concerns, a model of disability which ignored the contribution that medical science has to make to impairment would be imprudent, since many disabled people – though by no means all – benefit from some form of medical treatment. However, it can be difficult, particularly in light of the medical

32 Marks, D., *Disability: Controversial Debates and Psychosocial Perspectives*, London, Routledge, 1999 at p. 49.
33 Swain *et al.*, *op.cit.*, p. 81.
34 Barnes and Mercer, *op.cit.*, p. 21f.

profession's role in defining illness, to determine when an individual requires treatment. As Oliver notes:

> ... doctors can have a role to play in the lives of disabled people: stabilising their initial condition, treating any illnesses which may arise and which may or may not be disability related... The conceptual issue underpinning this dimension of the debate, therefore, is about determining which aspects of disabled people's lives need medical or therapeutic interventions, which aspects require policy developments and which require political action. Failure to distinguish between these up to now has resulted in the medicalisation of disability... [35]

Arguably the medical model has neither the theoretical resources nor the desire to support the type of detailed investigation that is necessary to differentiate between the aspects of disability which are primarily socio-political issues and those that legitimately require medical intervention. This suggestion is supported both by the concerns we have highlighted regarding medicalisation and also by the fact that the social justice issues which are raised by disability have largely been addressed by an alternative understanding of disability, namely, the social model. We will now turn to examine this approach before assessing the ramifications of the medical and social models for life-and-death decision-making.

The social model

The medical approach to disability was challenged during the mid-1970s by a model that crystallised within the disability community. This alternative 'social model' understood disability not as a direct consequence of impairment, but as the product of society's failure to accommodate the needs of people with impairments. This approach to disability was famously presented in 1976 by the Union of the Physically Impaired Against Segregation (UPIAS) when it published its *Fundamental Principles of Disability*.[36] In this document, disability is presented as 'a situation caused by social conditions'.[37] The UPIAS explains that in order to appreciate the nature of its thesis:

> ... it is necessary to grasp the distinction between the physical impairment and the social situation, called 'disability', of people with such impairment. Thus we define impairment as lacking part of or all of a limb, or having a

---

35 Oliver, M., 'Defining Impairment and Disability: Issues at Stake', in *Exploring the Divide*, Leeds, The Disability Press, 1996, 29–54.
36 UPIAS, *Fundamental Principles of Disability*, London: Union of the Physically Impaired, 1976 at p. 14.
37 *Ibid.*, p. 3.

defective limb, organ or mechanism of the body; and disability as the disadvantage or restriction of activity caused by a contemporary social organisation which takes no or little account of people with physical impairments and thus excludes them from participation in the mainstream of social activities.[38]

This distinction between impairment and disability allowed the UPIAS to present a radically different understanding of 'disability' from that associated with the medical model. Oliver emphasises that the unique contribution of the social model is its representation of disability as being '...wholly and exclusively social' and 'nothing to do with the body'.[39] The idea that societal restrictions, and not physical or mental impairments, are the cause of disability has developed into a central theme within Disability Studies.[40] The adoption of the social model signals a commitment within much of the disability community to the idea that the 'struggle against disability discrimination' should be based on the conviction that 'disability was a social problem rather than the outcome of a "natural" (f)law'.[41]

At the heart of the social understanding of disability is the claim that people with impairments are detrimentally affected by 'the impact of social and environmental barriers, such as inaccessible buildings and transport, discriminatory attitudes and negative cultural stereotypes'.[42] It is important to emphasise that proponents of the social model are keen to stress that the deep roots of the discrimination experienced by disabled people are:

> ... not simply a question of individual prejudice, although that clearly occurs. Rather, it is institutionalised in the structures of society. Institutional discrimination is evident when the policies and activities of all types of organisations result in sustaining the inequalities between disabled people and non-disabled people.[43]

Like the medical approach to disability, the social model has been critiqued on various grounds. A number of these criticisms will now be examined. We will then

---

38 UPIAS, *Fundamental Principles of Disability*, London: Union of the Physically Impaired, 1976 at p. 14.

39 Oliver, *op. cit.*, 29–54, Leeds, The Disability Press, 1996. [No page numbers given]

40 Barnes, C., Oliver, M. and Barton, L. (eds), *Disability Studies Today*, Oxford, Polity Press, 2002; Barnes and Mercer, *op. cit.*; Priestley, M., *Disability: A Life Course Approach*, Oxford, Polity Press, 2003; Oliver, M., *The Politics of Disablement*, Basingstoke, MacMillan, 1990; Abberley, P., 'The Concept of Oppression and the Development of a Social Theory of Disability', *Disability, Handicap & Society*, 2, 1, 1987, 5–19; Fickelstein, *op. cit.*; Barton, L. and Oliver, M. (eds), *Disability Studies: Past, Present and Future*, Leeds, The Disability Press, 1997.

41 Hughes, *op. cit.*, p. 64.

42 Barnes and Mercer, *op. cit.*, p. 1.

43 Johnstone, D., *An Introduction to Disability Studies* (2nd Ed), London, David Fulton Publishers, 2001 at p. 43.

move from these preliminary discussions of different understandings of disability to consider their potential ramifications for life-and-death decision-making.

Social model: impairment critique

One of the primary arguments raised against the social model is that it fails to address the negative attitudes that exist towards impairment *per se*. Swain and French, for example, state that 'the social model disassociates impairment from disability.'[44] It has been claimed that, rather than confront the problems and often negative attitudes which arise from impairment, the social model introduces an 'untenable separation between body and culture, impairment and disability'.[45] That is, the social model prioritises the socio-political aspects of disability over the experiential features of impairment.[46]

The omission of impairment from the social model has led to calls from within the disability community for the experiences associated with impairment to be acknowledged. In this respect Crow is keen to stress that the difficulties faced by disabled people can only be addressed if all of their causes, including impairment, are given adequate attention. Her comments are worth quoting at length. She states.

> ...our criticisms of the medical model of disability, have made us wary of acknowledging our experiences of impairment ... This silence prevents us from dealing effectively with the difficult aspects of impairment. Many of us remain frustrated and disheartened by pain, fatigue, depression and chronic illness, including the way they prevent us from realising our potential or railing against disability (our experience of exclusion and discrimination); many of us fear for our futures with progressive or additional impairments; we mourn past activities that are no longer possible for us; we are afraid we may die early or that suicide may seem our only option; we desperately seek some effective medical intervention; we feel ambivalent about the possibilities of our children having impairments; and we are motivated to work for the prevention of impairments. Yet our silence about impairment has made many of these things taboo and created a whole new series of constraints on our self-expression.[47]

44 Swain and French, *op. cit.*, p. 571.
45 Hughes, B. and Paterson, K., 'The Social Model of Disability and the Disappearing Body: Towards a Sociology of Impairment', *Disability and Society*, 12, 3,1997, 325–340 at p. 326.
46 Shakespeare, T. and Watson, N., 'Defending the Social Model of Disability', *Disability and Society*, 12, 2, 1997, 293–300; Morris, J., *Pride and Prejudice*, London, Women's Press, 1992.
47 Crow, L., 'Including All of Our Lives: Renewing the Social Model of Disability', in Barnes, C. and Mercer, G. (eds), *Exploring the Divide*, Leeds, The Disability Press, 1996, 55–72. This document is available at http://www.leeds.ac.uk/disability-studies/archiveuk but this edition has no page numbers.

In response to such concerns Oliver has explained that:

> This denial of the pain of impairment has not, in reality been a denial at all. Rather it has been a pragmatic attempt to identify and address issues that can be changed through collective action rather than medical or other professional treatment.[48]

That is, the allegations of Crow and others regarding the failure of the social model to acknowledge the experiential implications of impairment are legitimate. But the omission is part of an effort to address socio-political issues like justice and discrimination rather than problems associated with 'the personal restrictions of impairment' that are far less easy to change.[49] Oliver acknowledges that the social model does not:

> ... deal with personal restrictions of impairment but only the social barriers of disability ... it has been a pragmatic attempt to identify and address issues that can be changed through collective action rather than medical or other professional treatment.[50]

For the social justice claims of disabled people to hold, it is thought crucial that the social model of disability is able to make a convincing case for there being 'no causal relationship between impairment and disability'.[51] However, it is precisely the negative ramifications of impairment – the impact impairments *can* have on an individual's bodily experience – which must be at the kernel of properly grounded life-and-death decisions. Although the need to eliminate the impact of social discrimination against disabled people in clinical decisions at the beginning and end of life – and in other areas – is of paramount importance, the focus of the traditional formulation of the social model appears to jeopardise the possibility of a full consideration of the issues that should be fundamental to these areas, namely, the assessment of the actual or potential personal impact of impairment(s). That said, it is necessary to consider other criticisms which have been made in relation to the social model.

Social model: marginalisation critique

It has been argued that the social model does not distance itself sufficiently from the 'tragic' view of disability which sees disabled people as dependent and as individuals who are positioned on the margins of society. That is, although

48 Oliver, *op. cit.*, 1996, 29–54.
49 *Id.*
50 *Id.*
51 *Ibid.*

exponents of the social model certainly want to reject such ideas about disability:

> ...it can be argued that the social model has not, in itself, underpinned a non-tragedy view. First, to be a member of an oppressed group within society does not necessarily engender a non-tragedy view. There is, for instance, nothing inherently non-tragic about being denied access to buildings.[52]

This suggests that, despite the endeavours of those who employ the social model to move away from the idea that disability is a personal tragedy, disability is not in fact presented in a more positive light under this model. This is because shifting the blame for such difficulties does not, as Swain and French rightly highlighted, act as a catalyst for a more positive assessment of disabled lives.[53] Similarly, Anita Silvers has argued against trying to protect the interests of disabled people by presenting them as a social minority who need to have their rights protected. She explains the problems with this approach thus:

> Characterising a group as vulnerable further isolates its members from others in society. Doing so emphasizes their supposed fragility, which becomes a reason to deny that they are capable, and therefore deserving, of full social participation. So we must carefully avoid stereotyping and bias in depicting them as especially vulnerable.[54]

In the context of healthcare, the same concerns over the impotence of the social model hold. For example, drawing attention to the fact that within a traditional medical approach to impairment and health disabled people are viewed as 'abnormal' and dependent on professional assistance does not in itself propose an alternative ideology which allows for and generates a more positive assessment of disability and impairment.

Comparison: medical and social models

The primary difference which has emerged between the medical and social approaches to disability is that the social model prioritises the need to minimise or remove the social obstacles and the discrimination which the exponents of this model argue that disabled people face, and the medical model focuses on the need to prevent or treat physical or mental impairments which disable individuals.

---

52 Swain and French, *op. cit.*, p. 571.
53 *Ibid.*, 569–582.
54 Silvers, A., 'Protecting the Innocents from Physician-Assisted Suicide', in Battin, M.P., Rhodes, R. and Silvers, A. (eds), *Physician Assisted Suicide: Expanding the Debate*, London, Routledge, 1998, 133–148 at p. 134.

We have seen that the pursuit of normality is at the heart of the medical model but that this concept is ignored by the social model in its intense focus on issues concerning social justice, or rather, the social model understands impaired people as just one example of the diversity of the human community. The problem in the eyes of social modellists is that sometimes society does not embrace or support diversity as well as it could, a point which is evidenced by the ongoing debates in areas such as gender, race and sexuality.

Closely associated with the medical model's commitment to normality are various assumptions about disability that depreciate the value of impaired lives. Arguably amongst the most damaging of these are those that relieve disabled people of their autonomy and assume that an impaired life must be a bad life. To a large extent these ideas appear to be socially pervasive. Exponents of the social model are keen to reveal and to address such flawed assumptions, discriminatory attitudes and the poor treatment in which they can result. Indeed, we have seen that exponents of the social model focus exclusively on addressing the socio-political attitudes and policies that work against the interests of disabled people. They adopt this approach because they deem these issues to be amendable by social critique and political pressure. That is, exponents of the social model claim not to deny that impairment can lead to negative experiences but rather to focus on the social–political aspects of disability which can be changed. This is precisely because the negative bodily experiences of impaired individuals are often far more difficult to alter.

Life-and-death decision-making: relevant difference or discrimination?

The medical and social models of disability have different implications for the field of healthcare and for life-and-death decision-making. The concept of disability which apparently lends itself most easily to informing decisions at the beginning and end of life is the medical model, because it is so closely linked to the fundamental aims of clinical care. This approach ostensibly provides a clear, objective or 'factual' way to decide what treatment should, or should not, be provided in particular cases. That is, the treatment that individuals receive in their interaction with healthcare institutions is based firmly on their clinical diagnosis and prognosis. However, we have seen that such reputedly pure clinical judgements are influenced by value-laden assumptions about what constitutes a good or satisfactory life and by a power imbalance between medical professionals and their patients. Thus, the application of the medical model to life-and-death decisions involving disabled people can be problematic. These concerns are most satisfactorily illustrated by drawing on a number of examples.

As we will examine in Chapter 4, developments in biotechnology now provide us with the ability to decide whether to allow or prevent the birth of individuals who are thought likely to have disabilities. For example, prenatal genetic diagnosis (PGD) and embryo screening are techniques that provide medical professionals and prospective parents with the ability to choose to prevent the birth of children with a wide range of disabilities. From the perspective of the medical model, the rationale for utilising such procedures is essentially to ensure that infants are not born with impairments which would make their lives intolerable or at least less tolerable than the lives of other non-affected infants. The focus of such medical judgements is on the quality of life of the potential child and not only – as would be the case with abortions which are conducted for non-medical reasons – with the interests of the parent(s). That said, the ability of the potential parents to manage a child with severe impairments will also feature in decisions to not implant or to screen out an embryo or foetus on the grounds of disability (impairment). However, the medical model does not have the intellectual resources or the inclination to consider in detail the potential impact on such judgements of the negative social attitudes that exist towards disability. This makes it difficult to judge whether a decision to prevent a birth is grounded in a legitimate concern for the severity of impairment and concern for the potential child or in a deeply rooted prejudice which fallaciously assumes that a disabled life is 'not worth living' and will bring only difficulty and no pleasure to the child if born.

At the end of life, similar conflicts are evident between efforts to make decisions which truly prioritise the medical needs of patients and those which are based on assumptions that involve prejudice and discrimination. For example, the making of 'do not resuscitate' orders (DNR) is one area in which flawed assumptions about the value and quality of impaired lives may both override the opinions of disabled individuals themselves and their families, and also underestimate the value of 'disabled' lives. This topic along with other end-of-life issues will be examined in detail in Chapter 5.

What has gone before – and what follows – suggests that it is particularly important to ensure that genuine efforts to address the health needs of disabled people are not obstructed or undermined by bias and prejudicial perceptions of disability that should be irrelevant to the case in hand. This issue is an important one for our ethico-legal work because it dictates whether disabled people are treated fairly in the clinical decisions that are made concerning the beginning and end of their lives or whether they are discriminated against. As we have said, the medical model does not offer the theoretical resources to allow such concerns to be investigated in the detailed manner that an ethical and legal analysis of decision-making at the beginning and end of life requires. On the other hand, although the social model excels at the type of analysis in which the medical model lacks competency, it ignores or minimises the actual experience of people with impairment or disability.

In respect of the issues at the beginning of life, exponents of the social model would show no interest in medical judgements concerning the actual or potential impact of physical or mental impairments on an actual or potential life. Hence, social modellists would not be concerned with, or concede, suggestions that embryos or foetuses may lack crucial features of personhood or may suffer excessively if born. Rather, they would focus solely on the possibility that negative societal assumptions about the quality of disabled lives would implicitly or explicitly influence decisions in this area, that is, either prospective parents or medical professionals would decide that a nascent life should be prevented because it would be too burdensome for its holder. In this respect, exponents of the social model could point to a number of contentious decisions in which abortions have been performed for dubious reasons, including those involving infants with Down's syndrome and cleft palates.[55] Such cases, it could be suggested, show that clinical decisions are not always based on poor prognosis and severe impairment but on prejudices concerning disabled lives.

A similar concern exists concerning DNR at the end of life. That is, the social model would be concerned that the decisions in such cases are determined by prejudicial ideas about the capabilities and preferences of disabled people rather than on accurate diagnostic or prognostic judgements. Concerns over discrimination will hold in some cases and must be addressed. However, we have also seen in our critique of the social model that it fails to acknowledge the real difficulties that can be generated by impairment and it is crucial for clinical decisions to be able to focus on those experiential issues which the social model ignores or downplays.

Concerns about the application of both the medical and the social models make it difficult to determine when differential treatment crosses the threshold from being based on features which are relevant to the case at hand to those which are irrelevant and therefore a source of discrimination. In order to consider this distinction in greater detail it is necessary to assess briefly the nature of discrimination.

Discrimination

Discrimination arises when irrelevant criteria are used as if they were relevant. It can also occur when we reject or ignore the wishes and opinions of those who have the experience needed to make decisions, particularly if in doing so we are pushing an agenda, rather than listening to their voices. However, not all differentiation is to be equated with discrimination. Thus, the Disability Discrimination Act 1995 understands discrimination as biased, prejudicial treatment, but also allows for legitimate differential treatment which is proportionate to the circumstances of the case. In this respect, the Act states that a service provider discriminates against a disabled person if:

> (a) for a reason which relates to the disabled person's disability, he treats him less favourably than he treats or would treat others to whom that reason

---

55 See, for example, the following discussions of a late abortion for a cleft palate in the United Kingdom in 2001, Meikle, J., 'Cleft Lip Abortion Done in "Good Faith"', *The Guardian*, 17 March 2005; Jepson, J., 'Murder, even "in good faith"', is still murder, available at Telegraph.co.uk (accessed on 26 July 2005); Will, G.F., 'Eugenics by Abortion: Is Perfection an Entitlement?', 14 April 2005, available at Washingtonpost.com (accessed on 26 July 05).

does not or would not apply; and (b) he cannot show that the treatment in question is justified.[56]

Thus, it is not discriminatory to make separate and special arrangements to accommodate the fact of physical or mental disability or impairment. Differentiation does not inevitably imply discrimination. For example, to provide legislatively for wheelchair access to a building, while it recognises the physical limitations on the mobility of the person in the wheelchair, nonetheless does not discriminate against anyone. Rather, it differentiates the disabled person and the non-disabled person in a relevant and coherent way. While discrimination is always to be objected to, differentiation can be a positive and unobjectionable device aimed at achieving equality. Similarly, it could be legitimate not to sustain the life of an impaired adult because of severe impairment (for example, the patient in a Permanent Vegetative State, (PVS)), but in other cases careful consideration of whether decisions are based on impairments which really are severe or whether they are influenced by a predetermined dislike of disability is required. That is, the balancing of the benefits and burdens of treatment should be undertaken in the same way for people with impairment as would be the case for any other person.

A problem that persists for an ethico-legal treatment of disability is that literature in the area appears to lack a common language to enable us to differentiate between legitimate differentiation and discrimination. Efforts to overcome this theoretical shortcoming which has emerged from our assessment of the medical and social models of disability will form part of our focus in the remainder of this chapter and in the one which follows.

The issues which must be addressed by clinical decisions at the beginning and end of human life are neither purely social nor solely based on the experiences and problems which can be associated with mental, physical and sensory impairment. In this respect Oliver is correct to assert that we must not assume that the models of disability that we have examined 'can do everything'.[57] At the very least, to maximise the possibility that the wide range of issues raised by life-and-death decisions in the context of disability are addressed satisfactorily, it may be beneficial to utilise aspects of both the social and medical model. Thus, we will now turn to examining an alternative approach to disability which has recently been presented by the WHO.

Treading a middle path?: the biopsychosocial model

In 1980 the WHO published its *International Classification of Impairments, Disabilities and Handicaps* (ICIDH).[58] The ICIDH was intended to provide a

56 *Disability Discrimination Act 1995, Part III Discrimination in other Areas: Goods, Facilities, and Services*, 20, 1 (a), (b).
57 Oliver, *op.cit.*, 1996, 29–54.
58 WHO, *International Classification of Impairments, Disabilities, and Handicaps (ICIDH)* Geneva, WHO, 1980.

sound basis for public policy assessments of issues surrounding disability by moving away from the understanding of disability associated with the medical model and embracing key ideas derived from the social model.[59] The definitions used within the ICIDH were:

> Impairment: In the context of health experience, an impairment is any loss or abnormality of psychological, physiological or anatomical structure or function.
> Disability: In the context of health experience, a disability is any restriction or lack (resulting in impairment) of the ability to perform an activity in the manner or within the range considered normal for a human being.
> Handicap: In the context of health experience a handicap is a disadvantage for a given individual, resulting from an impairment or a disability, that limits or prevents the fulfilment of a role that is normal (depending on age, sex, and social and cultural factors) for that individual.[60] (original emphasis)

The definitions of impairment and disability used in the ICIDH received considerable amounts of criticism from disability theorists because they reproduced some of the most troubling features of the medical model.[61] As Barnes and Mercer state, in the ICIDH definition of disability the ' … stress is on functional limitations in the performance of daily living tasks'.[62] It has been claimed that this focus on the 'sick role' continued to disempower disabled people in exactly the same way as the medical model had.[63] The reliance of the ICIDH on this understanding of disability led it to overlook the contribution made by the social model. Indeed, one architect of the ICIDH classification, Mike Bury, has stated that the social model was seen to place too much emphasis on the social aspects of disability.[64] The team drafting the ICIDH thought that this emphasis risked obscuring the fact:

> … that chronic illness and disability are, in the majority of cases, closely related … one of the main reasons why the ICIDH in its original form created clear links between health and impairments, disabilities and handicaps, was not simply the prevalence of chronic disorders in modern societies. It was also that there was a concerted attempt, … to bring all

59 Bury, M., 'A Comment on the ICIDH2', *Disability and Society*, 15, 7, 2000, 1073–1077 at p. 1073f; Barnes and Mercer, *op. cit.*, p. 14; Marks, D., *Disability: Controversial Debates and Psychosocial Perspectives*, London and New York, Routledge, 1999 at p. 53.

60 WHO, *op. cit.*, 1980, p. 29.

61 Bury, *op. cit.*, p. 1074; Barnes and Mercer, *op. cit.*, p. 14; Pfeiffer, D., 'The ICIDH and the Need for its Revision', *Disability and Society*, 13, 4, 1998, 503–523.

62 Barnes and Mercer, *op. cit.*, p. 14.

63 Pfeiffer, D., 'The Devils Are in the Details: The ICIDH2 and the Disability Movement', *Disability and Society*, 15, 7, 2000, 1079–1082 at p. 1080.

64 Bury, *op. cit.*, p. 1074.

manner of social phenomena under the disability umbrella. So, for example, at one conference in the mid-1970s, arguments were put forward that unemployment and poverty should be regarded as a disability ... This struck us at the time to be quite untenable, and to introduce so many issues into the ICIDH that it would become almost meaningless.[65]

Thus, the drafting team was concerned that giving too much emphasis to the social aspects of disability risked overshadowing the idea that physical and mental impairments should be an important consideration for public policy work in this area. We have seen that some members of the disability community have also taken issue with the failure of the social model to focus on the experiences and issues associated with impairment. However, despite concerns regarding the overemphasis given to the social aspects of disability, Bury explains that the definition of handicap adopted by the ICIDH was intended as a tool to focus more attention on 'social exclusion' of disabled persons.[66] Nonetheless, as Thomas recently explained:

> ...despite this move in the direction of social consequences and determination, most social modellists have opposed the ICIDH on the grounds that it retains a medical model causal link between impairment and disability...and because the term 'handicap'...just does not do the job of re-centring the problems of disability in social arrangements and practices.[67]

In light of the reservations expressed over the ICIDH, the WHO began the job of redrafting the classification in the early 1990s.[68] The process came to fruition in 2001 with the publication of the WHO's *International Classification of Functioning, Disability and Health* (ICF).[69] The WHO promotes the ICF as a classification of disability which arguably takes the best elements of the social and medical models of disability, fusing these into what it terms the biopsychosocial model.[70] This development was thought necessary because, as the WHO stated:

> On their own, neither model is adequate, although both are partially valid. Disability is a complex phenomena [*sic*] that is both a problem at the level

---

65 *Id.*

66 *Id.*

67 Thomas, C., 'Disability Theory: Key Ideas, Issues and Thinkers', *Disability Studies Today*, Barnes, C. *et al.* (eds), Oxford, Polity Press, 38–57 at p. 42.

68 Pfeiffer, D., 'The ICIDH and the Need for Revision', *Disability and Society*, 13, 4, 1998, 503–523, at p. 506f; Hurst, R., 'To Revise or Not to Revise', *Disability and Society*, 15, 7, 2000, 1083–1087 at p. 1084f.

69 WHO, *International Classification of Functioning, Disability and Health*, Geneva, WHO, 2001.

70 WHO, *Towards a Common Language for Functioning, Disability and Health: ICF*, Geneva, WHO, 2002 at p. 9.

of a person's body, and a complex and primarily social phenomena [*sic*]. Disability is always an interaction between features of the person and features of the overall context in which the person lives, but some aspects of disability are almost entirely internal to the person, while another aspect is almost entirely external. In other words, both medical and social responses are appropriate to the problems associated with disability; we cannot wholly reject either kind of intervention.[71]

The ICF uses both the terms 'disability' and 'functioning' in a manner which is sufficiently general to allow for either of these features to be influenced by bodily functions, limitations of activity or social restrictions which place limitations on performance.[72] The WHO states:

> *Functioning* is an umbrella term encompassing all body functions, activities and participation; similarly, *disability* serves as an umbrella term for impairments, activity limitations or participation restrictions.[73]

This way of conceptualising disability and functioning – concepts that are key to our analysis – endeavours to do justice to the complexity which we have suggested is inherent in life-and-death decision-making.

More specifically, the ICF is divided into two main parts: (1) Functioning and Disability and (2) Contextual Factors.[74] The first of these corresponds loosely to the more desirable aims of the medical model and the second to the social model. Each of these parts is sub-divided into two additional sections. The first main section, Functioning and Disability, is concerned with (A) Functions of the Body and Structures (physiological and anatomical) and (B) Activities and Participation (mobility, social life, self-care).[75] The section concerned with Functions of the Body is intended to provide the tools to assess whether and to what degree the physiological functions of the body are impaired.[76] In this respect, impairments are understood to represent ' . . . a deviation from certain generally accepted population standards in the biomedical status of the body and its functions'.[77] The aim of the section on Activities and Participation is to measure both how the individuals are able to perform in their current environment and also their potential capacity for performance.[78]

---

71 WHO, *Towards a Common Language for Functioning, Disability and Health: ICF*, Geneva, WHO, 2002 at p. 9.
72 WHO, ICF: Introduction, Geneva, WHO, 2001 at p. 3.
73 *Ibid.*
74 *Ibid.*, p. 10 ff.
75 *Ibid.*, p. 12–17.
76 *Ibid.*, p. 12.
77 *Id.*
78 *Ibid.*, p. 15.

normal, and these must be resisted and challenged. As a rule, the more restrictive the range of normal human variation is conceived to be, the less likely that resources will be fairly distributed.[94]

Expanding the concept of what is normal within human experience in this way means that this model also provides a useful resource with which to resist the temptation, which we have identified in the medical model, to idealise 'able-bodiedness'.

The ICF has received a mixed reaction from disability theorists. While some maintain that it has been drafted in a manner which attends to the concerns of disabled people,[95] others reject it on the grounds that its 'functional' understanding of disability, long critiqued in the medical model, shows a '...disregard of the views of people labelled disabled'.[96] There does, however, appear to be some agreement that the ICF is better situated than its predecessor (the ICIDH) to ' ...open up new possibilities for a socio-medical analysis of disablement...'.[97] But this seems to be largely because it can be 'used as an international example of how the environmental impacts are the key to understanding the nature of disability/disablement and how solutions must come through social change.[98]

Hence it remains important to ensure that healthcare decisions – perhaps particularly at the beginning and end of life – draw on an understanding of disability that is sufficiently attentive to the ramifications of physical and mental impairment for a person's well-being or quality of life. Yet it is also imperative to appreciate the potential of negative social attitudes to influence detrimentally what are apparently value-free clinical decisions.

Conclusion

The issues raised by efforts to conceptualise disability are complex. Alone, neither the medical nor the social model is, we would argue, sufficiently nuanced to do justice to this complexity. This is because the medical model tends to overlook the role of bias and discrimination and the social model exhibits a tendency to deny that disability has any roots in physical and mental impairment. It may be the case that efforts to promote the rights of people with impairments in certain areas of life – for example, in respect of access to transportation or

94 Bickenbach, J.E. et al., op. cit., p. 1183.
95 Thomas, C., 'Disability Theory: Key Ideas, Issues and Thinkers', Disability Studies Today, Barnes, C. et al. (eds), 38–57, Oxford, Polity Press at p. 42.
96 Pfeiffer, D., 'The Devils are in the Details: The ICIDH2 and the Disability Movement', Disability and Society, 15, 7, 2000, 1079–1082 at p. 1079.
97 Barnes and Mercer, op. cit., p. 14.
98 Hurst, R., 'To Revise or Not to Revise?', Disability and Society, 15, 7, 2000, 1083–1087 at p. 1086.

access to buildings – are best couched in social rather than medical terms. However, this approach is not one that can be adopted exclusively in respect of life-and-death decision-making because the issues which *should* be at the heart of such debates are based firmly on the effects of physical and mental impairments. This is not, however, to deny the importance of critiquing the social discrimination that can unjustly influence such decisions.

The WHO's efforts to produce a framework for understanding disability that is able to harness the positive contributions of the medical and social approaches to disability is, we believe, to be welcomed. However, as the reservations of some disability scholars show, this approach is still associated with the worst aspects of the medical model. Thus, adopting this way of conceptualising disability could be a disadvantage because it may unnecessarily alienate crucial participants in the disability debate. That said, two aspects of this approach have particular value. First, its approach to 'disability' and 'functioning' is sufficiently general to allow us to see that many different features (physiological and social) are important. Second, its universal conceptualisation of disability is also to be welcomed. An important weapon in the crusade against discrimination and marginalisation is the ability to exhibit how difference and otherness are merely a different point on a continuum of universal human experience.

Finally, it must be emphasised that the commitments enunciated by the exponents of the medical and social models of disability fail to articulate the basic concerns which the two camps should share – such as the desire to support the well-being of people with impairments. One ramification of this apparent disunity is that it undermines efforts to determine which treatment at the beginning and end of life should be seen as justly differential and which as unjust discrimination. That is, because the different models fail to make explicit any ethical principles or concepts that they may share, it is difficult to compare and measure their different concerns about discrimination and impairment; there appears to be no common ground. In Chapter 3 we will argue that discourse on disability would benefit from drawing more explicitly on key bioethical principles, rather than focussing on a model of disability pure and simple.

Chapter 3

Towards ethical cohesion

Introduction: foundational principles of healthcare ethics

Healthcare ethics and other forms of applied ethics share a commitment to support the well-being of human beings. This commitment is often expressed by appeals to a range of foundational principles such as 'human dignity', the 'sanctity of life' and 'respect for persons'. These principles aim to provide a common language with which to articulate our convictions about what enables humans to flourish and the circumstances that denigrate human well-being. In this chapter we will investigate whether any of these basic ethical resources have the potential to give cohesion to an analysis of disability and impairment and in so doing minimise the difficulties that have been identified in the previous chapter. In addition we will outline other secondary ethical principles and concepts that help to support and facilitate any of the foundational principles that are found to be valuable for our argument.

Despite the practical benefits that may be gleaned from drawing on these different foundational and facilitating principles in discussions of disability and impairment, they also pose a range of problems which must be critically evaluated. First, while the foundational principles can be used to express a common commitment to human well-being, they can also be employed in different ways to allow each principle to highlight slightly different characteristics that make human life valuable. These differences need to be identified and their potential impact on our efforts to find common ground in the debates on disability and impairment analysed. Second, the foundational and facilitating principles are so fundamental to debates in healthcare ethics that they are often invoked by those who stand on opposing sides of the same debates. This is a concern that can undermine our endeavour to bring cohesion to disability debates by relying on ethical principles. In addition each foundational and facilitating principle has received criticism which must be assessed in order to test its significance for our overall framework. Finally, it must be borne in mind throughout the following examination that:

> ...the disability community has not thought very highly of the mainstream bioethics agenda. To be blunt, disability scholars and activists wonder why bioethicists are more concerned about preventing people with disabilities

from being born, or killing them off as soon as possible, than ensuring that people with disabilities are relieved from the burdens society imposes and which prevent their full participation in areas of life and living.[1]

Hence the assumption pervades much disability literature that the primary interest of bioethicists is to argue against the value of disabled lives and for the liberalisation of clinical practices that prevent or end impaired lives. However, drawing on a more sophisticated understanding of disability and impairment, our ethical analysis will investigate whether or not bioethics can in fact help to expose and reduce the discriminatory attitudes that may detrimentally influence life-and-death decision-making. This question will also underpin our consideration of the response of the law at the beginning and end of life.

Foundational principle: human dignity

We can begin to identify what is protected by an appeal to the principle of human dignity by noting that its etymological roots (Lat. *dignitas*, literally 'worth') point to the conviction that humans have a special value.[2] It is, therefore, easy to associate efforts to protect human dignity with initiatives to safeguard traits which are seen as characteristically human. However, Schachter states that the meaning and content of the human dignity principle have essentially been left to 'intuitive understanding' rather than being clearly conceptualised.[3] Additionally, Gaylin remarks, [c]ertain concepts – like certain books with cachet – are prominently 'displayed' and discussed in intellectual abodes, while remaining essentially unexplored. Human dignity is one such concept.[4]

Yet the importance of affirming human dignity is supported – and its aims further clarified – by its ubiquity in a wide range of ethical, legal and policy documents. As Schachter states, dignity:

> . . . has acquired a resonance that leads it to be invoked widely as a legal and moral ground for protest against degrading and abusive treatment. No other ideal seems so clearly accepted as a universal social good.[5]

---

1 Bickenbach, J., 'Disability Studies and Bioethics: A Comment on Kuczewski', *American Journal of Bioethics*, 2001, 1, 3, 49–50 at p. 49f.

2 The point made by some that historically the term 'dignity' was associated with the honour of elite groups need not impede this contemporary interpretation; a suggestion that is substantiated by the widespread use of the term in modern times as an egalitarian and not elitist manner. See Kass, L., *Life, Liberty and the Defense of Dignity*, San Francisco, Encounter Books, 2002 at p. 15ff.

3 Schachter, O., 'Human Dignity as a Normative Concept', *AJIL*, 77, 848–854, 1983 at p. 849.

4 Gaylin, W., 'In Defense of the Dignity of Being Human', *Hastings Center Report*, August 1984, 18–22 at p. 18.

5 Schachter, *op. cit.*, p. 849.

Arguably one of the clearest and most familiar uses of the principle appears in the Charter of the United Nations. This document highlights the need to support the 'inherent dignity...of all members of the human family'.[6] The UN also supports the idea of human dignity in its 1948 Universal Declaration of Human Rights. Article 1 of this document states 'All human beings are born free and equal in dignity...they are endowed with reason and conscience and should act towards one another in a spirit of brotherhood'.[7] The commitment of the UN to human dignity is explained by the context in which the organisation was established; namely, the aftermath of the Second World War and the legion of abuses that had deprived many of life. The need to affirm the principle of human dignity in biomedical ethics is explained by the fact that many of the abuses which took place during the Second World War were carried out under the umbrella of healthcare. For example, Pence explains that during this period:

> ...some medical experimentation took disturbing or even horrifying forms...Japanese physicians carried out deadly experiments on Chinese prisoners of war...These Chinese prisoners were injected with dozens of diseases to study the natural course of anthrax, syphilis, plague, cholera...It was Nazi Germany, though, which became – and remained – a symbol of the perversion of medical research...Physicians sympathetic to Nazi ideology participated in programs in which the disabled, insane, and comatose patients were involuntarily killed...In addition to 'euthanasia', there was also a great deal of experimentation on human subjects, much of which was at least irregular and at worst almost unimaginably savage and brutal.[8]

The commitment to protecting human dignity that followed in the wake of such exploitation was clearly intended to prevent its re-occurrence.[9]

In the contemporary world, ethico-legal debates and national and international policy documents continue to emphasise the need to support and respect human dignity but increasingly focus on the impact of peacetime developments in biomedicine. That is, developments in biomedicine and the provision of healthcare now aim to support human dignity without the torturous research methods that in the past ignored the wishes and interests of research subjects.

---

6 *Charter of the United Nations*, available at http://www.un.org/aboutun/charter/ (accessed on 1 August 2005).
7 *Universal Declaration of Human Rights*, available at http://www.unhchr.ch/udhr/lang/eng.htm (accessed on 1 August 2005).
8 Pence, G.E., *Classic Cases in Medical Ethics* (4th Ed), New York, McGrawHill, 2004 at pp. 270–271.
9 See also the UN's *International Covenant on Civil and Political Rights* (Art 10) and the *International Covenant on Economic, Social and Cultural Rights* (Art 13) both adopted in 1966 and which entered into force in 1976, available at http://www.ohchr.org/english/law/index.htm (accessed on 1 August 2005).

However, questions are still raised over whether biomedical techniques that are intended to benefit individuals always respect human dignity. As Bayertz comments:

> On the one hand, there can be no doubt that science and technology in their specifically modern interpretations are manifestations of human dignity. They have become (theoretically) perhaps the most unambiguous expression of human rationality, and (practically) decisive means within the process of human self-unfolding... There can be little doubt, however, that this success is profoundly ambivalent. Progress in science and technology... ha[s] begun to undermine the natural basis of human existence.[10]

Importantly, a variety of documents and other statements emanating from a range of sources have emphasised the importance of building on the UN's commitment to human dignity to help ensure that biotechnology developments and healthcare support do not denigrate the value (dignity) of human life. For example, in the Preamble to its 1997 *Convention for the Protection of Human Rights and Dignity of the Human Being with regard to the Application of Biology and Medicine: Convention on Human Rights and Biomedicine* the Council of Europe states signatories of the document declare themselves to be '[c]onscious that the misuse of biology and medicine may lead to acts endangering human dignity';[11] and Art 1 declares that 'Parties to this Convention shall protect the dignity and identity of all human beings...'[12] This enduring commitment to human dignity is important. Even more significant for our purposes is that many of the issues in biomedicine where the concept of human dignity is invoked concern the beginning and end of human life and have particular relevance for the treatment disabled (impaired) people receive in healthcare institutions.

Debates on ethical issues at the beginning of life that involve appeals to human dignity have traditionally focused on issues such as the termination of pregnancy. Developments in genomic technology have intensified concerns over the appropriate treatment of embryos and foetuses. In this respect, of particular interest are techniques such as preimplantation genetic diagnosis (PGD) and prenatal screening. These issues will be examined in detail in Chapter 4. Here, however, it is sufficient to note that such techniques are often seen to have the capacity to both threaten and to safeguard human dignity. That is, for some they are advances that help to support the dignity of human life because they promise

10 Bayertz, K., 'Human Dignity: Philosophical Origin and Scientific Erosion of an Idea', in Bayertz, K. (ed), *Sanctity of Life and Human Dignity*, Dordrecht and London, Kluwer Academic Publishers, 1996, 73–90 at p. 82f.
11 Council of Europe, 1997 at http://conventions.coe.int/treaty/en/treaties/html/164.htm (accessed on 1 August 2005).
12 *Ibid.*

to improve human health and alleviate suffering by, for example, minimising the number of infants born with impairments and genetic disease. Or, they may be seen as examples of respecting the human dignity of those already born, by respecting their reproductive liberty.[13] However, others express concern that eliminating or seeking to minimise the existence of people with genetic impairment actually offends human dignity. For example, the United States Conference of Catholic Bishops states:

> Experience suggests that widespread use of screening could raise abortion, or other violations of human dignity like forced sterilization, to the level of social tools... Genetic screens could allow misguided governments to employ abortion and sterilization not only to control the number of their citizens, but also to prevent the birth of people who might become a welfare 'burden'.[14]

The concern that advances in biotechnology may devalue human life is shared by many disability organisations. For example, Disabled Peoples International (DPI) question:

> How can we live with dignity in societies that spend millions on genetic research to eradicate disease and impairment, but refuse to meet our needs to live dignified and independent lives? We cannot. We will not. The genetic threat to us is a threat to everyone.[15]

In the context of such concerns, in 1997 the United Nations Educational, Scientific and Cultural Organisation (UNECSO) issued a *Universal Declaration on the Human Genome and Human Rights*. This document identifies the need to balance the positive and negative ramifications that may be associated with the use of genetic technology. It states:

> Article 1: The human genome underlies the fundamental unity of all members of the human family, as well as the recognition of their inherent dignity and diversity. In a symbolic sense, it is the heritage of humanity.
> Article 2: (a) Everyone has a right to respect for their dignity and for their rights regardless of their genetic characteristics.

---

13 For further discussion of this argument, see McLean, S.A.M., *Modern Dilemmas: Choosing Children*, Edinburgh, Capercaillie Press, 2006.
14 United States Conference of Catholic Bishops, Committee on Science and Human Values, 'The Promise and Peril of Genetic Screening', 1996, available at http://www.usccb.org/shv/ screening.htm (accessed on 1 August 2005).
15 Disabled Peoples International (DPI), *Disabled People Speak on the New Genetics: DPI Europe Position Statement on Bioethics and Human Rights*, London, 2000 at p. 4, available at http://www.dpieurope.org/htm/bioethics/ dpsngfullreport.htm (accessed on 1 August 2005).

(b) That dignity makes it imperative not to reduce individuals to their genetic characteristics and to respect their uniqueness and diversity.
Article 6: No one shall be subjected to discrimination based on genetic characteristics that is intended to infringe or has the effect of infringing human rights, fundamental freedoms and human dignity.[16]

This suggests that, while knowledge of the human genome holds great potential for humanity, the way in which this knowledge is used will determine whether it undermines human dignity. Of concern for our attempts to identify ethical convictions that may unify debates on disability is that the principle of human dignity appears so broad that it can be used to justify actions and positions which often conflict. This being so, invoking the principle of human dignity may do little to resolve debates in this area.

More recently, in 2005, the International Bioethics Committee of UNESCO promulgated the Universal Declaration on Bioethics and Human Rights which states in Art 3 that 'Human dignity, human rights and fundamental freedoms are to be fully respected.'[17] Thus, for UNESCO at least, there seems to be an enduring value in appealing to respect for human dignity as a benchmark and fundamental ethical commitment.

Appeals to human dignity are also frequently found in the debates that are conducted at the end of life. As Sandman states:

> ...in palliative care we often hear references to the idea of a 'death with dignity' or a 'dignified death' in different forms. Dignity is obviously one of the more central concepts in discussions on the topic of a good death...[18]

More specifically, in the seemingly intractable and long-running disputes over assisted suicide and voluntary euthanasia there are frequent reminders of the need to protect human dignity. Amongst those who argue that human dignity is supported by euthanasia and assisted suicide is the Voluntary Euthanasia Society (VES) which states '[o]ur vision is for everyone to be guaranteed choice and dignity at the end of their life, to help take away the fear of the process of dying.'[19] The human rights organisation Liberty quotes Diane Pretty as saying that her legal fight to ensure that her husband would be immune from prosecution if he assisted her to commit suicide was based on her desire to

---

16 UNESCO, *Universal Declaration on the Human Genome and Human Rights*, 1997, available at http://unesdoc.unesco.org/images/0011/001102/110220e.pdf#page=47 (accessed on 1 August 2005).
17 Available at http://portal.unesco.org/shs/en/ev.php-URL_ID=1879&URL_DO=DO_TOPIC&URL_SECTION=201.html (accessed on 5 July 2006).
18 Sandman, L., 'What's the Use of Human Dignity within Palliative Care?' *Nursing Philosophy*, 3, 177–181, 2002 at p. 177.
19 See http://www.dignityindying.org.uk/ (accessed on 1 June 2006).

secure '... the right to die at the time of my choosing, with dignity...'.[20] By contrast, the Catholic Church views euthanasia as an *attack* on human dignity:

> ...no one is permitted to ask for this act of killing, either for himself or herself or for another person entrusted to his or her care, nor can he or she consent to it, either explicitly or implicitly, nor can any authority legitimately recommend or permit such an action. For it is a question of the violation of the divine law, an offence against the dignity of the human person, a crime against life, and an attack on humanity at the beginning and end of life.[21]

Thus, in 2004, John Paul II could state:

> *Euthanasia* is one of those tragedies caused by an ethic that claims to dictate who should live and who should die. Even if it is motivated by sentiments of a misconstrued compassion or of a misunderstood preservation of dignity, euthanasia actually eliminates the person instead of relieving the individual of suffering.[22]

Debates at the end of life show that the principle of human dignity can be employed either to legitimise or to condemn a wide range of behaviour. Although the principle is employed in a number of prestigious documents, concerns have been expressed over its usefulness. Horton, for example, says that human dignity '... is a linguistic currency that will buy a basketful of extraordinary meanings'.[23] Macklin is even more dismissive in her assertion that '[d]ignity is a useless concept in medical ethics and can be eliminated without any loss of content'.[24]

In light of such concerns, others have tried to identify the nature of human dignity with more precision. Kilner, for example, suggests a number of more specific features associated with appeals to human dignity. He states that the concept is usually called on:

> ...in situations in which the worth of human beings is brought into question when they are used, forced, or injured. Human beings should not be used

20 Liberty, 'First Ever Right-to-Die Case Under the Human Rights Act', Press Release, 20 August 2001, available at http://www.liberty-human-rights.org.uk/press/press-releases-2001/first-ever-right-to-die-case-under-the-human-rig.shtml (accessed on 1 August 2005).

21 Sacred Congregation for the Doctrine of the Faith, *Declaration on Euthanasia*, 1980, available at http://www.vatican.va/roman_curia/congregations/cfaith/documents/rc_con_cfaith_doc_19800505_euthanasia_en.html (accessed on 1 August 2005).

22 Address of John Paul II to the Participants in the 19th International Conference of the Pontifical Council for Health Pastoral Care, Friday, 12 November 2004, available at http://www.vatican.va/holy_father/john_paul_ii/speeches/2004/november/documents/hf_jp-ii_spe_20041112_pc-hlthwork_en.html (accessed on 1 August 2005).

23 Horton, R., 'Rediscovering Human Dignity', *The Lancet*, 364, 1081–1085, 2004 at p. 1081.

24 Macklin, R., 'Dignity Is a Useless Concept', *BMJ*, 327, 2003, 1419–1420 at p. 1420.

because their dignity requires that they be treated as having intrinsic, not merely instrumental, worth. They should not usually be forced because their dignity mandates that their wishes be respected. They should not normally be injured because their dignity entails that their well-being be preserved.[25]

The association between autonomy and dignity has also been highlighted by Beyleveld and Brownsword who claim that:

> ... the essence of the dignity of agents resides in their capacity to choose, to set their own ends ... we respect ... dignity by creating the conditions and opportunities for choice and recognising agents as sources of informed choice.[26]

Similarly in his efforts to identify the content of the term dignity, Schachter draws on Kant's requirement that people should not be used solely as a means to another person's end.[27] On this basis he suggests that supporting human dignity requires respecting 'the will and consent' of individuals, avoiding coercion, recognising that an individual is 'entitled to have his or her beliefs, attitudes, ideas and feelings' respected and that 'respect for individuals and their choices also implies proper regard for the responsibility as individuals'.[28] Schacter goes on to list a range of behaviours that denigrate human dignity. Some of these are particularly relevant for our consideration of the treatment of disabled (impaired) people at the beginning and end of life:

> (3) Denial of the capacity of a person to assert claims to basic rights.
> (5) Dissemination of negative stereotypes of groups ... and implications that members of such groups are inferior.
> (12) Medical treatment or hospital care insensitive to individual choice or the requirements of human personality.[29]

In the context of disability and life-and-death decision-making the points raised by Schacter are reflected in a number of ways. Concerns exist over whether in healthcare environments disabled people are assumed to lack the ability (capacity) to make decisions about their treatment options because they have an impairment; assumed to have a poor quality of life and so receive inappropriate, inadequate or no treatment; bracketed together in a manner that does not allow

---

25 Kilner, J.F., 'Human Dignity', *Encyclopedia of Bioethics* (3rd Ed), Post, S.G. (ed) 1193–1200, New York, MacMillan Reference, 2004 at p. 1197–1198.

26 Beyleveld, D. and Brownsword, R., *Human Dignity in Bioethics and Biolaw*, Oxford, Oxford University Press, 2001 at p. 5.

27 Schachter, *op. cit.*, p. 849.

28 *Ibid.*, p. 849f.

29 *Ibid.*, p. 852f.

for their healthcare needs to be assessed on a case-by-case basis because they are viewed primarily through a lens which has predetermined ideas about the needs of 'disabled' people. This suggests that supporting the dignity of disabled and impaired people could help to resolve concerns that exist at the beginning and end of life.

However, efforts to avoid human dignity being applied in a wide variety of conflicting ways by adding further specification to the principle may result in it losing any distinctive content. Macklin, for example, suggests that efforts to flesh out the principle of human dignity invariably stray into areas that are more comfortably addressed by other ethical principles and concepts. She states '... appeals to dignity are either vague restatements of other, more precise, notions or mere slogans that add nothing to an understanding of the topic'.[30] Thus, in the context of requests to 'die with dignity' Macklin explains that '... dignity seems to be nothing other than respect for autonomy'.[31] This suggestion is partially supported by the efforts of Kilner and Schacter to explain the content of human dignity by drawing on concepts such as rationality, the capacity to choose and personal freedom.

Yet Macklin's concern does not hold in cases where we perceive that there is a need to protect a human quality that is hard to identify. The question of intrinsic worth is, for example, often at issue in cases at the beginning of life. In such cases, the dilemmas do not relate to the autonomy or rationality of the embryo or foetus – although they can invoke the potential of the embryo or foetus to develop such characteristic human features – but to a value or worth (dignity) which is difficult to discern. But we have seen that efforts to use vague normative concepts allow for a wide variety of interpretations to be placed on them. We will return to this later in our assessment of the sanctity of life.

This investigation of human dignity was inspired by its foundational status within bioethics and the endeavour to determine whether this (and similar) ethical principles could help us to highlight any common goals which may underlie the conflicts in disability studies between the medical and social models. The consensus that exists over the importance of protecting human dignity offered hope that this principle could be used to identify convictions shared by participants in debates concerning the appropriate understanding of disability and the most appropriate ways of responding to it. However, beyond this most basic agreement it seems that efforts to utilise the principle of human dignity to unify debates generates many problems which are difficult to overcome.

Finally in this section, it is important to note that the concerns which have been identified over the interpretation and application of human dignity replicate the conflicts which exist between the different interpretations of disability associated

30 Macklin, *op. cit.*, p. 1419.
31 *Id.*

with the medical and social models. That is, for some, biomedical technology is a testament to the worth of human beings and offers a way to promote our dignity. This position is one which can be associated with the medical model. For others, the application of such technological advances carries a risk that they will be utilised in a manner that disvalues human lives; a claim that mirrors the issues raised by exponents of the social model of disability. This suggests that the disagreements that we identified between the medical and social model may in fact be a facet of a more general conflict between competing world views. This being so, it could be the case that ethical principles will not help us to resolve the dispute between distinct philosophical perspectives but only enable us to identify with more precision what is at the heart of such disputes.

Foundational principle: sanctity of life

Another important foundational principle within biomedical and healthcare ethics is the sanctity of life. Most fundamentally, like human dignity, the sanctity-of-life principle holds that human life is unique and should be valued for its own sake. It follows from this that the treatment of human beings should revere and promote their special nature. Exponents of the idea that life is sacred hold that it is both necessary and possible to identify and prevent actions and policies that denigrate the special nature of human life. As Keenan suggests '... the term is not about what we ought to do, but, what we cannot do'.[32]

The claim that all human life is 'sacred' originated in a religious context and is particularly dependent on the conviction that life is a 'divine gift' and that human beings are fashioned *imago dei* (in the image of God). It is these dual claims that support the belief that humans have a special status in the world order. As theologian and bioethicist Norman Ford explains:

> In the light of God's creative design and absolute dominion over human life and persons' responsibility for it, there is an ethical duty to respect human life. The Bible portrays human life as sacred from conception. Put negatively from a biblical perspective, it is immoral to directly intend to terminate, or needlessly risk, God's gift of human life.[33]

Its religious associations have led the sanctity-of-life principle to be associated with 'vitalism', a philosophical stance that requires human life to be 'preserved at all costs'.[34] This position is based on the conviction that life is an absolute good and

---

32 Keenan, J.F., 'The Concept of Sanctity of Life and Its Use in Contemporary Bioethical Discussion', in Bayertz, K. (ed.), *Sanctity of Life and Human Dignity*, Dordrecht and London, Kluwer Academic Publishers, 1996, 1–18 at p. 3.

33 Ford, N., *The Prenatal Person: Ethics from Conception to Birth*, London, Blackwell, 2002 at p. 43.

34 Cf Keown, J., *Euthanasia, Ethics and Public Policy: An Argument Against Legalisation*, Cambridge, Cambridge University Press, 2002 at p. 39.

requires no particular qualities or abilities to give it value or meaning. If this position were used to direct public policy on life-and-death decision-making it would be deemed morally desirable – even necessary – to go to any lengths possible to sustain a human life. This is because vitalism holds that it is unethical actively or passively to end a human life. Thus, the difficult decisions which some doctors and family members face, such as whether to withdraw life-sustaining treatment or to provide treatment to an impaired neonate, would cease to be questions at all.

The unequivocal, absolutist nature of this position may appeal to some because of the certainty and clarity it brings to issues that are renowned for raising seemingly intractable dilemmas. Exponents of the social model might welcome the capacity of this approach to provide an obstacle to discrimination by its insistence that all life is of absolute value and should therefore be protected. Taking this approach it would, for example, be unethical to withdraw or withhold the treatment from an impaired person on the grounds that his or her life is thought to lack value, or to prevent the birth of a child likely to have an impairment. On the other hand, the medical model, we have suggested, assumes certain logical consequences of impairment or disability that can lead to a position which does not in fact value all lives, merely those which are 'normal', or 'healthy', or which can be 'repaired'.

Furthermore, it is important to emphasise, however, that vitalism would also require the endless resuscitation of patients, regardless of their age, condition or quality of life and irrespective of their wishes. This is because when life is an absolute value it must be preserved at *all* costs. Thus, vitalism does not prioritise the need to preserve particular characteristic features of human life, but life *per se*. Hence, ultimately, this approach seems unlikely to be welcomed by exponents of either a medical or social approach to disability. This is because, while it may protect the lives (existence) of disabled people, it also threatens to disempower them should they want to make decisions about how to end their lives. Furthermore, a vitalist reading of the sanctity of life would impose a severe strain on healthcare resources, such that lives could in fact be endangered. That is, substantial resources would have to be employed to sustain lives which would never regain an ability to flourish (and which may not be wanted by the people living them), often at the expense of other lives which could. A vitalist reading of the sanctity-of-life ethic would, therefore, present considerable problems and would often result in decisions which were counterintuitive and perhaps counter-productive. However, most appeals to the sanctity of life are not vitalist. As Reich points out:

> ...generally speaking, the sanctity-of-life principle depends on moral judgments concerning qualities of human life that go beyond mere biological life to embrace mental, social, religious, and other qualities...[35]

---

35 Reich, W.T., 'Life: Quality of Life', in *Encyclopedia of Bioethics*, Reich, W.T. (ed), New York, Free Press, 1978, 829–840 at p. 834.

In this version of the sanctity-of-life principle, life need not be sustained at all costs. Such is the position of the Roman Catholic Church. As the 1980 *Declaration on Euthanasia* issued by the Vatican's Sacred Congregation for the Doctrine of the Faith stated:

> When inevitable death is imminent in spite of the means used, it is permitted in conscience to take the decision to refuse forms of treatment that would only secure a precarious and burdensome prolongation of life, so long as the normal care due to the sick person in similar cases is not interrupted.[36]

It continues:

> Life is a gift from God, and on the other hand death is unavoidable; it is necessary, therefore, that we, without in any way hastening the hour of death, should accept it with full responsibility and dignity.[37]

Rachels also contends that it is possible to interpret the sanctity of life in a manner that does not attribute absolute value to human life. That is, only human life of a certain sort has intrinsic value or is sacred:

> The doctrine of the sanctity of life can be understood as placing value on things that are alive. But it can also be understood as placing value on *lives* and on the interests that some creatures, including ourselves, have in virtue of the fact that they are the subjects of lives.[38]

This approach acknowledges that it is not mere biological existence that is 'sacred', but rather values 'higher' features which are characteristic of human life. In this respect it concurs with some of the more detailed expositions of human dignity that we examined in the previous section. That is, it affords value to human traits such as rationality and free choice. In doing this, the principle of the sanctity of life, like human dignity, seems to function as a substitute for a collection of other, more specific, principles and concepts. Hence, despite the prominence of both principles in bioethics literature and in policy documents their derivative nature calls into question their foundational status.

Foundational principle: respect for persons

Like human dignity and the sanctity of life, respect for persons is a principle that points to the general conviction that individuals are valuable and so should be

36 Sacred Congregation for the Doctrine of the Faith, *op. cit.*, n. IV.
37 *Ibid.*, n. IV.
38 Rachels, J., *The End of Life: Euthanasia and Morality*, Oxford, Oxford University Press, 1986 at p. 25.

treated in a manner that respects or promotes this value. We will contend that the foundational principle of respect for persons offers one of the most satisfactory tools with which to identify a common purpose in the ongoing debates between exponents of the social and medical models of disability. In this section we will also return to the issue we raised at the end of the assessment of human dignity, namely, that the efforts to unite and so assess the disparate claims associated with the medical and social models will fail because the disunity is part of a wider philosophical dispute. We argue that the principle of respect for persons helps to clarify such disputes because it actually supports such disagreements.

The principle of respect for persons is most famously articulated in the work of Immanuel Kant.[39] In Kant's work the principle of respect for persons is presented most clearly in the second version of his categorical imperative. The different formulations of the categorical imperative are, most simply, moral injunctions derived solely from reason which amount to saying 'if you want to be moral do x'; no further explanation or justification for right action is necessary. Although all three expressions of the categorical imperative are related, for our purposes the first and second are of particular importance and so attention will be restricted to them.

Kant explains the first part of the categorical imperative thus:

> There is, therefore, only a single categorical imperative and it is thus: *act only on the maxim through which you can at the same time will that it be a universal law.*[40]

In the context of our discussion, this maxim serves as a way of determining the right course of action in particular cases, or what the participants *ought* to do under the circumstances when they are faced with life-and-death decisions. The 'rightness' of actions is determined by asking whether that same decision could logically be made universally by all persons in the same position without it resulting in a self-defeating conclusion. As Onora O'Neill explains, it requires that principles '... that cannot serve for a plurality of agents are to be rejected ... Morality begins with the rejection of non-universalizable principles'.[41] The example often given of behaviour it would not be possible to universalise is telling a lie. That is, it would not be possible to will that everyone should lie because truth-telling would be devalued if this happened. Thus, when universalised, the idea of telling a lie would become nonsensical.

In respect of healthcare this principle would require fairness of treatment, or – more importantly – it would prevent treatment that, if universalised for all

39 Kant, I., *Groundwork of the Metaphysics of Morals*, 1785, Gregor, M. (trans., and ed), Cambridge, Cambridge University Press, 1997.
40 *Ibid.*, para 4.421 at p. 31.
41 O'Neill, O., 'Kantian Ethics', in Singer, P. (ed), *A Companion to Ethics*, Oxford, Blackwell, 1993, 175–185 at p. 176f.

humans in a similar condition and with similar needs, would have an undesirable impact on human well-being. Thus, this expression of the categorical imperative requires that all persons receive equal treatment. As Raphael states, it:

> ...is a method of avoiding partiality. It says that when you are considering whether an action is morally right or wrong, you should ask yourself whether you would want everyone to act in that way. In other words it is not moral to make exceptions for yourself.[42]

In the context of life-and-death decisions the principal issues are whether it is acceptable to prevent or to end a particular human life. Following the universal law principle requires, as a matter of duty, rejecting as unacceptable any behaviour that would 'destroy, damage or undermine capacities for action for some or for many'.[43] Hence it would not be acceptable to universalise choices arbitrarily to euthanise a patient or abort a foetus. However, such policies could be permissible if it is possible to show that such actions are only taken in specific circumstances, particularly if the individuals concerned lack and will not gain or regain 'capacities for action'. However, impairment and disability are often used to justify decisions to prevent or end human life and so to avoid the duty to preserve life. The difficulty is to judge precisely when an individual's physical or mental prognosis is such that it is acceptable to treat him or her in a manner which would not be an acceptable way to treat the majority of individuals. Given this concern, the contribution of this version of the categorical imperative lies in the pressure it exerts on decision makers to justify any judgements that prevent or end a human life.

The second version of Kant's categorical imperative is usually directly associated with the principle of respect for persons. It states:

> So act that you use humanity, whether in your own person or in the person of any other, always at the same time as an end, never merely as a means.[44]

This maxim conveys the conviction that it is important to safeguard the interests of individuals by supporting their rationally formulated preferences or desires concerning what they want from certain situations, or indeed from their lives as a whole. As O'Neill explains, individuals should act '... in ways that respect, so leave intact, others' capacities to act (and so, in effect, leave them able to act on the maxims we ourselves adopt)'.[45] This suggests that the important features of personhood include the abilities to make decisions and consciously follow through a course of action. Raphael explains that to '... treat a person as an end,

---

42 Raphael, D.D., *Moral Philosophy* (2nd Ed.), Oxford, Oxford University Press, 1994 at p. 56.
43 O'Neill, O., *Autonomy and Trust in Bioethics*, Cambridge, Cambridge University Press, 2002 at p. 88.
44 Kant, *op. cit.*, para 4.429, p. 38.
45 O'Neill, *op. cit.*, p. 178.

then, is to help fulfil his desires and to allow or enable him to carry out his decisions'.[46] Thus, the principle of respect for persons requires that we show regard for the interest of others and do not merely use them as tools to fulfil or satisfy our own interests. It would be morally wrong for decisions in healthcare (as in other areas) to be made in a manner that did not pay heed to the interests of the subject.

This principle, like the others we have examined, affords value to human lives that have decision-making capacities and disvalues lives which lack such abilities. In the context of debates on disability this again complicates efforts to ensure that persons are respected by the decisions which are made in healthcare at the beginning and end of life. Importantly, it is not strict adherence to the principle that is problematic but the tendency to rely on stereotypical assumptions concerning the impact of impairments – even relatively minor physical impairments – on an individual's rational capacities. This position in turn allows for paternalistic decisions regarding an individual's quality of life. Yet it is also true that philosophy has done little to correct such exclusivity as part of its pursuit of fairness and equality. That is, the Kantian concept of the person is, in the very least, inattentive to the interests of impaired individuals. As Ford explains, in Kant's theory:

> Only beings who possess the capacity for autonomy, or 'moral agency', are morally valuable, are 'persons' in the Kantian sense. Such beings can have moral obligations towards one another. The rest are non-persons . . . [47]

Similarly, Kittay raises concerns that Kant's position on personhood is based on:

> . . . a fiction that the incapacity to function as a fully cooperating societal member is an exception in human life, not a normal variation; that the dependency is normally too brief and episodic to concern political life, rather then constituted by periodic, and often prolonged, phases of our lives whose costs and burdens ought to be shared.[48]

This concern regarding the tendency to denigrate the value of impaired lives has recently been investigated in the work of one of the most well-known contemporary exponents of Kantian thought, philosopher John Rawls. However, one aspect of Rawls' work has received criticism for omitting consideration of impairment and dependency, his well-known theory of justice.

46 Raphael, D.D., *Moral Philosophy* (2nd Ed.), Oxford, Oxford University Press, 1994 at p. 57.
47 Ford, M., 'The Personhood Paradox and the "Right to Die"', MLR, 13, Spring 2005, 80–101 at p. 84.
48 Kittay, E.F., *Love's Labour: Essays on Women, Equality, and Dependency*, London, Routledge, 1999 at p. 92.

In *A Theory of Justice*, Rawls presents an egalitarian theory in which he portrays 'justice as fairness'.[49] One of the key aims of Rawls' theory is to provide an alternative to the utilitarian concepts of justice which were dominant at the time.[50] His concern is that within utilitarianism:

> ...there is no reason in principle why the greater gains of some should not compensate for the lesser losses of others; or more importantly, why the violation of the liberty of a few might not be made right by the greater good shared by many.[51]

Rawls is keen to reject the negative consequences that this theory can have for social minorities and to ensure that persons receive the respect they deserve. Thus, he formulates a concept of justice that is intended to overcome this difficulty by prioritising equal liberty and requiring that social policy is made in a manner which favours 'the greatest benefit of the least advantaged'.[52] Rawls argues that the interests of the least advantaged would be prioritised if social rules were made on a fair and impartial basis. However, we do not live in this type of social environment, so he creates what he terms the 'veil of ignorance' to represent such conditions. The veil of ignorance – a version of Kant's universalising principle – is a device that Rawls uses to provoke consideration of which social policies would be chosen if individuals were ignorant of their social roles. Rawls holds that only in such conditions would it be possible to identify social rules that do not aim disproportionately to benefit one social group or cause. He explains:

> Somehow we must nullify the effects of specific contingencies which put men at odds and tempt them to exploit social and natural circumstances to their own advantage. Now in order to do this I assume that the parties are situated behind a veil of ignorance. They do not know how the various alternatives will affect their own particular case and they are obliged to evaluate principles solely on the basis of general considerations.[53]

Rawls argues that when formulating policies from behind this veil of ignorance individuals will not make decisions that treat any group unfairly because they could themselves be a member of that group. Although we do not live in Rawls' ideal world, his theory provides a useful resource for determining the type of policies that should exist and with which to identify and confront discrimination against disabled people.

49 Rawls, J., *A Theory of Justice*, Oxford, Oxford University Press, 1971 at p. 11ff.
50 *Ibid.*, p. 22.
51 *Ibid.*, p. 26.
52 *Ibid.*, p. 302.
53 *Ibid.*, p. 136f.

Despite his intentions, the relevance of Rawls' work in respect of disability has been questioned.[54] At the root of such criticism is the fact that Rawls does not take account of disability and dependency within his work. Rather, he states at the beginning of *A Theory of Justice* that his aim is to present a theory that is a more generalised and abstract version of a social contract theory.[55] That is, it develops the efforts of enlightenment writers such as Kant and Locke to manage social relations on the basis of a *quid pro quo* agreement that is to the mutual advantage of all members of society. The original position, then, is an effort to recreate the 'state of nature', the starting point for the work of earlier social contract theorists, in which humans in a pre-political world were thought to be naturally free and equal.[56]

Kittay suggests that the implication of this position is that the partners within this contract are not dependent, frail, impaired or disabled.[57] Similarly, Nussbaum explains that:

> Rawls explicitly omits from the situation of basic political choice the more extreme forms of need and dependency human beings may experience. His very concept of social cooperation is based on the idea of reciprocity between rough equals and has no explicit place for relations of extreme dependency.[58]

It is certainly true that many people with disabilities and impairments are not dependent. However, many individuals who find themselves the subject at the heart of life-and-death decisions *will* be dependent on others. Furthermore, people with impairments may be incorrectly assumed to be dependent and, therefore, are not permitted to be active participants in their treatment plans or life decisions. Hence it is important that the Western philosophical tradition – and indeed other traditions – has the capacity and the desire to consider such issues in detail. Unfortunately, as MacIntyre has recently commented:

> From Plato to Moore and since there are usually, with some rare exceptions, only passing references to human vulnerability and affliction and to the connections between them and our dependence on others...And when the ill, the injured and the otherwise disabled *are* presented in the pages of moral philosophy books, it is almost always exclusively as possible subjects of benevolence by moral agents who are themselves presented as though they were continuously rational, healthy and untroubled.[59]

54 Kittay, *op. cit.*; Nussbaum, M., 'Disabled Lives: Who Cares?' *The New York Review of Books*, 11 January 2001.
55 Rawls, *op. cit.*, p. 11.
56 *Ibid.*, p. 12.
57 Kittay, *op. cit.*, p. 76.
58 Nussbaum, M., 'Long-Term Care and Social Justice: A Challenge to Conventional Ideas of the Social Contract', in World Health Organisation, *Ethical Choices in Long-Term Care: What Does Justice Require?* 31–65, Geneva, WHO, 2002 at p. 47.
59 MacIntyre, A., *Dependent Rational Animals: Why Human Beings Need the Virtues*, London, Duckworth, 1999 at p. 1f.

Kittay advances what she refers to as a 'dependency critique' in which she notes how pervasive dependency is within human life.[60] She claims that:

> Theories which do not consider dependency at their heart may be based on the concept of persons as moral equals, but they will result in a society in which the claim to equal moral worth cannot be realized for *all*.[61]

This emphasises that efforts to utilise the principle of respect for persons to unify debates on disability need to be self-critical and based on a more inclusive understanding of personhood than that which has traditionally dominated the Western philosophical tradition. It will also remain necessary to consider the severity of impairment in cases which concern life-and-death decisions.

As exponents of the social model of disability have highlighted, many of the problems disabled people encounter are not directly associated with their impairment(s). It is imperative that these insights are incorporated into, and analysed within, mainstream ethico-legal work. Only in this way will it be possible to employ valuable ethical principles like respect for persons in a manner that is attentive to the interests of people with impairments – some of whom are also dependent – without impeding their right to equal treatment. Mere lip service to respect for persons, without an honest attempt to interrogate its nuanced meaning, may simply reinforce division and prejudice, disguising unacceptable assumptions, as we will see in the following chapters.

Foundational principles: summary

The foundational principles of biomedical ethics share a conviction that human life is something special and should, therefore, usually be protected. Yet the ethical dilemmas that exist in the field of healthcare are testament to the fact that a commitment to these foundational principles often marks the beginning of an ethical debate rather than its end. This is because sometimes the principles employed are too vague to produce definitive solutions to complex problems since they leave room for disagreement over the best way to protect human well-being. However, disagreements also persist because debates are conducted in an ethico-legal milieu that values pluralism. That is, the importance of allowing individuals to make choices about how to direct their own lives is an important feature of the Western philosophical tradition, but it can lead to disagreement. This suggests that it could be perfectly legitimate to allow two competing positions, like the medical and social models of disability, to co-exist.

---

60 Kittay, *op. cit.*, p. 76f.
61 *Ibid.*, p. 77.

However, the foundational principles we have examined are associated with the claim that there are some minimum standards which humans should respect. At times, particularly in our assessment of human dignity and the sanctity of life, it was difficult to ascertain what form these standards might take. Furthermore, we also argued that the detailed content of both principles is derived from other ethical principles that are more precise and central to the liberal philosophical tradition. Hence in what follows the account of foundational values on which we will rely will be taken directly from the principle of respect for persons. We claimed that the principle of respect for persons, though not unproblematic, provides a more satisfactory account of these minimal standards providing it is interpreted and applied in a manner which is alert to the potential difficulties which it can pose in cases involving impairment. That is, not only does the principle of respect for persons allow for a degree of pluralism, but it also requires that we value the decisions, opinions and interests of others, including those who are dependent or impaired.

In light of the basic values associated with the principle of respect for persons, another feature of the conflict between the medical and social models of disability returns to the fore, namely, the assertion by the proponents of the social model that the medical model has a tendency to discriminate against people with impairments. While appeals to the principle of respect for persons can require that we accommodate the diverse opinions and preferences of others, the principle is not so broad that it permits individuals to be discriminated against or treated unfairly. The commitment to minimal ethical requirements associated with the need to respect persons must become an explicit feature in the debates on life-and-death decision-making between those who claim that disability is primarily a problem of social discrimination and those who hold that it is a consequence of impairment that can only be remedied by medical interventions. This is because only such an explicit commitment to common moral standards will provide a common framework which will allow disputes in this area to be assessed using the same appeal to the same normative yardstick. However, it remains possible for participants to disagree over the acceptable ways of interpreting the requirements of these minimal standards. This concern can be minimised by adding further detail to the requirements of the respect-for-persons principle.

Facilitating ethical principles and concepts

Biomedical and healthcare ethics present a range of normative principles that help both to clarify and to facilitate the attainment of the foundation ethical commitments we have associated with the principle of respect for persons. An exposition of some of these principles will provide more detail with which to identify and critique any legitimate concerns that exist within debates on life-and-death decision-making in the context of disability regarding discrimination.

Facilitating principle: autonomy

It is central to the Western philosophical tradition that human well-being is best promoted and persons are allowed to flourish when they can act freely. In this respect pre-eminent amongst the facilitating principles is autonomy (literally, self-rule). As Young explains:

> In a health-care setting, when a patient exercises her autonomy she decides which of the options for dealing with her health-care problem (including having no treatment at all) will be best for her, given her particular values, concerns and goals. A patient who makes autonomous choices about her health care is able to opt for what she considers will be best for her, all things considered.[62]

Thus, autonomy emphasises the importance of individuals being self-determining or being able to choose and pursue their own life plan. Key aspects of autonomy are freedom from coercion (liberty) and the capacity for free thought, reasoning and action (agency).[63] Autonomous individuals are able to understand the nature of the issues they face and the options that are open to them in the short and long term. Comprehension of this information forms the basis for the decisions and choices taken by the person in question. On the basis of the decisions they make, moral agents then take action. In this way, autonomy is essentially 'the running of one's own life according to one's own lights'.[64] As Downie and Calman note, '... the most appropriate way of treating [patients] will most often be leaving them alone – not harming them but respecting their liberty'.[65]

However, it is important to note that contemporary theories of autonomy also suggest that there is a positive duty to actively help people to exercise their autonomy. As Beauchamp and Childress explain:

> To respect an autonomous agent is, at a minimum, to acknowledge that person's right to hold views, to make choices, and to take actions based on personal values and beliefs. Such respect involves respectful *action*, not merely a respectful *attitude*. It also requires more than non-interference in others' personal affairs. It includes, at least in some contexts, obligations to build up or maintain others' capacities for autonomous choices while helping allay fears and other conditions that destroy or disrupt their autonomous actions.[66]

---

62 Young, R., 'Informed Consent and Patient Autonomy', in Kuhse, H. and Singer, P. (eds) *A Companion to Bioethics*, Oxford, Blackwell, 1998, 411–451 at p. 442.

63 Beauchamp, T.L. and Childress, J.F., *Principles of Biomedical Ethics* (5th Ed), Oxford, Oxford University Press, 2001 at p. 58.

64 Harris, J., *The Value of Life: An Introduction to Medical Ethics*, London, Routledge, 1985 at p. 199.

65 Downie, R.S. and Calman, K.C., *Healthy Respect: Ethics in Health Care*, Oxford, Oxford University Press, 1994 at p. 54.

66 Beauchamp and Childress, *op. cit.*, p. 63.

They further clarify that this means that respecting an individual's autonomy:

> ...can be stated as a positive or negative obligation. As a *negative* obligation: *Autonomous actions should not be subjected to controlling constraints by others*...As a *positive* obligation, this principle requires respectful treatment in disclosing information and fostering autonomous decision-making.[67] (Italics in original)

Thus, efforts to respect patient autonomy in healthcare can require a wide range of responses. For example, they may require that patients should be left to make their own decisions (and that these decisions should be respected), or the provision of active assistance by way of information or resources to enable the patient to make truly autonomous decisions.

Despite the weight that is afforded to autonomy within the Western bioethical tradition, it is important to acknowledge that it is rarely possible to attain complete autonomy. This is because it is difficult, for example, to avoid choices being implicitly influenced by past or present events and circumstances. In addition, we will often lack the full and detailed information that we would need to make our decisions and actions truly autonomous. As Harris states:

> Full autonomy and even fully autonomous individual choices, are in a sense ideal notions, which we can at best only hope to approach more or less closely. This is because all sorts of things tend to undermine the individual's capacity for autonomous choice.[68]

Similarly, Beauchamp and Childress claim:

> Even autonomous persons with self-governing capacities sometimes fail to govern themselves in particular choices because of temporary constraints caused by illness or depression, or because of ignorance, coercion, or other conditions that restrict their options.[69]

Thus, although autonomy is often endorsed as one of the most important principles within biomedical ethics, and is a key vehicle in affirming the foundational commitment to respect for persons, its attainment is restricted to some extent by the complexity and rich detail of human life. This qualification does not detract from the importance of utilising this principle as an ideal with which to protect and support the interests of individuals. However, Barnes suggests the principle of autonomy is interpreted in such an idealistic manner that in the context of disability there is a tendency to assume that even people

67 *Ibid.*, p. 64.
68 Harris, *op. cit.*, p. 195.
69 Beauchamp and Childress, *op. cit.*, p. 58.

with physical impairments cannot exercise their autonomy. He states that such assumptions fail to acknowledge that:

> Independence does not refer to someone who can do everything themselves, a feat that no human being can achieve whether they have an impairment or not, but indicates someone who is able to take control of their own life and to choose how that life is to be led. It is a thought process not contingent upon physical abilities.[70]

The problem to which Barnes' remark points concerns the fact that disabled people are often *ex hypothesi* assumed to lack autonomy. As Ells states:

> People living with disabilities are particularly vulnerable to the failure of others to recognize their authority to make and act on decisions, thus impeding the ability of disabled people to govern important aspects of their lives. Numerous factors can contribute to this vulnerability. Because authority in health care contexts depends in part on competence, an incorrect assessment of competence contributes to the failure to recognise authority. For example, communication barriers, caused either by physical processes (e.g. aphasia), attitudinal processes (e.g. bias), or confounding conditions (e.g. depression), may suggest the presence of incompetence and non-authority when someone is actually competent and has authority. Further, a lack of ability to enact one's decisions might be falsely assumed to indicate a lack of authority.[71]

Thus, Ells suggests, there is a tendency within healthcare to assume falsely that because some 'disabled' individuals do have impaired rational abilities which restrict their autonomy, all other disabled and impaired individuals must also have restricted abilities to exercise their autonomy. This tendency to undermine the decision-making abilities of impaired individuals plays a key role in disabling them. Furthermore, this issue takes us to the heart of the tension which exists in debates at the beginning and end of life concerning justly differential treatment and unjust discrimination. This is because it highlights the danger of basing our decisions and assumptions about the capacities of others on stereotypes and false assumptions which unfairly discriminate, rather than on information which legitimately allows – even necessitates – that we treat people in different ways. Thus, despite the difficulties with trying to affirm the autonomy ideal, appealing to the principle can help to protect the interests and

---

70 Barnes, C., *Disabled People in Britain and Discrimination*, London, Hurst and Co., 1994 at p. 129. Quoted in Johnstone, D., *An Introduction to Disability Studies* (2nd Ed), London, David Fulton, 2001 at p. 62.

71 Ells, C., 'Lessons About Autonomy from the Experience of Disability', *Social Theory and Practice*, 27, 4, 599–615, 2001 at p. 605.

freedoms of individuals. This claim can be given further support by other facilitating principles.

Facilitating principle: consent

Another way in which healthcare professionals can facilitate efforts to respect persons is by gaining their consent or authorisation prior to performing a medical procedure on them. This helps to ensure that any treatment individuals accept or decide to forego is in keeping with their decisions about their wider life plans. In this respect, consent is an important pragmatic tool which helps prevent individuals from receiving treatment which ignores or strips them of their decision-making powers. Beauchamp and Childress explain that there are generally thought to be five related elements to a legitimate consent; these are competence, disclosure, understanding, voluntariness and consent.[72] Together these features require that:

> ...any justifiable analysis of informed consent must be rooted in autonomous choice by patients and subjects. An act is increasingly recognised in this literature as informed consent only if (1) a patient or subject agrees to an intervention based on an understanding of material information (2) the agreement is not controlled by influences that engineer the outcome; and (3) an authorization for an intervention is given by the patient or subject with the understanding that it is an authorization.[73]

These different facets of consent are likely to be features on which exponents of the medical and social models of disability already implicitly agree. For those who employ a medical approach to disability, consent is an ethical (and legal) requirement which medical professionals must respect and indeed from which they receive a degree of professional protection.[74] Equally, those who argue that disability is largely or exclusively a social problem are also keen to promote the autonomy of disabled (impaired) citizens. Given that consent is a device which makes it easier to ensure that the interests and opinions of disabled people are placed at the centre of clinical decisions, the importance of consent will, like the related goals to respect persons and support autonomy, be a principle to which proponents of either model are committed.

At the heart of a legitimate consent or authorisation is an autonomous, competent patient who is able to exercise the features of agency and liberty identified above. However, in the previous section we have identified concerns that

---

72 Beauchamp and Childress, *op. cit.*, p. 79ff.

73 Beauchamp, T.L. and Faden, R.R., 'Informed Consent: Meaning and Elements', in Post, S.G. (ed), *Encyclopedia of Bioethics*, New York, Macmillan Reference, 2004, 1277–1280 at p. 1279.

74 BMA, *Medical Ethics Today: The BMA's Handbook of Ethics and Law* (2nd Ed), London, BMJ Books, 2004 at p. 71f.

the capacities of some disabled people for autonomous decision-making – including their abilities to consent to treatment – may be underestimated. Thus, although healthcare professionals are committed to securing the consent of competent patients, the importance of consent in safeguarding the interests of disabled patients may be reduced by failure to determine accurately which patients are able to authorise or refuse treatment. This concern seems to be rooted in the negative attitudes towards disability that we identified in the previous chapter as pervading biomedicine and healthcare. An appropriate response to this can be made by drawing on other ethical principles, namely, respect for persons and autonomy. This is because failure to determine accurately the intellectual capacities of individuals suggests that insufficient attention has been given to seeing them as an end in the clinical decision-making process. As a result it is likely that such uninformed decisions have not given sufficient importance to the need to respect persons as autonomous moral agents.

Finally, one limitation of consent is that it is only useful for helping individuals either to avoid treatment they do not wish to have or to empower them to acknowledge and accept that a certain course of treatment is in keeping with their wishes. Thus, in terms of preventing discrimination against disabled people in healthcare the principle of consent helps to ensure that a recommended treatment does not work against the interests of the patient. Examples of such unwanted treatment might be pain relief measures which may hasten the end of life, or recommendations to terminate a pregnancy where the infant is likely to be severely impaired. However, consent is of no use in cases in which medical professionals decline to offer treatment on the grounds of disability. In such cases efforts to ascertain whether such decisions are discriminatory can be made by appealing to another facilitating principle associated with respect for persons and autonomy, namely, rights language.

Facilitating concept: rights

Many debates in healthcare ethics are conducted with reference to the language of 'rights'. Like the other facilitating principles we have outlined, the aim of appeals to rights in healthcare (and other contexts) is to support human well-being. The major contribution of rights language is to arm individuals with the moral (and legal) tools to secure the treatment necessary to safeguard and promote their autonomy and well-being. Thus, the concept of rights is particularly closely related to the principle of autonomy. As O'Neill has commented, 'no themes have become more central in large parts of bioethics, and especially in medical ethics, than the importance of respecting individual rights and autonomy.'[75]

---

75 O'Neill, *op. cit.*, p. 2.

Despite the considerable attention that is afforded to the discussion of rights within healthcare there is a lack of clarity over what rights individuals have and whether all persons and potential persons have access to the same rights. Hence the nature and role of rights language requires further investigation.

Rights claims are supported by either a moral principle (moral rights) and/or a legal rule (legal rights). Moral and legal rights can, but do not necessarily, overlap: legal rights can be based on fundamental moral rights, but not all legal rights are moral rights, and not all moral rights have legal support. The impetus for both legal and moral rights claims within healthcare ethics can be traced – as was the case with human dignity – to the formation of the United Nations. As the BMA has said:

> The United Nations' Universal Declaration of Human Rights of 1948 ushered in an era in which ideas of personal autonomy and 'rights' came to be seen as central in many parts of the world, including Britain and Europe. The international and legal concepts about human dignity, self determination, freedom from interference, and welfare protection articulated in the UN Declaration were defined further in international conventions in the 1970s...[76]

The UN Declaration mandates that all people have access to basic rights that protect their dignity and well-being. Article 2 of the Declaration states 'Everyone is entitled to all the rights and freedoms set forth in this Declaration, without distinction of any kind, such as race, colour, sex, language, religion...'[77] Amongst the rights in the Declaration that have the greatest impact in healthcare and life-and-death decision-making are the:

- right to life, liberty and security of the person (Art 3);
- right not to be subjected to cruel, inhuman or degrading treatment (Art 5);
- right to equal protection before the law (Art 7);
- right to have privacy protected from arbitrary inference (Art 12);
- right to found a family (Art 16);
- right to freedom of thought (Art 18).[78]

In addition, Art 12 of the UN's 1966 International Covenant on Economic, Social and Cultural Rights says that states must '... recognize the right of everyone to the enjoyment of the highest attainable standard of physical and mental health'.[79] Although people with disability are not explicitly mentioned in

76 BMA, *op. cit.*, p. 5.
77 United Nations, Universal Declaration of Human Rights, adopted and proclaimed by the General Assembly resolution 217 A (III) on 10 December 1948.
78 *Id.*
79 International Covenant on Economic, Social and Cultural Rights adopted and opened for signature, ratification and accession by General Assembly resolution 2200A (XXI) of 16 December 1966 *entry into force* 3 January 1976, in accordance with Art 27.

these human rights instruments the provisions of such documents are intended to apply to all. The European Convention on Human Rights, which was incorporated into UK law by the Human Rights Act 1998, also means that rights language is now an integral part of domestic jurisprudence. In addition, in the introduction to this book we outlined a number of other international legal instruments that focus specifically on the interests and rights of disabled people.

However, there are questions over the ability of disabled people to claim the rights to which they are entitled as persons. Barron has suggested that despite the legal and ethical commitment to the need to respect persons and individual rights 'some disabled people are prevented from exercising this autonomy'.[80] She continues that:

> Individual rights operate as a mechanism of both inclusion and exclusion. For those who are in a position to (e.g. can themselves take care of their own interests and/or have adequate assistance) apply for the services of one's choice and, if necessary, appeal, this kind of individual rights legislation can be of great value ... However ... individual rights have for some little or no bearing on their everyday lives. There are those, for example, women and men with learning difficulties, who are in no position to by themselves find out about legal rights nor, if familiar with these, apply for them ...[81]

The contribution of rights language to efforts to help identify and prevent the discrimination that disabled people experience, like the other principles we have outlined, is not unproblematic; that is, rights tools are most needed by precisely those individuals who may find it most difficult to invoke them or gain access to the remedies they offer. This is perhaps particularly true of individuals who while at their most frail – either at the beginning or end of life – need the protection and perhaps resources provided by basic rights claims. However, the point at issue here does not relate to the capabilities of moral rights but rather the abilities of the legal system to ensure that even the most vulnerable members of society have their interests protected and can gain access to rights instruments easily.

Conclusion

Ethico-legal debates that are conducted without drawing on a common language are unlikely to cultivate an understanding of the issues involved, let alone forge agreement on them. In this respect, the ongoing disputes between those who

---

80 Barron, K., 'Autonomy in Everyday Life, For Whom?' *Disability and Society*, 2001, 16, 3, 431–447 at p. 445.
81 *Ibid.*, p. 445f.

claim that disability is either a medical or a social issue are marked by failures to articulate explicitly the shared goals of these otherwise disparate positions. This is not to deny that much ethical literature has been produced on the topic, but is rather to emphasise that those involved have not succeeded in elucidating (or resolving) conflicts by highlighting the issues over which there may be agreement.

In this chapter we have articulated a set of principles over which there is wide consensus within bioethics, biomedicine and law. Importantly, these principles are intended to protect the interests of all members of society, but particularly to support the well-being of individuals who are most at risk of having their interests overridden. However, we have also noted that some of these basic principles and concepts can be problematic when employed in the context of disability. This is not least because their full and accurate application risks are being obstructed precisely by the prejudicial attitudes and assumptions that such principles are meant to defeat. This appears to support the concerns expressed at the beginning of this chapter regarding the reputation of bioethics for working against the interests of disabled people. However, we contend that such claims about the intentions of 'bioethics' or 'bioethicists' should only be made if they are carefully targeted, because dismissing the discipline as a whole threatens to discard a valuable set of resources. It is critical, however, that application of such principles are subjected to self-criticism.

It is also important to understand the limitations of bioethics. The role of the principles we have articulated is not necessarily to solve the disputes over the treatment or nature of disability but rather to ensure that debates at the beginning and end of life are informed by a set of accepted minimum standards for the treatment of human persons, whether or not they have impairments. The concerns raised by exponents of the social model regarding the discriminatory treatment of disabled people makes the need to affirm such standards particularly urgent. More specifically, it is important to ensure that clinical decisions are based on the needs and interests of particular individuals rather than on prejudicial assumptions about 'disabled people'. One valuable element of liberal devices such as autonomy and rights is that they recognise and foster the diversity which exists within the human community. Efforts to squash this diversity – whether or not they are intentional – work not only against the interests and well-being of particular individuals but against the whole liberal tradition.

However, we have also seen that even the vaguest of ethical precepts (such as human dignity and the sanctity of life) operate on the assumption that in order to be of value human life requires certain characteristics, or in the very least the potential to gain or regain such characteristics. If human life permanently lacks key traits then the principles which we have outlined will be of no importance and no value to them. It is in such circumstances that discrimination ceases to be of concern and legitimate differential treatment commences. The difficulty in making such clear-cut distinctions within a clinical environment is suggested both by the concerns which have been raised over the application of the facilitating ethical principles in the context of disability and by the large number of cases which come to court each year seeking help to resolve disagreements over treatment decisions. Given that the courts often act as the final arbiter in such difficult cases, it is necessary to consider whether the law is equipped with the theoretical resources to overcome the difficulties we have encountered to date in attaining fair and non-discriminatory treatment for disabled people at the beginning and end of their lives.

Chapter 4

Decisions at the beginning of life

Introduction

Impairment and disability can have profound effects on individuals and their families; many of them positive. However, modern capacities to make predictive decisions about the health status of embryos and potential children, advances in prenatal screening and controversial choices about treatment provision in the period following birth, can lead to decisions being taken which are essentially about who should live. The right to life is one of the most significant rights we can claim, and how that right is interpreted – as well as who or what is entitled to its protection – is clearly vital to our ability to experience the entire range of other human rights, like those guaranteed by the European Convention on Human Rights, whose terms were incorporated into UK law by the terms of the Human Rights Act 1998. It is also vital for the application of our foundational principle of respect for persons that who is a 'person' is identified.

From a legal perspective, although arguably not necessarily from an ethical one, the right to life becomes meaningful on live birth. The status of a rights bearer is not accorded until then. In terms of our argument, this means that – legally at least – the principle of respect for persons cannot be applied to the human embryo or foetus. That is not to say that entities before birth are not of some legal relevance. For example, there is a legal prohibition on conducting research on *ex vivo* embryos after 14 days,[1] which is substantially based on the view that the embryo of the human species is worthy of some respect.[2] Equally, the abortion debate is – rightly or wrongly – often couched in terms which relate to the viability of the developing foetus, so that the more mature the foetus the more protection it is offered in law. As we will see later, however, there is an exception to this general rule in the case of foetuses likely to be born with serious handicap.

---

1 Human Fertilisation and Embryology Act, s 3 (4).
2 See, for example, the conclusions of the Report of the Committee of Inquiry into Human Fertilisation and Embryology (Warnock report) Cmnd. 9314/1984, para 11.17, p. 63 'the embryo of the human species ought to have a special status...'.

Preimplantation genetic diagnosis (PGD)

Before turning to the question of abortion, it is instructive to consider technological developments which can be undertaken at the embryonic stage. For most – but by no means all – people, the human embryo (especially when it is not implanted) is of less moral worth than the already implanted, developing foetus. Failing to implant an embryo is less morally troubling than terminating an established pregnancy. The combination of developments in assisted reproduction and genetics (widely referred to as reprogenetics) means that intending parents undergoing assisted reproduction can in some circumstances choose which embryo(s) to implant. Regulations contained in the most recent Code of Practice issued by the Human Fertilisation and Embryology Authority (HFEA), which has responsibility for licensing clinics and assisted reproductive techniques, limit PGD to specific circumstances. Primarily, this means that there should be a significant risk of a serious genetic condition,[3] and it is anticipated that practice will mimic that in respect of prenatal screening.[4] In addition, account must be taken of

1   the view of the people seeking treatment of the condition to be avoided;
2   their previous reproductive experience;
3   the likely degree of suffering associated with the condition;
4   the availability of effective therapy, now and in the future;
5   the speed of degeneration in progressive disorders;
6   the extent of any intellectual impairments;
7   the extent of social support available; and
8   the family circumstances of the people seeking treatment.[5]

More recently, the HFEA has agreed that it will license PGD for so-called late onset conditions; that is, conditions which are serious (such as inherited breast cancer) but which the child if born may never have.[6] In addition, the HFEA has authorised the creation of so-called saviour siblings by allowing PGD both to identify an embryo which will not develop the condition[7] and, by means of the additional process of tissue typing, to identify which embryo(s) will be compatible with an existing, ill child. The aim is to try to save the life of the existing child by using cord blood from the selected child.[8] Interestingly, these restrictions on PGD are inconsistent with our argument that respect for

---

3 HFEA Code of Practice 6th edition, 2003 at p. 124, para 14.22.
4 *Ibid.*, para 14.21.
5 P. 124, para 14.23.
6 http://news.bbc.co.uk/1/hi/health/4756697.stm (accessed on 7 July 2006).
7 See *R. (on the application of Quintavalle) v Human Fertilisation and Embryology Authority* (2005) 83 BMLR 143; for further discussion, see Kanavakis, E. and Traeger-Synodinos, T., 'Preimplantation Genetic Diagnosis In Clinical Practice', *Journal of Medical Genetics*, 39, 2002, 6–11.
8 Post Whittaker change of mind.

persons should be the guiding principle, since legally there is no person to respect other than the intending parent who wishes to make the choice. What they show, however, is that ethically some account is taken of the human embryo, although on what basis is not entirely clear.

Although PGD is relatively rare – there are only about 200 tests per year in the United Kingdom[9] – for families who are aware of a genetic condition, or for those who are concerned to avoid suffering for themselves and any future child and who are undergoing In Vitro Fertilisation (IVF), the availability of PGD means the opportunity to screen out affected embryos. The President's Council on Bioethics asks a pertinent question here:

> What father or mother does not dream of a good life for his or her child? What parents would not wish to enhance the life of their children, to make them better people, to help them live better lives? Such wishes and intentions guide much of what all parents do for and to their children.[10]

Indeed, it goes further saying that '[n]o one would *wish* to be afflicted, or to have one's child afflicted, by a debilitating genetic disorder, and the new technologies hold out the prospect of eliminating or reducing the prevalence of some of the worst conditions.'[11] Although it is difficult to argue against the freedom of individual intending parents to exercise maximum choice to ensure that they have healthy children (or children who are as healthy as possible), many do object.

Concerns about PGD

For some people any selection of embryos is inherently wrong. For them, an embryo is an actual or a potential person, and must be given the right to live by being implanted rather than destroyed. Others object to the selection of embryos on different grounds. One important objection, from the point of view of our discussion, is that which suggests that it is a clear form of discrimination to select out potential people just because of their impairment. However, Harris argues that it makes no sense to talk of discrimination in this context. For him:

> Choosing between existing people for whatever reason always involves the possibility of unfair discrimination because there will, inevitably, be people who are disadvantaged by the choice. Choosing which sorts of people to

---

9 'Very Early Detection? British Group Gauges Public Interest in Embryo testing for Cancer', *Journal of the National Cancer Institute*, 98, 3, 1 February 2006, 156–157.

10 *Beyond Therapy: Biotechnology and the Pursuit of Happiness*, A Report of the President's Council on Bioethics, Washington, DC, October 2003, http://www.bioethics.gov at p. 27.

11 *Ibid.*, p. 44.

bring into existence or choosing which embryos or fetuses to allow to become persons can never have this effect because there is no one who suffers adversely from the choice.[12]

A second order version of the discrimination-based argument suggests that, even if Harris is correct, selecting out embryos with a particular condition risks disrespecting those who already live with the condition. However, this presumes that because I do not wish to have a child with, for example cystic fibrosis, I will not respect those who have it and who are already born. This contention is fallacious. There is no logical link between my consideration of unimplanted embryos and existing people. Neither legally nor ethically, we would argue, is any respect due equivalent, nor is it linked. I may prefer to avoid suffering for a future child, while at the same time treating all born people – irrespective of their health or other status – with utmost respect. In any case, as Petersen notes, 'arguments against PGD tend to focus only on possible harms to disabled people. Such opposition ignores, or vastly underestimates, the increase in welfare of other individuals that might be gained from PGD.'[13] Even if there were evidence that PGD was intimately linked to discrimination against existing people, as Petersen says:

> If sound empirical studies were to show that many disabled people were being harmed by PGD (for example, by serious employment discrimination; barriers to obtaining health insurance; cutbacks in public support programmes; or a rising suicide rate because of demoralisation or hostile attitudes), then we will have a strong reason to abandon the use of PGD. However, if studies showed that the use of PGD would have no, or only limited, harmful effect on disabled people, then we will have a weak reason not to use PGD.[14]

At present, we have no evidence that discrimination against people is linked to the availability of PGD. Yet, for DPI, the threat to people with disabilities from reprogenetics is real:

> DPI Europe is greatly concerned about the threat posed to our human rights by developments in human genetics research and practice and by the fact that our voice struggles to be heard in the ethical and scientific debates. In general we have been considered as little more than the passive subjects both of these debates and of genetic research. This has been a profoundly disabling experience. We are also concerned that the new genetics is fostering

12 Harris, J., 'One Principle and Three Fallacies of Disability Studies', *JME*, 27, 2000, 382–387 at p. 386.
13 Petersen, T.S., 'Just Diagnosis? Preimplantation Genetic Diagnosis and Injustices to Disabled People', *JME*, 31, 2005, 231–234 at p. 233.
14 *Ibid.*, p. 234.

a biologically reductive vision of the world which not only undermines what it is to be human but also devalues the importance of social factors, relationships, mutual respect and the environment in determining everyone's quality of life.[15]

This view is common in literature in this area. The fact that there is increasing capacity to make such decisions is of concern to many disability rights activists for whom the elimination of disabilities is far from easily acceptable. The arguments against selection are wide and varied. As we have seen, for many, they hinge on the fear of a return to negative eugenics;[16] for others, the critical issue is the effect that accepting selection will have on those who are currently living with impairment.[17] Still others, like the DPI, point to the absence of the views of disabled people in making policy, arguing that their voice is vital to bridge the gap between those living with impairment and those who are not. As Chapman says:

> ... lay and scientific understandings and experiences of genetic disorders are different.... This mismatch is of considerable importance in bioethical issues generally, and the practice of genetic counselling specifically since those people approaching a clinic for information and perhaps guidance may make different decisions if given both types of information. If information about the lives of people currently living with genetic conditions is somehow incorporated into genetic counselling, then reproductive decisions taken by lay people can be based on information generated from personal experiences and from a lay perspective. This then stands as a counterpoint to the over-deterministic, biomedically oriented or socially structured views of health, illness and quality of life that also exist.[18]

Tom Shakespeare also notes the irony that advances in genetic testing have arisen at virtually the same time as the disability rights movement has become a 'significant political player in many Western societies'.[19] Calling for a balanced debate, he warns that what he calls 'genetic hyperbole' can fail 'to respect the

---

15 Disabled Peoples International (DPI), *Disabled People Speak on the New Genetics: DPI Europe Position Statement on Bioethics and Human Rights*, London, DPI, 2000 at p. 5.

16 See Chapman, E., 'The Social and Ethical Implications of Changing Medical Technologies: The Views of People Living with Genetic Conditions', *Journal of Health Psychology*, 7, 2, 2002, 195–206.

17 See, for example, Gollust, S.E., Apse, K., Fuller, B.P., Miller, P.S. and Biesecker, B.B., 'Community Involvement in Developing Policies for Genetic Testing: Assessing the Interests and Experiences of Individuals Affected by Genetic Conditions', *American Journal of Public Health*, 95, 1, 2005, 35–41.

18 Chapman, *op. cit.*, p. 203.

19 Shakespeare, T., ' "Losing the plot?" Medical and Activist Discourses of Contemporary Genetics and Disability', *Sociology of Health and Illness*, 21, 5, 1999, 669–688 at p. 669.

diversity of human embodiment, and the moral value of disabled people, as well as overstating the power of genetic intervention'.[20]

However, a balanced debate needs to take account of the difference between how we view an embryo and how we view a person. In particular, people who are already born have other rights which could be seriously infringed were we to emphasise the embryo rather than the person. One lasting legacy of the negative eugenics polices already referred to briefly was state-enforced intervention in people's reproductive choices. As a consequence, the right to make free reproductive decisions has come to be seen as one of the most important that people can aspire to, and is intimately linked to our concern with respect for persons. Thus, when we select out certain embryos because of their characteristics, we do so in support of reproductive liberty (and respect), as well as in line with the facilitating principles of autonomy and respect for human rights.

One of the disability rights movement's most thoughtful commentators, Shakespeare, also picks up this point. As he says, '[t]he role of prospective parents has largely been ignored by disabled radicals.'[21] He also concedes that

> there are reasons to want to prevent the birth of a child affected by impairment which do not reflect discrimination against disabled people: for example, the desire to avoid the early death or suffering of a loved child, or a feeling that a family will be unable to cope with the strain of looking after a very impaired member.[22]

Thus, arguably, to emphasise concern about discrimination against those embryos which are not implanted because of their genetic condition is to deny the value of being born free from impairment.

Indications for genetic screening and diagnosis seem likely to expand, and as the President's Commission pointed out '[t]he use of IVF and PGD to move from disease avoidance to baby improvement is conceptually simple, at least in terms of the techniques of screening, and would require no change in the procedure.'[23] The possibility, therefore, of widening the use of the availability of these techniques towards enhancement rather than disease avoidance – while very much in the future – nonetheless becomes one more potential matter for anxiety, particularly for those concerned about the impact of the rapid progress of genetic technology on people with impairment or disability. One feared consequence of this could, of course, be increased pressure to conform to 'desirable' norms, further alienating those who are in some way different. Paradoxically, however, extending choice to include characteristics regarded as desirable would render virtually all of us subject to the possibility of rejection which informs the debate at present; unless, for example, we all conform to whatever the desirable norm is

20 Shakespeare, T., ' "Losing the plot?" Medical and Activist Discourses of Contemporary Genetics and Disability', *Sociology of Health and Illness*, 21, 5, 1999, p. 685.
21 *Ibid.*, p. 681.
22 *Id.*
23 *Beyond Therapy: Biotechnology and the Pursuit of Happiness, op. cit.*, 41.

judged to be, we would all become potential victims of precisely the same kinds of decision which have in the past generally been confined to those with impairment. In this way, it is likely that the arguments currently advanced by the disability community regarding their rights will become more widely applicable as more and more people feel themselves threatened by medical capacity.

Prenatal screening

PGD is – for the moment – relatively unusual. Much more common, however, is the prenatal screening of pregnancies for potential impairment. In fact, it is more accurate to say that such screening is commonplace, and advances in genetic screening seem likely to increase the range of conditions which can be detected pre-birth. Henn[24] says:

> Prenatal diagnosis is one of the ethically most problematic applications of genetics, at least as far as it is aimed at conditions which, if detected in the fetus, are incurable and thus may lead to selective abortion. In particular, prenatal diagnosis of genetic traits typically can only provide information to assist the prospective parents in their decision making whether to carry the pregnancy to term or to terminate it.[25]

Virtually every pregnancy in the United Kingdom is screened for the presence of, for example, Down's Syndrome,[26] and the UK Government seems set on expanding both the numbers screened and the range of conditions for which screening is offered.[27] As the British Medical Association (BMA) says:

> Prenatal screening might be by family history, serum screening, molecular tests, or ultrasound. Ultrasound scanning is currently offered routinely to all pregnant women in the UK and, although it is undertaken to monitor the development of the fetus, it can also detect both major and minor defects.[28]

Although it is theoretically the case that such screening implies no outcome – that is, it does not necessarily imply the termination of an affected pregnancy – in reality some doctors have in the past been reluctant to provide screening to women who indicate that they would not elect to terminate.[29] This may

24 Henn, W., 'Consumerism in Prenatal Diagnosis: A Challenge for Ethical Guidelines', *JME*, 26, 2000, 444–446.
25 *Ibid.*, p. 444.
26 British Medical Association (BMA), *Human Genetics: Choice and Responsibility*, Oxford, Oxford University Press, 1998.
27 *Our Inheritance, Our Future: Realising the Potential of Genetics in the NHS*, London, Department of Health, June 2003, Cm 5791-II.
28 BMA, *op. cit.*, p. 38.
29 The BMA, *op. cit.*, indicated that 'a 1993 study of obstetricians found that one-third still generally required an undertaking to terminate an affected pregnancy before proceeding with prenatal diagnosis' at p. 52.

remain the case, despite the BMA's express disapproval of any such assumption being made.[30] Moreover, Marteau and Drake have concluded from their own study that:

> ...less help will be given to parents who decline testing because the outcome, giving birth to a child with a condition for which prenatal screening and selective termination are available, is seen as preventable. Initial support from health professionals following the birth of a child with a disability seems to be an important factor affecting early adjustment.[31]

The Human Genetics Commission also notes concerns that reproductive decisions may be 'made against a background of inadequate social support for, and widespread discrimination against, disabled people and people with genetic disorders'.[32] The possible combination of prejudice and inadequate support is of real concern; obviously particularly for people with impairment or disability.

Further, knowledge of health status places additional stress on those who have to make decisions. As Robertson and Shulman say:

> Developments in obstetrics, genetics, fetal medicine and infectious diseases will continue to provide knowledge and technologies that will enable many disabled births to be prevented. While most women will welcome this knowledge and gladly act on it, others will not. The ethical, legal, and policy aspects of this situation require a careful balancing of the offspring's welfare and the pregnant woman's interest in liberty and bodily integrity.[33]

The President's Council on Bioethics reinforces concerns around prenatal screening and its implications, saying:

> ...the practice of prenatal screening establishes the principle that parents may choose the qualities of their children, and choose them on the basis of genetic knowledge. This new principle...may already be shifting parental and societal attitudes toward prospective children: from simple acceptance to judgment and control, from seeing a child as an unconditionally welcome gift to seeing him as a conditionally acceptable product.[34]

---

30 The BMA, *op. cit.*, indicated that 'a 1993 study of obstetricians found that one-third still generally required an undertaking to terminate an affected pregnancy before proceeding with prenatal diagnosis' at p. 52.

31 Marteau, T.M. and Drake, H., 'Attributions for Disability: The Influence of Genetic Screening', *Social Science and Medicine*, 40, 8, 1995, 1127–1132 at p. 1130.

32 *Choosing the Future: Genetics and Reproductive Decision Making*, London, Human Genetics Commission, July 2004 (discussion paper) at p. 23, para 5.8.

33 Robertson, J. and Shulman, J., 'Pregnancy and Prenatal Harm to Offspring: The Case of Mothers with PKU', *Hastings Center Report*, 17, 4, 1987, 23 at p. 32.

34 *Beyond Therapy: Biotechnology and the Pursuit of Happiness, op. cit.*, p. 37.

What is undeniable is that screening programmes – in searching for the existence of potential disorders or impairments – rest clearly, at both a theoretical and a practical level, on the assumption of the legitimacy of preventing the birth of children with certain identifiable health problems.[35] For the DPI:

> Human genetics poses a threat to us because while cures and palliatives are promised, what is actually being offered are genetic tests for characteristics perceived as undesirable. *This is not about treating illness or impairment but about eliminating or manipulating foetuses which may not be acceptable for a variety of reasons. These technologies are, therefore, opening the door to a new eugenics which directly threatens our human rights.*[36]
>
> (emphasis added)

Saxton also notes the potential hazards associated with screening, saying:

> Disability rights activists have begun to articulate a critical view of the practice of prenatal diagnosis with the intent to abort if the fetus appears to be destined to become a disabled person. Some people with disabilities, particularly those who are members of the disability rights community, perceive that selective abortion may be based on the assumption that any child with a disability would necessarily be a burden to the family and to society, and therefore would be better off not being born.[37]

Shakespeare, on the other hand, rejects the homogeneity that the DPI (and others) claims for people with impairment, noting that they will have different views on screening. As he argues, 'some will welcome screening, because of the suffering they have personally experienced.'[38] Equally, however, he is clear that '[o]thers will oppose screening, because it is very difficult to support a practice which would have prevented one's own existence.'[39] He concludes by emphasising the importance of engaging in 'rational arguments about the value of disabled people's lives and their views, which are likely to be varied and reflective.'[40]

While it is clear that the possibility of impairment in a future child may form an important plank of the decision-making of potential parents, and that

35 For discussion of the UK Government's proposals to expand screening and testing, see McLean, S.A.M. and Mason, J.K., 'Our Inheritance, Our Future: Their Rights?', *The International Journal of Children's Rights*, 13, 2005, 255–272.

36 DPI, *op. cit.*, p. 3.

37 Saxton, M., 'Why Members of the Disability Community Oppose Prenatal Diagnosis and Selective Abortion', in Parens, E. and Asch, A. (eds), *Prenatal Testing and Disability Rights*, Washington, DC, Georgetown University Press, 2000, 147–164 at p. 147.

38 Shakespeare, T., 'Choices and Rights: Eugenics, Genetics and Disability Equality', *Disability and Society*, 1998, 13, 665–682 at p. 274.

39 *Id.*

40 *Id.*

awareness of the possibility of impairment is encouraged by current government policy, it is less clear on what basis the superficially benign enhancement of the choices available to intending parents can be resisted. Reproductive liberty is generally valued, and people may legitimately take that liberty to include the right to make informed choices about their offspring.[41] Of course, not everyone would choose to avoid what others see as impairment. Indeed, in one case in the United States a couple deliberately chose to have a child who was congenitally deaf, believing that deafness was not a disability and that the child would benefit from being introduced to the rich world of deaf culture. The power of the assumption that disability is a tragedy was evident in some of the responses to this decision, which was widely – albeit not universally – criticised.[42] However, this is not the sole reason for objecting to such decisions. Doyal and McLean, for example, have argued that the obligation of intergenerational justice[43] requires consideration of the objective well-being of future children.[44] 'Objective well-being' is taken not as a judgement of life with impairment *in se*, but rather as 'a right of access to the goods and services required for them to do their best to be good citizens in terms of those commitments.'[45] This approach incorporates the social as well as the physical environment in which future children are to be raised. It would, however, not endorse the deliberate creation of children designed to have an impairment which would entail denial of objective well-being. In the case of the deliberate creation of deaf children, their conclusion was that:

> ... we would not support using a reproductive technology like IVF to ensure the birth of a child that was congenitally deaf, on the grounds that deafness would enhance the child's future through introducing it to the rich world of deaf language. While it may be true that such children would have increased objective well-being as regards interaction within a deaf family, the fact remains that outside of this family, their potential for social participation would be considerably constrained, along with the range of choices about themselves and their future. These same constraints would be placed on any descendants who inherited the same disability.[46]

More commonly, debate rests on the decision of a woman (and her partner, if available) to terminate a pregnancy because of the health status of the foetus.

41 For further discussion, see McLean, S.A.M., *Modern Dilemmas: Choosing Children*, Edinburgh, Capercaillie Press, 2006.
42 See discussion in Savulescu, J., 'Deaf Lesbians, "Designer Disability" and the Future of Medicine', *BMJ*, 325, 2002, 771–773.
43 See the Declaration on the Responsibilities of the Present Generations Towards Future Generations, UNESCO, 1997.
44 Doyal, L. and McLean, S.A.M., 'Choosing Children: Intergenerational Justice?', *Ethics, Law and Moral Philosophy of Reproductive Biomedicine*, 1, 1, March 2005, 119–124.
45 *Ibid.*, p. 121.
46 *Ibid.*, p. 123.

As we have seen, abortion is allowed in certain circumstances, most of them permitted only to the point at which the foetus is 'viable'.[47] For our purposes, the major exception to this rule relates to the availability of abortion up to full term where there is a 'substantial risk that if the child were born it would suffer from such physical or mental abnormalities as to be seriously handicapped.'[48] There is no doubt that this provision differentiates the 'handicapped' foetus from the non-handicapped, and for many this merely points to the very concerns they have been arguing should be taken seriously. However, two things need to be restated. First, people in existence are not logically discriminated against by this provision, and second the reproductive liberty of the woman is protected by her ability to make such decisions. Of more concern, arguably, is the law's vagueness. For example, a challenge was recently (albeit unsuccessfully) raised by the Reverend Joanna Jepson to the decision to authorise termination of a late foetus apparently on the basis that it had a cleft palate.[49] As Douglas points out:

> A ... problem is in deciding what amounts to a 'substantial' risk. The Royal College of Physicians describe a risk of more than 10% of producing a seriously abnormal child as a 'high' risk. Presumably, where the abnormality is less severe, a greater degree of probability would be classed as high. A one in 10 chance of a foetus carrying spina bifida may indeed be regarded as a substantial risk, but a further complication is that it is not generally possible to determine from pre-natal screening the degree of handicap a affected foetus may suffer. Parents may therefore be faced with the possibility of aborting a normal, or mildly affected foetus.[50]

Although application of our preferred principle of respect for persons is problematic when considering embryos or foetuses, so too is the position adopted by proponents of the medical and social models. If the medical model is applied to the embryo or foetus, then the fact of impairment would be sufficient to select out, irrespective of other considerations, since the impairment itself would be the source of disability. In the social model, no selection would be permissible because the impairment (however severe) only becomes disabling because of society's attitudes, ignoring the very real consequences for the individual him or herself. Applied to pre-implantation or pre-birth decisions, each of these can be seen as coercive on the respect due to intending parents.

---

47 For the moment, this means a cut-off point at 24 weeks' gestation.
48 Human Fertilisation and Embryology Act 1990, s 37 (1) (d).
49 *Jepson v The Chief Constable of West Mercia Police Constabulary* [2003] EWHC 3318.
50 Douglas, G., *Law, Fertility and Reproduction*, London, Sweet & Maxwell, 1991 at p. 94.

Legal consequences

The law's approach to the birth of a disabled child also merits consideration. If disability is indeed, as some assume, always a 'tragedy', might not the law offer compensation for birth with impairment? Is life with a disability of less value than another, different, non-disabled life, and how are we to answer this question, when the alternative would have been no life at all? There are three possible legal actions which might take account of impairment as a compensable issue. The first of these is called a wrongful life action. In this case, the child is claiming that it would have been better off not being born, because of its impairment.

Courts in the United Kingdom have routinely withstood pressure to allow recovery of damages for the fact of having been born. Indeed, in England and Wales it is widely assumed that the terms of the Congenital Disabilities (Civil Liability) Act 1976 preclude wrongful life actions. Additionally, in a case relating to a child who had been born before the terms of this Act could apply, the common law position was clarified. In *McKay v Essex Area Health Authority*,[51] the policy issues behind rejection of wrongful life actions were considered. Particular emphasis was laid on the fact that the alternative would be effectively to require doctors to terminate pregnancies, and that this obligation:

> ... would mean regarding the life of a handicapped child as not only less valuable than the life of a normal child, but so much less valuable that it was not worth preserving, and it would even mean that a doctor would be obliged to pay damages to a child infected with rubella before birth who was in fact born with some mercifully trivial abnormality. These are the consequences of the necessary basic assumption that a child has a right to be born whole or not at all, not to be born unless it can be born perfect or 'normal', whatever that may mean.[52]

However, despite what this case says about not wanting to devalue life with impairment, there are wider policy reasons, such as the purported impossibility of calculating the harm caused by impairment as opposed to not being born at all, which have been influential in rejecting wrongful life actions.

On the other hand, while rejecting compensation in wrongful life cases, the second action – for prenatal damage – may result in compensation being awarded against any person implicated in causing that impairment. For example, the children who were impaired because their mothers ingested thalidomide were able personally to obtain financial compensation, albeit without succeeding in a court of law.[53] The law is now settled that damage sustained either preconception

---

51 [1982] 2 All ER 771.
52 *Ibid.*, p. 781.
53 Teff, H. and Munro, C., *Thalidomide: The Legal Aftermath*, Aldershot, Saxon House, 1976.

or prenatally can legitimately form the basis of legal action. In Scotland this is achieved by using the provisions of the common law,[54] and in England and Wales an action is available in terms of the Congenital Disabilities (Civil Liability) Act 1976.

Finally, failures in genetic counselling, the failure to provide indicated screening[55] and so on, may allow parents to take what is known as a wrongful birth action. In this case, the birth of a child with impairment is perceived by the law as being a harm worthy of compensation. Although traditionally parents have been able to obtain compensation in these circumstances, in the case of *McFarlane v Tayside Health Board*,[56] the compensation made available was restricted to the extent of parental pain and suffering. In apparent contradiction of earlier case law, the court declined to provide financial compensation for the additional costs associated with rearing (in this case a non-disabled) child. In a later judgement, the courts *did* award additional compensation, but this was based on the disability of the mother of the child.[57] The *McFarlane* judgement did not specifically address the question of whether additional compensation might be available when the child is born disabled. However, this question was addressed in the case of *Parkinson v St James and Seacroft University NHS Trust*,[58] which decided that additional damages could be awarded in these circumstances. In *Mason and McCall Smith's Medical Law and Ethics*, the authors suggest that:

> Admitting damages limited to the restitution of costs beyond those involved in bringing up a normal child gave no offence to those with disability and simply acknowledged that the costs in the event of disability were greater than in the case of normality – put another way, the 'deemed equilibrium' between the benefits derived from and the costs of maintaining an uncovenanted healthy child that underpins the *McFarlane* decision is distorted to an extent that is determined by the degree of disability in an unhealthy child.[59]

Thus, even given the *McFarlane* decision, it seems that birth with impairment can be the basis of the award of compensation. It may also have consequences which are non-financial, as we will see in the final section of this chapter. In recognising the 'harm' associated with the birth of a child with an impairment the law is not concerned with distinctions between medical and social models,

---

54 Scottish Law Commission, *Liability for Antenatal Injury*, SLC No 30 (1973) Cmnd 5371.
55 See, for example, *Anderson v Forth Valley Health Board* (1998) 44 BMLR 108; *McLelland v Greater Glasgow Health Board* 1999 SC 305.
56 *McFarlane v Tayside Health Board* [2000] AC 59.
57 *Rees v Darlington Memorial Hospital NHS Trust* [2002] 2 ALL ER 177.
58 [2001] 3 All ER 97.
59 (7th Ed), London, Oxford University Press, 2006, p. 179, para 6.26.

nor does it appear concerned about stigmatisation. Rather, it has long recognised that physical and/or mental problems *which result from someone else's fault* are compensable in law. The focus then is on fault, rather than overtly on the actual condition of the child once born. However, implicit in the desire to right legal wrongs is the possible conclusion that it is impairment rather than fault that is being compensated for. Moreover, decisions about compensation are dependent on the *presence* of impairment; not on how the person is subsequently treated. In other words, the medical model – perhaps inevitably – dominates when fault is brought into the equation. However, the availability of compensation in the presence of fault arguably also sits comfortably with the principle of respect for persons. Once born, every individual is entitled to compensation when someone else's fault (negligence) harms them; people with impairment are simply being accorded the same rights as anyone else would have.

We do, therefore, on occasion treat embryos and foetuses differently based on their genetic or other characteristics. However, for the reasons we have advanced this is not evidence of discrimination *in se*, as there is no person against whom discrimination can be practised. Once born, at least in terms of the consequences of negligence, they are accorded the same rights as others. Additionally, as we have argued, there are other important rights which might trump any 'rights' claimed for the embryo/foetus.

Reproductive liberty

Protecting parental preference for an embryo or foetus free from identifiable impairment might be seen by intending parents (and others) as an aspect of respect for persons, supported by our facilitating principles of autonomy, consent and human rights. Although no positive right to reproduce exists,[60] considerable value is invested in people's reproductive freedoms, and this is reflected in the law's facilitation of the provision of contraception, and even abortion in certain circumstances. Indeed, the recent report from the House of Commons Select Committee on Science and Technology firmly restated the value of reproductive liberty.[61]

In addition to this, prospective parents may argue that their rights to procreative choice – including arguably what kind of children to have – is protected by Art 8 of the European Convention on Human Rights which broadly guarantees the right to private and family life. The positive element of this right is the ability to make decisions both about whether or not to establish a pregnancy and whether or not to continue with it; basically, the right to autonomy or self-determination. However, these rights are not absolute and their exercise is sometimes a cause of concern,

60 For discussion, see McLean, S.A.M., 'The Right to Reproduce', in Campbell, *et al.* (eds), *Human Rights: From Rhetoric to Reality*, Oxford, Basil Blackwell, 1986, chapter 6.
61 *Human Reproductive Technologies and the Law*, House of Commons Select Committee on Science and Technology, Fifth Report of Session 2004–2005, HC 7–1, 2005.

most specifically that what appears to be a choice is actually either inadequately informed, or subject to pressure. As the President's Council says:

> ...the very availability of these [pre-natal screening] tests – accompanied in many cases by subtle pressures applied by counselors (and others) to prospective parents, to abort any abnormal fetus – strongly implies that certain traits are or should be disqualifying qualities of life that justify prevention of birth.[62]

The DPI, whose doubts about screening have already been referred to, maintains that it is not opposed to reproductive liberty, rather it deplores:

> ...the context in which these choices are made.

- There can be no informed choice as long as genetic counselling is directive and misinforms parents about the experience of disability.
- There can be no free choice as long as the myths, fears, stereotypes of and discrimination against disabled people continues.
- There can be no free choice if women are under social pressure to accept routine tests.
- There can be no real choice until women feel able to continue with a pregnancy knowing that they will be bringing their child into a welcoming society that provides comprehensive systems of support.[63]

The value of life with impairment

The fact that so much financial and professional energy is invested in seeking to identify ill health or impairment preconception or pre-birth can easily be seen as symptomatic of an underpinning (negative) mindset in respect of impairment or disability. Shakespeare, for example, says that '...a clear set of values does emerge from the literature, which is implicit and subtle, but undoubtedly reflects a consensus that disability is a major problem, which should be prevented by almost any means necessary'.[64] In addition, the law – either by default or in some situations directly – appears to endorse this mindset, for example in the case of late abortion which we have already discussed. The House of Lords Select Committee in its report for 1987–1988, noted that there are few terminations on this basis, but that 'they comprise most of the abortions performed after 24 weeks...'[65] It has been suggested that '...the law in most countries

---

62 *Beyond Therapy: Biotechnology and the Pursuit of Happiness, op. cit.*, p. 36.
63 DPI, *op. cit.*, p. 6.
64 Shakespeare, T., *op. cit.*, 1999, p. 673.
65 *Report of the Select Committee on the Infant Life (Preservation) Bill*, HL Paper No 50, 1987–1988, London, HMSO, 41.

discriminates against disabled people by allowing termination of pregnancies after a specified time, if the prospective child might be disabled, yet such discrimination is widely outlawed on the grounds of race and gender. This medicalisation of the quality of life diminishes the value of disabled people's lives and those of everyone.'[66]

Moreover, as Gollust says:

> Prenatal genetic testing elicits special concerns for individuals who have genetic conditions. These individuals may perceive the availability of prenatal testing as evidence of pervasive negative attitudes toward life with a disability, because termination of affected fetuses remains the predominant option when a condition is detected.[67]

Doubtless this is so, but it is not clear that dividing the issue into medical versus social will help to resolve this situation. Screening out every compromised pregnancy (the medical model) will not lessen this concern; equally, compelling the implantation and birth of children destined for short or unhappy lives, is scarcely a better solution (the social model). Moreover, if either of these positions is taken to its logical limit, questions would also need to be asked about the provision of *in utero* therapy. That is, in some cases it may be possible to correct a health-related impairment before birth; is it always or ever wrong, or judgmental, to seek cures for impairments, thereby reducing, if not eliminating, the number of such people in the community? Is this demonstrating the same kinds of prejudice towards impairment as the selection of 'good' embryos or the termination of certain pregnancies? Is it merely a legitimate goal of medicine or, as DPI put it, is it reflection of a:

> ...utilitarian ideology which informs much of the new human genetics, particularly the assumption that society would be better off without the inconvenience and expense of disabled people. In contrast, we want to see all clinical practice based on strong principles of justice, ethics and non-discrimination with a respect for diversity, autonomy and fully informed choice.[68]

Alderson, Scott and Thapar conclude that:

> Screening policies are influenced by the medical model of disability which identifies disability with the individual's physical or intellectual impairment, and correlates levels of impairment with the quality of life which that

66 Available at http://freespace.virgin.net/dpi.europe/downloads/bioethics-english.pdf at p. 6 (accessed on 2 August 2005).
67 Gollust, S.E. *et al.*, *op. cit.*, p. 36.
68 *Id.*

person will experience. The aims of this model are to make precise diagnoses and prognoses, and to provide effective cure or relief. These therapeutic aims are inestimably beneficial to people with conditions that can be treated effectively, but they raise problems for people with conditions that cannot be corrected or alleviated medically.[69]

On the other hand, in a small study of people with Down's Syndrome Alderson found that the 'interviewees tended to attribute problems to negative attitudes and social barriers rather than to their congenital condition, and most were frustrated at not having the opportunities, employment, income and social acceptance to enable them to live their lives as fully as they thought they could.'[70] Limitations associated with impairment in such cases are firmly linked to social restrictions and not to physical or mental characteristics.

However, there is arguably one further important factor that needs to be considered. Not only, as we have seen, will people have different views about the choices intending parents want to make, it is not clear what priority – if any – should be given to their own experience of life with disability. In other words, their experience will be personal to them; whether or not it should have direct bearing on the lives of people yet to be born is moot, even if we were wholeheartedly to endorse the social model of disability. First, although it is 'important...to develop rational arguments about the value of disabled people's lives',[71] it is unclear precisely what impact this will or should have on those who are not yet alive. Of course, if there is evidence that decisions taken at the pre-implantation or prenatal stage actually result in cognisable harm to those living with disability or impairment, this may well be relevant. At least from a legal perspective, any decisions, for example, to avoid the birth of children with certain characteristics, are bounded by the legal rights accorded to intending parents and the constraints imposed by legislation such as the Abortion Act 1967 (as amended) and the Human Fertilisation and Embryology Authority, as well as by the fact that the embryo or foetus enjoys no legal personality.

As we have seen in Chapter 2, a number of disability scholars are concerned that the social model fails to take sufficient account of the experiences that are associated with impairment. Shakespeare, for example, contends that the social model fails 'to take account of the salience of impairment in the lives of many disabled people. There is a danger, in the stress laid on social and environmental barriers and practices, of ignoring the impact of physical and intellectual

69 Alderson, P., Scott, P. and Thapar, N., 'Living with a Congenital Condition: The Views of Adults Who Have Cystic Fibrosis, Sickle Cell Anaemia, Down's Syndrome, Spina Bifida or Thalassaemia', in Ettore, E. (ed), *Before Birth: Understanding Prenatal Screening*, Aldershot, Ashgate, 2001, 156 at p. 156.
70 Alderson, P., 'Down's Syndrome: Cost, Quality and Value of Life', *Social Science and Medicine*, 53, 627–638, 2001 at p. 635.
71 Shakespeare, *op. cit.*, 1998, p. 674.

limitation and suffering on people (*sic*) lives.'[72] In addition, he points out that since the people making the decisions 'are predominantly non-disabled people, it is likely that they will hold some of the prejudicial attitudes to disability which are common in society.'[73]

No claim to reproductive liberty, however, is likely to ease the concerns that some people have about the impact of our increasing capacity to identify genetic or other compromise, both on those who may be born and on those already living. For the moment, reprogenetics is likely to exacerbate already difficult decisions in this area by facilitating increased diagnostic capacity in the absence of therapeutic options. As the House of Commons Science and Technology Committee pointed out:

> While genetics is likely eventually to transform medicine, it may take some while before treatments based on genetic knowledge become available... [i]n the short term, the most widespread use of medical genetics will be, as now, in diagnosis and screening.[74]

Scientific advances will, for the foreseeable future, find their primary impact in facilitating the ability of individuals to choose to avoid genetically compromised offspring. Consequently, this will impact on the numbers of people born with particular impairments. As we have suggested, for prospective parents a right to reproductive choice might be invoked to justify the availability of information both about the likely existence of impairment and the ways of avoiding certain births. Rights, by and large trump mere interests, so if it could be said that potential people also have rights there would – in law at least – be an argument for equivalence. However, for the potential persons there is – as we have indicated already – a real question as to what 'rights' might be invoked on their behalf.

Despite some of the rhetoric in this area, both the law and some mainstream ethical positions are clear that no rights are attributable to a potential person not currently in being. Although both the *Report on the Review of the Guidance on the Research Use of Foetuses and Foetal Material*[75] (Polkinghorne Report) and the *Committee of Inquiry into Human Fertilisation and Embryology*[76] (Warnock Report) concluded that the embryo of the human species was worthy of some respect from an ethical perspective, this is not the same as requiring full legal protection. McCullough and Chervenak say:

> ...the fetus cannot be thought to posses subjective interests. Because of the immaturity of its central nervous system, the fetus has no values and beliefs

72 Shakespeare, *op. cit.*, 1999, p. 682.
73 *Ibid.*, p. 681.
74 House of Commons Select Committee on Science and Technology, Third Report, Session 1994–1995, 41-1, London, HMSO, paras 71–72.
75 Cm 762/1989.
76 Cm 9314/1984.

that form the basis of such interests. It obviously follows from this that the fetus cannot possess deliberative interests, since these, in turn, are based on subjective interests and reflection on subjective interests. The latter is a task no fetus can accomplish. Hence, there can be no autonomy-based obligations to the fetus. Hence, also, there can be no meaningful talk of fetal rights, the fetus's right to life in particular, in the sense that the fetus itself generates rights.[77]

Equally, the law's position can be identified from a series of important cases – often dealing with attempts to compel women into certain behaviour in order to protect the developing foetus[78] – and is clearly expressed in the case of *Re MB*,[79] where it was said that '[t]he fetus up to the moment of birth does not have any separate interests capable of being taken into account...'.[80]

Thus, the 'rights' of the embryo or foetus will not be protected either by national law or by the terms of Art 2 of the European Convention on Human Rights.[81] Nonetheless, the President's Council has said that:

> ...we think it important to observe that the existence and normalization of prenatal diagnosis and abortion for genetic defect have already had significant effects on our thinking: about our genetic endowments, about reproductive choice and responsible parenthood, and about what constitutes a good or 'good enough' child.[82]

Expectations of health and freedom from impairment undoubtedly inform virtually all preconception and prenatal decisions. It is the search for the 'perfect' or non-impaired child that drives medical intervention in these pregnancies. This may well seem insulting to those who live with impairment, although we have argued that there is no logical link between preventing impairment and our attitude to those who currently exist in similar circumstances. However, even if this is so, prevention of birth with impairment *does* – like it or not – reflect our preference for 'ability' over 'dis-ability'. Whether this is pure and unacceptable prejudice or simply the (acceptable) desire to spare future children possible suffering (clinical or social) is a question which requires to be answered, however difficult it may be. The balance to be struck seems to be between reproductive liberty on the one hand and concerns

---

77 McCullough, L.B. and Chervenak, F.A., *Ethics in Obstetrics and Gynaecology*, Oxford UP, 1994 at p. 102.
78 See, for example, *Re S.* 9 BMLR 69 (12 October 1992); *Re MB* [1997] 8 Med LR 217; *Re F (in utero)* [1998] 2 All ER 193; *St. George's Healthcare N.H.S. Trust v S* [1998] 3 All ER 673.
79 Cited earlier.
80 Per Butler-Sloss at p. 227.
81 *Vo v France* (2004) 79 BMLR 71.
82 *Beyond Therapy: Biotechnology and the Pursuit of Happiness, op. cit.*, p. 35.

about possible discrimination on the other. What seems clear, however, is that forcing people to abandon reproductive liberty by removing choice is unlikely to resolve the problems of discrimination that undoubtedly exist for those born with impairment.

This is an issue that pervades the whole of life, but one particularly vulnerable group is the one in the very early stages of life.

The neonatal period and the early years of life

Decisions about treatment in the early days or months of life are choices made about people who are especially vulnerable, yet cannot make their own views heard. It is thus necessary – assuming that such decisions need to be taken at all – that they are set against some kind of principle.

In the ordinary course of events, the birth of a child raises few ethical or legal dilemmas. A child not in need of unusual medical care and presenting with no impairment will seldom, if ever, be a source of conflict between doctors and parents or indeed of difficult and sensitive medical or social decisions. However, for the child born with an impairment, particularly where it is severe, there may well be conflicts of interest and difficult decisions to be taken about whether or not treatment should be made available. In some cases parents and/or doctors may find themselves making judgements about whether or not an individual child should receive treatment which can sustain life. Light identifies the scale of this problem by noting that:

> There is a particularly high incidence of death amongst disabled children, which appears to reflect the still prevalent assumption that disabled lives are 'not worth living', such that newborn children with impairments are denied medical treatment or simply left to die.[83]

The UK law's approach to this question is evidenced by a series of cases, which are worth brief consideration. Although not the first case to consider this issue, the first criminal prosecution came in 1981 in the case of *R v Arthur*.[84] In this case, a child suffering from what appeared to be uncomplicated Down's Syndrome was born to parents who indicated their preference that the child should not survive. The doctor marked the child's medical records accordingly and prescribed 'nursing care only'. The child was not, therefore, provided with sustenance and died some 69 hours later. Dr Leonard Arthur, a respected paediatrician, was subsequently charged with the child's murder. In the course of the trial, evidence from an expert pathologist indicated that the child had suffered from additional clinical problems and that, in fact, death could have

---

83 Light, R., 'A Real Horror Story: The Abuse of Disabled People's Human Rights', *Disability Awareness in Action Human Rights Database*, Disability Awareness in Action, 2002 at p. 13.
84 (1981) 12 BMLR 1.

been caused by one of them. In these circumstances, the charge was reduced to attempted murder, of which the jury found Dr Arthur not guilty. This somewhat perverse judgement can be interpreted as demonstrating a number of phenomena. First, juries are reluctant to convict respected professionals such as doctors of criminal offences, particularly when the doctor is acting according to his or her conscience and in what he or she perceives to be the best interests of the child. Second the judge's directions to the jury clearly invited such a verdict. Although the judge claimed that no special rules applied to medical professionals, he nonetheless, in referring to the weight of evidence from fellow paediatricians that they also might have made the same decision as Dr Arthur, said, 'I imagine that you will think long and hard before concluding that doctors, of the eminence we have heard...have evolved standards that amount to committing a crime.'[85] Evidence given by experts at trial indicated that 'no paediatrician takes life but we do accept that allowing babies to die is in the baby's best interests at times.'[86]

In a case heard in the same year – the case of *Re B (a minor)*[87] – a Down's Syndrome child was born suffering from an intestinal blockage. The life-saving surgery to remove the blockage was relatively straightforward and certainly would have been indicated in the case of a child not diagnosed as Down's. The parents declined to provide their consent to the surgery, and the case was taken to court for resolution. Dunn, L.J. declared that this child should be '...put in the position of any other mongol child and given the opportunity to live an existence.'[88] This judgement, unlike the *Arthur* judgement, seemed to uphold the values overtly espoused by the courts when they refer – as they often do – to the importance of erring on the side of life where possible. However, Templeman, L.J. did say in the same case:

> There may be cases...of severe proved damage where the future is so certain and where the life of the child is so bound to be full of pain and suffering that the court must be driven to a different conclusion.[89]

In this case, therefore, we actually see movement *away* from a commitment to an ethic which affords value to life *per se*, *towards* an approach which values certain human characteristics or qualities. In Chapter 2 we found that a number of fundamental ethical principles – human dignity, sanctity of life and respect for persons – also tend, in their more sophisticated formulations, to prioritise these 'higher' traits of human life, but also that respect for persons offered the most solid basis from which to consider what is appropriate treatment of a person.

85 *Ibid.*, p. 22.
86 *Ibid.*, p. 18.
87 [1981] 1 WLR 1421.
88 *Ibid.*, p. 1425.
89 *Ibid.*, p. 1424.

In seeming recognition of this, following the *Arthur* case the Attorney General indicated that in his view the law of murder had not been changed, and held out the possibility that anyone who had a duty towards a child would still be guilty of murder or attempted murder if they fail to fulfil that duty.[90] However, in the *Arthur* case it would seem that professional decisions about quality of life, or potential quality of life, particularly when endorsed by parents, are unlikely to lead to a successful criminal prosecution. Moreover, the case of *Re B* suggests that the civil law also does not offer blanket protection to all of those who are legally 'persons'.

It should be acknowledged here, however, that not everyone agrees that a baby or very young child is in fact a 'person'. Although we do not adopt this position, it is espoused by a number of commentators. At the heart of such claims is the conviction that newborn infants do not possess any capacities that enable them to be rationally – not just emotionally – distinguished from a viable but unborn foetus that is legally not taken to be a person. Glover, for example, acknowledges the temptation to think that infants change in some significant way upon birth to assume the status of legal personhood that they lacked moments earlier.[91] However, he argues that allocating personhood on the basis of such life-events is artificial and unsound.[92] Thus, he proposes that it is:

> ...more defensible to abandon the view that there is an abrupt transition to the status of a person and to replace it by the view that being a person is a matter of degree. A one-year-old is much more of a person than a new-born baby or a foetus just before birth, but each of these is more of a person than the embryo.

Similarly, Tooley has more recently explained that debates on the allocation of personhood must focus on:

> ...the type of mental life that an entity is capable of enjoying at present, it seems likely that any criterion of personhood that classified newborn human infants as persons would also classify adult animals of *many* other species as persons as well, and so would necessitate a very significant revision of our ordinary moral opinions.

At least theoretically, the law does not accept this position and purports to provide equal rights and respect irrespective of characteristics such as age, sex, race and disability. This is not to say that treatment must always be given, as we must also recognise that some conditions are incompatible with life, or may be unduly burdensome for the person concerned. Respecting them might also

---

90 19 HC Official Reports (6th series) written answers, col 349, 8 March 1982.
91 Glover, J., *Causing Death and Saving Lives*, London, Penguin Books, 1977 at p. 126.
92 *Ibid.*, p. 126f.

include allowing them to die in as dignified a manner as possible, and a number of legal cases have done just that. Again this reflects the fact that the actual impact of impairment on the individual should not be ignored. Some of these cases will be considered briefly below.

The case of *Re C (a minor) (Wardship: Medical Treatment)*[93] concerned a moribund child. In this case, the hospital was given the authority to provide palliative care, but was not obliged to use additional care – for example antibiotics – should the child become ill. The decision was said to be based on the welfare of the child. The case of *Re J (a minor) (Wardship: Medical Treatment)*[94] concerned a brain damaged child, subject to fits and occasional cessation of respiration. This case differs somewhat from *Re C* because in this case the child was not dying, although clearly it was very ill. Ventilation would result in the child's life being saved and failure to treat would guarantee the child's death. The Court of Appeal held that '...it would not be in J's best interest to reventilate him in the event of his stopping breathing unless to do so seems appropriate to the doctors caring for him given the prevailing clinical situation.'[95] In other words, the decision as to whether or not this child should live was one which appeared to lie firmly within the ambit of the judgement of the medical profession. However, Lord Donaldson emphasised a number of things which must be present when such decisions are being taken. First, he suggested that whoever makes the decision should try to take the perspective of the individual child in reaching a conclusion. Second, he indicated that the possible distress or pain that might be caused by imposing treatment should be taken into account. Third, the decision as to whether or not to treat in these circumstances should be a shared decision, either between parents and doctors or between doctors/parents and the court. Fourth, the decision should be in the best interests of the child. Finally, the decision should not be the direct cause of death. In other words, the choice not to treat is couched in terms of allowing death to happen as a result of underlying illness or impairment rather than actively causing death. In this way, courts are able to convince themselves that they do not sanction deliberate killing, even although it is clear that the actions (or omissions) in question are expected (even intended?) to cause the death of the individual child. In this respect Lord Donaldson said:

> The Court never sanctions steps to terminate life. That would be unlawful. There is no question of approving, even in the case of the most horrendous disability, a course aimed at terminating life or accelerating death. The Court is concerned only with the circumstances in which steps should not be taken to prolong life.[96]

93 [1989] 2 All ER 782.
94 [1990] 3 All ER 930.
95 *Ibid.*, p. 933.
96 *Ibid.*, p. 943.

This apparent sophistry will be returned to later, but it merits brief consideration at the moment. In an effort to avoid legitimising even voluntary euthanasia[97] the courts effectively permit what Glover calls non-voluntary euthanasia.[98] In other words, they selectively endorse the death of an individual without being able to ascertain his or her views, albeit purportedly in his or her best interests. In the case of *Re J (a minor) (Medical Treatment)*[99] a mother tried to force clinicians to provide intensive care for her child. In the clear view of the doctors, such treatment would have been either futile or overly intrusive. In this case, Balcombe, C.J. said:

> I can conceive of no situation where it would be proper . . . to order a doctor, whether directly or indirectly, to treat a child in the manner contrary to his or her clinical judgement. I would go further. I find it difficult to conceive of a situation where it would be a proper exercise of the jurisdiction to make an order positively requiring a doctor to adopt a particular course of treatment in relation to a child.[100]

This case clearly demonstrates another set of tensions which differ from those identified in the first section of this chapter. In this case, the professional judgement of the clinicians – rather than the parents – is held to be of paramount importance. This is something which on the one hand could be applauded, since it certainly is not for the courts to make clinical decisions. Nor, indeed, is it for patients or relatives to make them. However, the tension emerges when we accept that the result of endorsing professional choice is the medicalisation of decisions about life-and-death.[101] This is perhaps less troublesome in circumstances where the prognosis is in any event hopeless, but more controversial in circumstances where a life could be saved, but quality of life judgements become of critical importance. Smith, for example, has said that in the United States:

> Although generally considered unlawful, non-treatment of disabled newborns is probably not a rare event. One study, for example, found that 14 per cent of all infant deaths in the studied hospital were related to withdrawal or withholding of medical treatment.[102]

97 That is, causing the death of someone at their request and in their best interests. See Glover, J., *Causing Death and Saving Lives*, Harmondsworth, Penguin, 1977.

98 *Ibid.*, p. 192.

99 [1992] 4 All ER 614.

100 *Ibid.*, p. 625.

101 For further consideration, see McLean, S.A.M., *Old Law, New Medicine*, London, Rivers Oram/Pandora, 1999, chapter 6.

102 Smith, S.R., 'Disabled Newborns and the Federal Child Abuse Amendments: Tenuous Protection', *The Hastings Law Journal*, 37, May 1986, 765 at pp. 767–768.

Where life sustaining treatment is withheld from a child born with impairment, the courts are at pains to indicate that their only concern is the welfare of the child and not the interests of the state or of the parents or of the doctors. However, it is obviously difficult to identify any subtle external influences, although it is easy to assume that they are there.

For some, of course, the very decisions themselves are unacceptable, no matter how we try to justify them. Rhoden, for example, notes that:

> Withholding treatment based on quality of life decisions has been roundly condemned by many courts and legal commentators and has been deemed nearly as reprehensible as denying care to an infant born in a ghetto because it is likely to grow up in poverty, ignorance and squalor.[103]

In the case of *Re C (a baby)*[104] a premature infant, who had suffered from meningitis, had become blind and deaf and was suffering from convulsions, required ventilation. With ventilation, it was anticipated that the child could have lived for months, perhaps even longer. However, in the circumstances the court agreed that the ventilation could be discontinued. In the case of *Re C (a minor)*[105] the parents of the disabled child were Orthodox Jews who held all human life to be sacred. In this case, the child suffered from a progressive condition for which there was no cure. The child was conscious and did evidence some reactions, seeming, for example, to recognise the parents. The doctors proposed to conduct a trial of ventilation. In other words they intended to remove the ventilation and, should the child suffer respiratory problems, she would not be reventilated but would be allowed to die. While the parents were prepared to permit the doctors to undertake the first part of this plan – namely the removal of the ventilation – they were not comfortable with the second part which would result in the child's death. In this case, the Court agreed with the doctors' proposals, against the wishes of the parents.

This run of cases resulted in the Royal College of Paediatrics and Child Health issuing in 1997 a document entitled *Withholding or Withdrawing Life Saving Treatment in Children: A Framework for Practice*.[106] This document provided guidance for clinicians about the circumstances in which it would be legitimate to withhold or withdraw treatment from children born with illnesses or impairment ostensibly requiring treatment. These guidelines are not uncontroversial, perhaps most so in respect of two cases. The first is referred to as the 'no purpose' situation; that is, a situation where a child could be saved, but the 'degree of physical or mental impairment will be so great that it is

---

103 Rhoden, N., 'Treatment Dilemmas for Imperiled Newborns: Why Quality of Life Counts', *Southern California Law Review*, 58, 1985, 1283 at p. 1331.

104 (1996) 32 BMLR 44.

105 (1997) 40 BMLR 31.

106 'A Framework for Practice', available at www.rcpch.ac.uk/publications/recent_publications/witholding.pdf (accessed on 18 October 2006).

unreasonable to expect them to bear it.'[107] The second, is the 'unbearable' situation; namely that the child or (more commonly and controversially, the family) feel that further treatment cannot be borne.

In the case of *National Health Service Trust v D*,[108] the Courts had the opportunity not only to review the precedents derived from the cases that have already been discussed, but also of contemplating the practice of selectively allowing some children to die against the backdrop of the European Convention on Human Rights. In this case, the child had been born with irreversible lung disease and multi-organ failure. The Trust concerned applied for a declaration that it would be lawful not to resuscitate the child if he suffered cardio-respiratory arrest and that only treatment which would allow him to end his life peacefully need be given. The case reached court, as is commonly the case, because the parents opposed this plan. In the clearest statement yet of the value to be given to the interests of the child and others, the Court said:

> ...the Court's primary and paramount consideration must be the best interests of the child. This of course involves...consideration of the views of the parents concerned...However...those views cannot themselves override the Court's view of the ward's best interests.[109]

Additionally, the Court opined that there was no breach of Art 2 of the Convention on Human Rights ('the right to life') in permitting doctors to fail to resuscitate, providing that the decision was in the best interests of the child. This position was adopted most recently in the sad case of Charlotte Wyatt, whose parents have fought two court battles to require resuscitation should she require it. Their most recent petition was unsuccessful, as had been the earlier one, based on a clear acceptance by the court of the clinical judgement of the doctors concerned.[110] In October 2005, as Charlotte reached the age of two years, her parents won a revision of these earlier declarations in the High Court.[111] Despite the extremely gloomy prognosis from her doctors at the beginning of her life, Charlotte seems to have defied the odds. Her life may be impaired, but her parents have ensured that she still has it.

In March 2006, The High Court in England heard the case of *An NHS Trust v MB*.[112] In this case, MB was diagnosed at a few weeks old as having spinal muscular atrophy (SMA). Although some people may live for many years with this condition, MB's case was particularly serious and death reasonably imminent. At 18 months, the child was very ill, but according to his parents, able to respond to some stimuli. A dispute arose between doctors and parents about

107 RCPH, *op. cit.*, 2004, p. 11.
108 (2000) 55 BMLR 19.
109 *Ibid.*, p. 28.
110 *Re Wyatt (a child) (medical treatment: parents' consent)* (2004) 84 BMLR 206.
111 http://news.bbc.co.uk/1/hi/programmes/law_in_action/4364774.stm (accessed on 7 July 2006).
112 [2006] EWHC 507 (Fam) (15 March 2006) (transcript).

whether or not further ventilation should be offered should it become necessary. Expressing the law's position, Mr Justice Holman said that while '[t]he views and opinions of both the doctors *and* the parents must be carefully considered', they may not reflect the 'objective best interests' of the child.[113] Identifying these interests is the job of the courts. In this case, the court was prepared to authorise treatment to the point at which he might require CPR; at that point, although he might possibly be saved, he was in effect dying and should be permitted to do so with dignity. This judgement seems to have sought a balance between the wishes of the parents and the judgement of the doctors.

One further case merits consideration, since it seems to go against the trend which has emerged from the cases already discussed. In the case of *Re T (a minor)(Wardship: Medical Treatment)*[114] the Court of Appeal followed the wishes of parents rather than those of clinicians in a situation where in fact potentially a child could have been saved. In this case, the child was born with biliary atresia. Although this condition was likely to be fatal without a transplant, the doctors believed that a transplant had a good chance of success. A consultant acting for the child's mother, however, opposed the surgery, on the basis of the pain and suffering which the child would undergo were a transplant to be undertaken, and based on the fact that an earlier attempt at surgery had resulted in just such pain and suffering and had been unsuccessful. Although the trial judge had overridden the views of the parents that the child should not be forced to undergo this treatment, the Court of Appeal felt that the trial judge had given insufficient attention to the views of the parents (who interestingly were described as health professionals). In addition, it was asked whether – if the surgery went ahead – the mother would not find considerable difficulty in looking after the child, given her opposition to the treatment. This in itself would be harmful for the child. As has been pointed out:

> Despite the protestations of all three judges, and despite the court's repeated assurances as to the responsibility and devotion of the parents, an unavoidable impression remains that their interests weighed heavily in the balance at the expense of the paramountcy of those of the child.[115]

From what has gone before, then, it can be seen that children born with certain kinds of conditions will not necessarily receive equal treatment to those not suffering from them. Harris, for example, says:

> Selective treatment of severely handicapped children is calculated to result in their deaths... Such a policy has been justified on the basis of the

---

113 Transcript at p. 4.
114 [1997] 1 All ER 906.
115 *Mason and McCall Smith's Law and Medical Ethics*, Oxford, Oxford University Press, 2006, at p. 571, para 16.79.

hypothesis that it is reasonable to conclude that the child would be better off dead. This paradoxical sounding conclusion means simply that it is judged to be in the child's best interests to die.[116]

We have already discussed the deliberate creation of a child with what those outside of the deaf community would almost certainly see as an impairment, in the case where parents deliberately created a child who was congenitally deaf. Interestingly, a court in the Republic of Ireland recently took arguably a somewhat puzzling view on preventable impairment. In this case, the child was diagnosed at birth as suffering from phenylketonuria (PKU). Children born with this condition can develop severe learning disabilities, but treatment at birth and throughout life can stave off these effects. All children are now tested at birth for this condition, and this has largely been seen as uncontroversial. However, in the case of *North Western Health Board v W (H)*,[117] a court in the Republic of Ireland permitted parents to reject the heel prick test for PKU. As the Irish Constitution explicitly regards the family as the fundamental unit of society, the decision was taken not solely from the perspective of the child's best medical interests (which everyone agreed would be served by accurate diagnosis and treatment) but rather – perhaps in a similar way to the judgement in *Re T* already referred to – by evaluation of his holistic best interests. Laurie says that, '[o]n one analysis this decision represents a triumph for the view that the best interests test does not simply mean best medical interests...'.[118] However, it also suggests that one potential outcome of widening the interests to be evaluated beyond the purely medical might lead to decisions which can be seen as perverse (as arguably was also the case in *Re T (a minor)(Wardship: Medical Treatment)*, which we discussed above.

Medical considerations have, by and large, dominated the judgements of UK courts. As we suggested at the beginning of this chapter, this may be intelligible given that the decision-makers are often medical. However, even where others – such as parents and courts – have been involved, it would appear that the medical model predominates when decisions are made about the child's future. Corker and Davis argue that '...the dominant discourse of law in relation to disabled children is one that sees disability or children, but not disabled children, and views disability itself in terms of dependency.'[119] Yet it has been said that:

One's options in life as a person with a disability may indeed, in some ways, be limited, but oppressive social conditions have so distorted the public's

---

116 Harris, J., *The Value of Life*, London, Routledge and Kegan Paul, 1985 at p. 33.
117 [2001] IESC 70 (8 November 2001).
118 Laurie, G., 'Better to Hesitate at the Threshold of Compulsion: PKU Testing and the Concept of Family Autonomy in Eire', *JME*, 28, 2002, 136–138 at p. 137.
119 Corker, M. and Davis, J.M., 'Disabled Children: (Still) Invisible Under the Law', in Cooper, J. (ed), *Law, Rights and Disability*, London, Jessica Kingsley Publishers, 2000, 217–238 at p. 233.

perceptions, as well as how disabled individuals themselves might internalize these perceptions, that it is difficult to assess the true impact of disability on the individual's life experience.[120]

Decisions in this area are inherently ethically problematic, but it does appear that the courts are heavily influenced by the medical assessment of quality of life, despite the fact that judgements about quality might arguably be taken to involve relevant considerations which are wider than diagnosis and prognosis. As has been said:

> Medicine may well have created or exacerbated the problems faced in the paediatric wards, but the resolution of these problems requires assessments which transcend the clinical. Certainly, courts will wish to take account of parental views and clinical prognoses, but these cannot be treated as definitive. The issues involved are too significant to be left to partial decision making, however well intentioned...These are dilemmas for all of us and not simply for the doctors or for the unfortunate parents.[121]

In light of such concerns it is important to examine in more detail whether the approaches that are generally employed to inform surrogate decisions are able to fairly represent the interests of disabled infants by avoiding partial decisions which may work against the interests of disabled people.

Assessing the value of disabled infant lives: best interests and the quality of life

Best-interest judgements are employed in cases where it is necessary to make a treatment decision regarding a patient whose views and general mindset are unknown; often such cases involve infants who have not been able to formulate such preferences.[122] As we noted at the beginning of this section, the birth of healthy infants presents few, if any, treatment dilemmas. Therefore, the infants at the heart of best-interest decisions are more often than not those with impairments, or to use the language of the medical model, infants who are disabled. Given the ubiquity of best-interest decisions in cases we have examined involving neonates it is necessary to examine this concept in more detail.

---

120 Saxton, M., 'Why Members of the Disability Community Oppose Prenatal Diagnosis and Selective Abortion', in Parens, E. and Asch, A. (eds), *Prenatal Testing and Disability Rights*, Washington, DC, Georgetown University Press, 2000, 147–164 at p. 150.

121 McLean, *op. cit.*, pp. 136–137.

122 Beauchamp, T.L. and Childress, J.F., *Principles of Biomedical Ethics* (5th Ed), Oxford, Oxford University Press, 2001 at p. 100; Elliott, C., 'Patients Doubtfully Capable or Incapable of Consent', in Kuhse, H. and Singer, P. (eds), *A Companion to Bioethics*, Oxford, Blackwell Publishers, 2001, 452–462 at p. 454.

Issues which must be identified in relation to best-interests decisions are: the factors which determine whether something is in an infant's best interests, the perspective from which such decisions are made and the relationship between such decisions and impairment or disability. Cantor identifies the elements which influence whether treatment or even continued existence is thought to be in an infant's best interest as '...physical and mental suffering, chances of recovery, nature of patient interaction with his or her environment, regaining of function, indignity...'[123] That is, it is necessary to determine whether the infant will experience more pain than pleasure (burden/benefits) as a result of any proposed treatment (or treatment omission). [124] As Brock notes:

> ...the best interest principle instructs us to determine the *net* benefit for the patient of each option, assigning different weights to the options to reflect the relative importance of the various interests they further or thwart, then subtracting costs or 'disbenefits' from the benefits for each option. The course of action to be followed, then, is the one with the greatest net benefit to the patient. The mere fact that a treatment would benefit the patient is not sufficient to show that it would be in the individual's best interests, or the costs of the option to the patient – in suffering and disability – may exceed the benefit.[125]

Hence, it lies at the heart of best-interest evaluations that disability is a cost. This suggests that best-interest assessments are based on a predetermined attitude towards impairment which perceives the experience of such people in a negative way, and quality of life considerations appear to reflect the concerns of those who espouse the social model of disability.

There is agreement that best-interests decisions can be made by endeavouring to determine what either most rational people would want if they were in the position of the infant (or other never competent person) or by considering what the impaired child would choose for him or herself.[126] Brock states that making a best-interests decision:

> ...requires the surrogate to make the treatment decision that best serves the patient's interests...it applies the choice of most persons to the patient in question because in the absence of any information to establish that the patient's relevant preferences and values are different than most people's, the

123 Cantor, N.L., 'The Bane of Surrogate Decision-Making: Defining the Best Interests of Never-Competent Persons', *The Journal of Legal Medicine*, 26, 2005, 155–205 at p. 158.
124 *Ibid.*, p. 160.
125 Brock, D.W., *Life and Death: Philosophical Essays in Biomedical Ethics*, Cambridge, Cambridge University Press, 1993 at p. 123f.
126 Cantor, *op. cit.*, p. 161; Arras, J.D., 'Toward an Ethic of Ambiguity', *Hastings Center Report*, 14, 4, 1984, 25–33 at p. 29.

most reasonable presumption is that the patient is like most others in relevant respects and would choose like others.[127]

However, Cantor adds to this by noting that it is not only the requirements of most rational people which should be borne in mind:

> At the same time that a conscientious surrogate must use the reasonable person perspective in fixing the level of suffering that should be deemed intolerable, that surrogate must scrupulously adhere to the disabled person's perspective in discerning the levels of suffering and gratification actually present (or foreseeable) in any individual case. The object is to discern the benefits and burdens from the point of view of the profoundly disabled patient.... The question is whether the particular patient would be better off dead than alive in the circumstances facing the patient, not whether the surrogate (or even the average capacitated person) would want to live in those conditions...[128]

Arras, on the other hand, succinctly argues that any efforts to use either the preferences of most rational people or those which the surrogate thinks would be chosen by the incompetent infant present 'staggering problems of interpretation'.[129] First, making best interests decisions based on the perspective of most rational adults is problematic because it is likely their perspectives will be '...biased in favour of normalcy. Being normal themselves, competent adults have naturally pitched their value systems on the solid ground of normalcy.'[130] This concern is substantiated by our analysis in Chapter 1 where we identified the negative ramifications of the normal-abnormal dichotomy that can be associated with a medical approach to disability. Arras continues that decisions made from the perspective of rational adults:

> ... will necessarily be prejudicial to the best interests of impaired children. In contrast to the point about the inevitability of abuse, this objection assumes the appropriateness of a best interests standard but insists that any criterion based on the values of normal adults is bound systematically to distort our judgements of what is truly in the child's best interests.[131]

Second, another option for surrogate decision-makers is to make decisions based on some notion of what the incompetent child would choose for him or herself. However, problems also exist in respect of this '...inherently difficult'

---

127 Brock, *op. cit.*, p. 290f.
128 Cantor, *op. cit.*, p. 161f.
129 Arras, *op. cit.*, p. 26.
130 *Ibid.*, p. 30.
131 *Id.*

alternative for determining what is in an infant's best interest.[132] There is, for example, the possibility that a:

> ...surrogate will undervalue the simple benefits that the disabled patient derives from existence and project negative feelings (such as frustration flowing from incapacity or embarrassment from posing a burden to others) to the disabled patient.[133]

This is, because the competent surrogate necessarily lacks first hand experience of the value and pleasure that can be gained from the *most basic* human capacities, the decisions they make could assume that such experiences are not worth having. In addition it is also possible that they will apportion pain and frustration to a life where none exists, as Robertson states:

> One who has never known the pleasures of mental operation, ambulation, and social interaction surely does not suffer from their loss as much as one who has. While one who has known these capacities may prefer death to a life without them, we have no assurance that the handicapped person, with no point of comparison would agree.[134]

Alternatively, a best-interests assessment could decide that if an infant's life is free from pain, sustaining it is necessary even when it expresses no characteristics which are distinctly human. In such cases involving severely disabled children Arras notes that '...it is difficult to understand in what sense such a child can have any interests to which a best-interest standard might apply.'[135] Cases which give us no clear idea whether a child benefits from what seems to be merely a vegetative existence raise wider questions about what features a life must exhibit for us to consider it 'worth living'. In this respect, it is necessary to note that the best-interests standard is in essence a way of determining an actual or prospective patient's quality of life.[136] A more detailed investigation of quality of life judgements will help us assess whether the concerns which have been expressed about the treatment of infants with impairment in respect of surrogate decision-making are valid.

Quality of life

Assessments of the value of human life made within a quality of life framework are based on the conviction that 'the really important thing is not to live, but to

132   Cantor, *op. cit.*, p. 162.
133   *Id.*
134   Robertson, J., 'Involuntary Euthanasia of Defective Newborns', *Stanford Law Review*, 27 January 1975, 213–269 at p. 254.
135   Arras, *op. cit.*, p. 31.
136   Beauchamp, T,L. and Childress, J.F., *Principles of Biomedical Ethics* (5th Ed), Oxford, Oxford University Press, 2001 at p. 102.

live well.'[137] Thus, like the foundational and facilitating principles we examined in the previous chapter, the aim of quality of life judgments is to promote a particular type of human life. Yet amidst the diversity of human experience it is notoriously difficult to assess the quality of another person's experiences, or to determine whether what is 'good' for one person is 'good' for another. The difficulties of employing quality of life as a tool to evaluate healthcare decisions, as Nussbaum and Sen point out, concern questions such as: 'How do we determine this? What information do we require? Which criteria are truly relevant to human "thriving"?'[138]

Quality of life judgements reputedly provide reliable markers to prevent the value-laden judgements which may detrimentally impact on the interpretation of impaired and disabled lives – whether incompetent or competent. There is a wide range of frameworks within which such decisions are made. One fairly detailed approach to assessing the quality of a human life is provided by Nussbaum, who employs a list of what she terms 'capabilities' to set standards for human flourishing in respect of basic areas of life.[139] She suggests that the aim of society should be to enable its members to live well by supporting them in the following spheres:

1. Life – Being able to live to the end of a human life of normal length; not dying prematurely, or before one's life is so reduced as to be not worth living.
2. Bodily Health – Being able to have good health, including reproductive health; to be adequately nourished; to have adequate shelter.
3. Bodily Integrity – Being able to move freely from place to place; to be secure against assault, including sexual assault, child sexual abuse; having opportunities for sexual satisfaction.
4. Senses, Imagination, and Thought – Including adequate education to permit the use of these functions.
5. Emotions – Being able to have attachments to things and people outside ourselves; in general, to love, to grieve, to experience longing, gratitude and justified anger. Not having one's emotional development blighted by overwhelming fear and anxiety, or by traumatic events of abuse and neglect.
6. Practical Reason – Being able to form a conception of the good and to engage in critical reflection about the planning of one's life.
7. Affiliation – a) To engage in various forms of social interaction.

137 Socrates in Plato's Crito in *The Last Days of Socrates*, trans. Tredennick, H., London, Penguin Classics, 1954 at p. 87.
138 Nussbaum, M. and Sen, A., 'Introduction', in Nussbaum, M. and Sen, A. (eds), *The Quality of Life*, Oxford, Oxford University Press, 1993, 1–6 at p. 1.
139 Nussbaum, M., *Women and Human Development: The Capabilities Approach*, Cambridge, Cambridge University Press, 2000.

 b) Having the social bases of self-respect and non-humiliation; being able to be treated as a dignified being whose worth is equal to that of others. This entails, at a minimum, protections against discrimination on the basis of race, sex, sexual orientation, religion, caste, ethnicity, or national origin.
 8. Other Species – Being able to live with concern for and in relation to animals, plants, and the world of nature.
 9. Play – Being able to enjoy recreational activities.
 10. Control Over One's Environment – a) Political. Being able to participate in political choices that govern one's life.
 b) Material – Being able to hold property.[140]

Nussbaum claims that a life that lacks capabilities in these areas, which cannot be redressed by social support, cannot be identified as a good human life. Rather, it could be too 'bestial' for it to be regarded as a human life at all.[141] The principles in Nussbaum's list that are relevant to disability, impairment and life-and-death decision-making lead to the conclusion that some human lives will not be worth living. For example, the quality of life is questionable if people are impaired in such a way that: movement is restricted (bodily integrity), their lives are expected to end before those of their more 'normal' peers (Life) or they lack what could be termed 'good health' due to disease, trauma or impairment. Nussbaum is surely right to suggest that most people are likely to flourish if they are able to function in all the areas she identifies. As Morreim suggests:

> . . . there may be disagreement about the particular elements on such a list, yet the important point is that there are at least some circumstances of life which, judged in and of themselves, are undesirable for any human being and some which are desirable.[142]

One positive aspect of this way of assessing disability and impairment is that Nussbaum's approach to quality of life imposes positive and negative obligations on others – nation states and other agencies – to ensure that, where possible, individuals are helped to attain an adequate quality of life; a proposal that could help to address the concerns of some disabled people that social factors are equally as disabling as physical and biological impairments.[143] Arguably a primary concern raised by this type of approach to assessing the quality of

---

140 Nussbaum, M., *Women and Human Development: The Capabilities Approach*, Cambridge, Cambridge University Press, 2000, p. 78f.
141 Nussbaum, M., 'Aristotelian Social Democracy', in Douglass, B., Mara, G.M. and Richardson, H.S. (eds), *Liberalism and the Good*, London and New York, Routledge, 1990, 203–252 at p. 218f.
142 Morreim, E.H., 'Computing the Quality of Life', in Agich, G..J. and Begley, C.E. (eds), *The Price of Health*, Dordrecht and Lancaster, Reidel Publishing Company, 1986, 45–69, at p. 47.
143 Banfalvy, C., 'The Paradox of the Quality of Life of Adults with Learning Difficulties', *Disability and Society*, 11, 4, 1996, 569–577 at p. 576. We will examine the influence of social and physical factors on disability in the following chapter.

a person's life is that it could still be used to impose negative judgements on individuals with physical and mental impairments who cannot be helped by the provision of additional resources.

This concern has not surprisingly led to criticism of decisions based on quality of life judgements from within the disability community. Indeed, Johnstone suggests there is a 'looming crisis of confidence around the concept of the quality of life',[144] and Morris claims that part of this crisis relates to the fact that despite assumptions to the contrary:

> The quality of our lives, and our life chances, are not inevitably determined by what our bodies can't do, or look like, or how our minds function. Like the women's movement, we say that 'anatomy is not destiny'.[145]

Another question is raised by Asch, who takes issue with the tendency to assess the quality of disabled lives by assuming that if a person requires assistance with basic day to day tasks his or her 'dignity and adulthood' are compromised,[146] while Wolfensberger suggests that individuals with impairments are assumed to have a poor quality of life merely because they are different from their 'able-bodied' peers.[147] Finally, it is also important to note that it has been claimed that research on the life experience of people with impairments constantly finds a 'paradox' in the high levels of quality of life that are reported by disabled people as opposed to the assumptions of third parties. The fact that disabled people reporting that they have a good quality of life is regarded as a paradox highlights the extent to which negative ideas of disability are deeply entrenched within society.[148] As Albrecht and Devlieger say, '[i]n practice, the anomaly is that patients' perceptions of personal health, well-being and life satisfaction are often discordant with their objective health status and disability.'[149]

Despite these claims, Asch emphasises that disciplines such as medicine and bioethics have not 'fully absorbed' this information and so continue to underestimate the quality of disabled lives.[150] One of the concerns that underpins

144 Johnstone, D., *An Introduction to Disability Studies* (2nd Ed), London, David Fulton, 2001 at p. 64.

145 Morris, J., 'Impairment and Disability: Constructing and Ethics of Care That Promotes Human Rights', *Hypatia*, 16, 4, 2001, 1–16 at p. 2.

146 Asch, A., 'Distracted by Disability', *Cambridge Quarterly of Healthcare Ethics*, 7, 1998, 77–87 at p. 79.

147 Wolfensberger, W., 'Lets Hang Up "Quality of Life" as a Hopeless Term', in Goode, D. (ed), *Quality of Life for Persons with Disabilities: International Perspectives and Issues*, Cambridge, MA, Brookline Books, 1994, 285–321 at p. 290f.

148 Albrecht, G.L. and Devlieger, P.J., 'The Disability Paradox: High Quality of Life Against all Odds', *Social Science and Medicine*, 48, 1999, 977–988; Banfalvy, *op. cit.*, p. 576; Brock, D.W., 'Two Moral Issues about Disability', *American Journal of Bioethics*, 1, 3, 2001, 1–2 at p. 1.

149 Albrecht, G.L. and Devlieger, P.J., 'The Disability Paradox: High Quality of Life Against all Odds', *Social Science and Medicine*, 48, 1999, 977–988 at p. 978.

150 Asch, *op. cit.*, p. 79.

the problems we have identified with quality of life judgements is that their quasi-objective nature may allow the life-and-death decisions made by healthcare professionals to be unwittingly influenced by any negative assumptions they hold towards disability. At the heart of the concern is what has been identified as:

> ...the fallacy of believing that we can take our own life experiences and translate them into someone else's reality. The child born with Down's Syndrome will never have known anything else and cannot blindly be presumed to have an unacceptable quality of life simply because we know what we would lose if our situation changed.[151]

As Marks claims:

> ...the concept of quality of life has been used not as an objective value-free measure of the extent to which the needs of a *population* are met, but rather as one laden with cultural prejudices that justify the removal of *individuals* deemed to be a burden.[152]

In light of the concerns which have been raised regarding this method of assessing the quality of life it is useful to consider a more simple account. At the centre of Richard McCormick's thesis is the idea that human life is given value by relationships. Therefore, to be valuable, a life must have 'the potential for human relationships'.[153] He suggests that creatures who are unable to live a full, biographical life do not have the intrinsic value or worth that is attributed to those who do.[154] On the basis of this claim, McCormick finds treatment that threatens human relationships to be an 'excessive hardship for the individual.'[155] By implication, treatment that is unable to generate recovery or provide individuals with the capacity to restore their relational sensibilities would be unwarranted. In making this point, McCormick refers to a case in which an infant with Down's syndrome was allowed to die without undergoing surgery to correct a duodenal atresia. McCormick suggests that commentators on the case were almost unanimous that it was wrong to withhold treatment from the child because there was a possibility of it providing a standard of life sufficient to incorporate a relational aspect.[156] McCormick concludes that human life

---

151 McLean, S.A.M., *Old Law, New Medicine: Medical Ethics and Human Rights*, London: Pandora Press, 1999 at p. 118.

152 Marks, D., *Disability: Controversial Debates and Psychological Perspectives*, London, Routledge, 1999 at p. 42.

153 McCormick, R., 'To Save or Let Die', *America*, 131, 1974, 6–10. All references to reprinted edition in Walter, J.J. and Shannon, T.A. (eds), *Quality of Life: The New Medical Dilemma*, 26–34, New York, Paulist Press, 1974 at p. 32.

154 *Ibid.*, p. 32f.

155 *Ibid.*, p. 31.

156 *Ibid.*, p. 26f.

'is a value to be preserved precisely as a condition for other values, and therefore insofar as these other values remain attainable. Since these other values cluster around and are rooted in human relationships, it seems to follow that life is a value to be preserved only insofar as it contains some potentiality for human relationships.'[157]

This approach provides a clearer basis from which to assess whether a particular individual exhibits key human traits in sufficient abundance for his or her life to be a valuable human life; that is, a life which is of value to the individual living it because of its characteristically human features. It also allows for the fact that some lives may not be worth sustaining. This way of assessing the quality of life is useful because it acknowledges that a life with even the most basic feature – the ability to engage in relationships – should be valued and respected. In cases concerning life-and-death decision-making that often – though not exclusively – involve individuals who are severely impaired, this approach encourages us not unnecessarily to denigrate the value of impaired experience. Similarly, it would also encourage individuals with even severe impairments not to denigrate the value of their lives within an 'able-ist' society; but encourage them to see value in basic human relationships.

The concerns that have been identified over the use of best interests and quality of life decisions in the context of disability and impairment suggest that they provide a dubious foundation for life-and-death decisions. If disciplines such as medicine, ethics and law continue to use such concepts without endeavouring to address the problems they appear to raise for people with disability or impairment then the work of these disciplines may also be undermined.

Conclusion

Modern science undoubtedly facilitates reproductive choice, even if there are sometimes reasons to doubt the basis on which such choices are articulated and formed. However, as Shakespeare says:

> There is a marked disparity between the generally upbeat, confident rhetoric of the genetics establishment and its media apologists, and the gloomy, hostile and suspicious reaction of disabled people and their organisations.[158]

This dissonance may stem from a variety of sources; ignorance about the effects of impairment or disability, fear of eugenics, the medicalisation of life-and-death decisions and the failure to listen to the voices of those who live with impairment or disability. We concede that historically, the existence of disability

---

157 *Ibid.*, p. 32.
158 Shakespeare, *op. cit.*, p. 671.

or impairment has been used to justify unacceptable, discriminatory practices. As DPI points out:

> Disabled people have faced enforced sterilisation, pre-natal termination, infanticide, euthanasia and wholesale elimination. We were left out on the hills of Sparta to die, sterilised by 'caring' doctors in the US, Scandinavia and Germany and were the first to be driven into the Nazi gas-chambers. We testify to the historic and continued links between genetics and eugenics.[159]

'These links' they conclude 'pose dangers for everyone, not just disabled people.'[160] On our argument, where such decisions are free, uncoerced and distanced from negative state policies, the right to reproductive liberty trumps any purported interests that might be attributed to embryos or foetuses. As non-persons they cannot be harmed by respecting reproductive choice. We noted in Chapter 3 that ethically some limitations may be placed on the vagaries of individual choice to satisfy the need to ensure that such decisions can be universalised, but it does not follow that these limitations should also be legally enforced, or indeed that individuals with dubious rational capacities will be protected.

Once born, we have argued that the underpinning assumptions about the quality of life with impairment may – deliberately or inadvertently – result in making choices detrimental to individual children. For this reason, we restate our belief that the principle of respect for persons has a more direct and meaningful role to play than is recognised in the argument between proponents of the medical and the social model. Measuring treatment decisions against this principle avoids negative presumptions, and begins from the prima facie position that life is to be valued, irrespective of its perceived quality. This would not require the provision of aggressive treatment in all cases; where the children's condition is incompatible with life or unduly burdensome for them, it is respectful rather than disrespectful to ease their lives to their end.

This chapter, we believe, illustrates a number of additional points. First, there is considerable effort invested in discovering the existence of impairment and facilitating the non-implantation or termination of affected embryos or foetuses. The range of conditions for which screening is available is likely to continue to expand out of proportion to the availability of cure or palliation; therefore, the number of pregnancies not established or terminated on these grounds seems likely to expand. This may be seen as a direct and undesirable consequence of a simplistic adherence to the notion that cure or 'normalisation' is the most important goal in such situations.[161] On the other hand, it may reflect the

159 DPI, *op. cit.*, p. 5.
160 *Id.*
161 For further discussion, see Chapter 2.

importance to be attached to the very real interests – even rights – that prospective parents have in reproductive freedom and choice. These interests are protected at common law and also by the Human Rights Act 1998. Absolute emphasis on the wrong of discarding or aborting embryos or foetuses with disabilities directly confronts the important reproductive liberties to which people legitimately aspire and which they rightly value. It remains moot whether or not the elimination of societal discrimination against people with disabilities would change the decisions currently taken by some (perhaps most) people to avoid the birth of a particular child. In other words, neither the social nor the medical models *simpliciter* provide clear guidance as to the 'right' answer on how to assess actual or potential discrimination against potential people who would be born with impairment.

Moreover, once born, the infant with impairment can become the subject of (life-threatening) decisions which would not be contemplated in other cases. The question as to whether or not these decisions are correctly labelled as discriminatory, however, is not so easy to answer as it might at first appear. As we have suggested, it is not inevitably discriminatory to differentiate; in other words, it is not discrimination to use specific characteristics in a relevant manner. Thus, the case of *Re C (a minor)* the decision not to attempt aggressive treatment does not sit comfortably with the notion of discrimination, as it was clear that the child was already dying. The imposition of additional treatment was likely only to cause additional suffering; treatment would be both burdensome and futile. In this case, the child was being treated in precisely the same way as would any other moribund child.

More troubling, however, are the cases in which life could have been saved, but 'quality of life' decisions were taken, resulting in an early death. Even here, however, there are shades of grey. In some cases, such decisions might spare the child in question dreadful suffering which it would endure only for the sake of maintaining it in the condition of being alive, which, we have suggested, is of prima facie but not inevitable value. Although some people might disagree with this proposition, for others – possibly the majority – it is counter-intuitive to suggest that *all* life is inevitably better than none. In these cases, therefore, it might be argued that the decisions themselves are not inherently discriminatory. Rather, the problem may be that they are dishonestly described, in order to avoid admitting that what is happening is *in fact* a form of euthanasia. The effect of this dishonesty may be to condemn the child to a protracted death (bear in mind that the child in the *Arthur* case took 69 hours to die), when a quicker, less distressing death could be made available. To accept this, however, would require us – and the law – to dispense with the distinction between act and omission, which will be discussed in more depth in our consideration of end-of-life decisions.

Finally, the judgements in *Re T (a minor)* and the Irish case are perhaps the most disturbing of those considered, since in one it seems that the interest (actual or postulated) of the child in life was subjugated to the wishes of its parents that it should not survive, while in the other the importance of the family was put ahead of the very real potential to ensure a healthy life for the child in question.

It is a consequence of our argument, then, that the foundational principle of respect for persons cannot be attributed to entities before birth. If they are to be offered some form of protection, it must be derived from another principle, such, for example, as our *own* interest in respecting the human embryo or foetus. For children already born, however, we have proposed that serious consideration needs to be given to respect for persons before any decision not to sustain life is made.

Chapter 5

Decisions at the end of life

Introduction

The reality of modern life – or rather death – is that increasingly medicine and healthcare professionals are involved. People no longer die at home, surrounded by their family. Very often, they die in hospital, surrounded by clinicians armed with an extraordinary array of techniques and technologies to help prolong life. Kass paints a gripping – if depressing – picture of the modern death as a process during which the patient is '...kept company by cardiac pacemakers and defibrillators, respirators, aspirators, oxygenators, catheters, and his intravenous drip. Ties to the community of men are replaced by attachments to an assemblage of machines'.[1]

Although modern death may be alienating, as Kass suggests, the process of dying can, of course, also be eased by modern healthcare and the availability of increasingly powerful analgesia. However, what has been called the 'medicalisation of death'[2] raises problems as well as benefits. The availability of treatment, or palliation of symptoms, particularly when coupled with limitations on available resources, means that decisions about whether to offer treatment and when to withdraw it will arise with relative frequency. These must be amongst the most difficult decisions for healthcare professionals and often involve a consideration of issues which go beyond the purely clinical. Additionally, as we will see in the next chapter, the capacity to prolong dying may provoke concern that people will be inappropriately kept alive against their own wishes.

Of particular interest in this chapter, however, are those situations in which third party involvement results in decisions which directly or indirectly result in the death of an individual. As Kuhse has argued:

> The question is not *whether* decisions to end human lives ought to be made but, rather, *who* makes these decisions, and on the basis of what principles

---

1 Kass, L.R., *Toward a More Natural Science: Biology and Human Affairs*, New York, The Free Press, 1985 at p. 32.
2 Capron, A., 'Legal and Ethical Problems in Decisions for Death', *Law, Medicine and Health Care*, 14, 3–4, 1986, 141 at p. 141.

or values. For the fact is that such decisions are already being made, and inevitably must be made, in modern hospitals.[3]

Furthermore, while the issues discussed in Chapter 4 concerned the interests and well-being of an identifiable, albeit loosely defined, group everyone will potentially be affected by the manner in which end-of-life decisions are made. That is, we are all vulnerable to proxy decisions about our death, irrespective of whether or not we had previously been described as impaired or disabled, because we all become impaired or disabled when we are in the kind of condition that triggers such decisions. It is essential, therefore, to cast the net of this chapter rather more widely than was necessary in the previous chapter. Indeed, the Disability Discrimination Act 2005 has recognised that disability is equivalent to more than traditional concepts of impairment by extending the definition of disability to include 'a person who has cancer, HIV infection or multiple sclerosis...'.[4] The number of people who legally qualify as disabled has therefore been increased, and of course in common sense terms it is likely that everyone who is facing end-of-life decisions will perceive him or herself as disabled in some way, or as suffering from impairment. However, although the focus of this chapter is more broad than the previous ones, this is not to say that there are no consequences at the end of life flowing from a previous categorisation as disabled or impaired.

Decisions not to make resources available for those whose quality of life is thought to be inferior to that of others are a routine part of healthcare provision, albeit that they generally remain implicit or hidden.[5] There is no principle of law, nor indeed arguably of ethics, that endorses the deliberate negative selection of people based on the extent to which they can be subsumed into a model of what is 'normal.' Nonetheless, the suspicion – however well or ill-founded – remains that inappropriate assessments of quality of life can and do influence treatment decisions in healthcare, especially when the person concerned is disabled or impaired. Indeed, the Council of Canadians with Disabilities, in its submission to the Canadian Human Rights Act Review Panel (October 1999)[6] reinforced this, by noting that – irrespective of the rhetoric of equality – disabled people are indeed regarded as having lives which are somehow less worthy or valuable than those of the able-bodied. This perception, they say, 'reinforces rationalizations for treating them prejudicially'. We have already suggested that the evaluation

3 Kuhse, H., 'The Case for Active Voluntary Euthanasia', *Law, Medicine and Health Care*, 14, 3–4, 1986 at p. 145.
4 s 18 3(1).
5 See 'Minister Puts a Price on the Right to Life', 19 May 2005, available at http://timesonline. co.uk (accessed on 19 May 2005).
6 *Taking the Lead: Council of Canadians with Disabilities Proposals for Amending the Canadian Human Rights Act* (submission to Canadian Human Rights Act Review Panel, October 1999), available at http://www.ccdonline.ca/law-reform/submissions/humrightsactreview.htm (accessed on 18 June 2003).

of 'quality of life' (QoL) is an important, albeit arguably dubious, basis on which to decide about whether or not a person should be allowed to continue living. There is a wealth of literature on this subject, and often a real dissonance between the opinions of professionals, lay people and – most acutely – people with impairment or disability as to what amounts to an acceptable quality of life. Wyatt, for example, says that belief that a quality of life is poor, or low, 'can perpetuate negative prejudices about the experiences of disabled people and may encourage a eugenic desire to eliminate any QoL-reducing impairment from our community'.[7]

In what follows, we will explore end-of-life decisions in general, but interrogate them also from the basis of the ethical principles we identified in Chapter 3, with specific attention to those situations where it appears that a previous impairment might be given unusual or disproportionate attention. Before doing so, however, it is informative to consider briefly how perceptions and assumptions about the relevance of impairment or disability can have an impact throughout life, not least because they seem likely to inform, directly or indirectly, our attitudes at the end of such a life.

A parallel example

It is self-evident that, in many areas, decisions that are taken seem to assume that certain individuals have less interest in the freedoms which are valued by others on the basis that they are impaired in some way or are disabled. Most significantly, perhaps, this can be seen in decisions about reproductive freedom. In Chapter 4, we concluded that assumptions about disability or impairment can be used to prevent some embryos and foetuses from being born, and we described this as a reflection of the value of reproductive rights. However, if such rights are conceded to exist, it is important to our argument that they are attributed equally and without discrimination, thereby satisfying the principle of respect for persons, and the facilitating principles of consent, autonomy and rights. However, in seemingly direct contravention of these principles, some people with disabilities are prevented from exercising the reproductive liberty which, we have suggested, is also of great importance.

This brief diversion from consideration of issues at the beginning and end of life is relevant because it addresses the extent to which there is a propensity to treat people equally in matters which are about respect for their inherent value and the decisions they are free to make about their lives. Although we have suggested that it is problematic to use the language of human rights before birth (and some would argue also in the early stages of life[8]), it is accepted in national

7 Wyatt, J., 'What's Wrong with Quality of Life as a Clinical Tool?', *American Medical Association Policy Forum*, available at http://www.ama-assn.org/ama/pub/category/14554.html (accessed on 16 June 2005).

8 See, for example, Glover, J., *Causing Death and Saving Lives*, Harmondsworth, Penguin, 1977 (reprinted 1984).

and international law that, once born, people are entitled to have their human rights respected.[9] If not, there is overt discrimination.

In the case of people with impairment or disability, however, it seems that the fact of impairment is in itself sufficient to trigger situations where principles such as respect, autonomy or self-determination are not prioritised,[10] rather, the value to be given to reproductive rights is profoundly informed by evaluations about what is 'good' for people, or what we think they would want, which are, sadly, reflective of a rather casual approach to reproductive rights. This is perhaps most clearly seen in the (admittedly) rather dated US case of *Buck v Bell*.[11] Heard at a time when eugenic policies in the United States were at their height, the words of Mr Justice Oliver Wendell Holmes nonetheless, can still give us pause, fuelling fears that the eugenics agenda is at the same time deeply rooted yet never too far beneath the surface. In granting permission for the non-consensual sterilisation of a young woman on the grounds of her alleged mental disability he said:

> We have seen more than once that the public welfare may call upon the best citizens for their lives. It would be strange if it could not call upon those who already sap the strength of the State for these lesser sacrifices, often not felt to be such by those concerned, in order to prevent our being swamped with incompetence. It is better for all the world, if instead of waiting to execute degenerate offspring for crime, or to let them starve for their imbecility, society can prevent those who are manifestly unfit from continuing their kind. The principle that sustains compulsory vaccination is broad enough to cover cutting the Fallopian tubes....Three generations of imbeciles are enough.[12]

Although no self-respecting contemporary judge would ever overtly endorse such a view, cases have arisen recently which show a worrying set of assumptions about the link between sexuality, parenting and impairment. In the United Kingdom, courts have been prepared on a number of occasions[13] to conclude that there is no loss to women with disabilities from being stripped

9 For further discussion, see Chapter 1.
10 For further discussion of these and other relevant ethical principles, see Chapter 3.
11 274 US 200 (1927).
12 At p. 207.
13 Cf *re D (a minor) (wardship: sterilisation)* [1976] 1 All ER 326; *Re B (a minor) (wardship: sterilisation)* [1987] 2 All ER 206, HL; *Re M (a minor) (wardship: sterilisation)* [1988] 2 FLR 497; *Re P (a minor) (wardship: sterilisation)* [1989] 1 FLR 182; *F v West Berkshire Health Authority* [1989] 2 All ER 545; *Re HG (specific issue order: sterilisation)* (1992) 16 BMLR 50; *Re W (mental patient: sterilisation)* [1993] 1 FLR 381; *Re LC (medical treatment: sterilisation)* [1997] 2 FLR 258; *Re S (medical treatment: adult sterilisation)* [1998] 1 FLR 944; *Re X (adult patient: sterilisation)* [1998] 2 FLR 1124; *Re E (a minor) (medical treatment)* (1992) 7 BMLR 117; *Re Z (medical treatment: hysterectomy)* (1999) 53 BMLR 53; *L (Petitioner)* 1996 SCLR 538.

non-consensually of their reproductive capacities, even – it must be said – without establishing whether or not the young women concerned were in fact fertile. Of course, the sexuality of people with impairment is something with which people were historically uncomfortable, although Shaw[14] suggests that this may be less true now. Nonetheless, commenting on the case of *F v West Berkshire Health Authority*,[15] Shaw makes an important point:

> The sexuality of mentally disabled persons, like any other aspect of sexual behaviour, is a socially constructed phenomenon....We may be at ease with F and others like her, but we make her freedom a conditional freedom: conception must be avoided at all costs.[16]

British courts, as we have indicated, have been prone to making assumptions that sterility is to be preferred where (admittedly usually significant) mental impairment is present. Interestingly, however, in a Canadian case, the court was very much less willing to reach this conclusion.[17] This court was unprepared to agree to the sterilisation of a young woman unless it could be shown to be in her interests, rather than the interests of those around her, and was unwilling to make the simplistic assumption that sterility was inevitably preferable because of her impairment. Although this judgement has found no favour in UK courts, and although it overtly rests on the concept of best interests which we have already criticised, it arguably addresses precisely the most important question. Deprivation of rights, such as reproductive liberty, is arguably unconscionable unless it is clear that harm will be caused *to that person* by failing to act. People should not be assumed to have no interests or rights which defeat the interests of the people caring for them, or society's prejudices. Indeed, the Law Reform Commission of Canada endorses this, by concluding that '[s]ex and parenthood hold the same significance for them [people with mental disabilities] as for other people...'.[18]

Of course, there may be cases where sterilisation (even when it has to be done without the consent of the person concerned because of his or her mental impairment) may be legitimate (just as it could be when a non-disabled person asks for sterilisation). However, arguably the 'searchlight of critical moral reasoning'[19] is seldom shone on decisions which deprive (usually) women with impairment of their reproductive capacities. As has been said:

> The reported cases have shown... that the medical willingness to sterilise, especially when coupled with parental approval, has been a critical predictor

---

14 Shaw, J., 'Sterilisation of Mentally Handicapped People: Judges Rule OK?', 53 *MLR*, 91, 1990.
15 Cited above.
16 At p. 98.
17 *Re Eve* 31 DLR (4th) 1 [1986].
18 *Sterilisation*, Law Reform Commission of Canada, Working Paper 24 (1979) at p. 50.
19 Gillon, R., 'On Sterilising Severely Mentally Handicapped People', *JME*, 1987, 13(2), 59–61.

of the outcome, even if the woman is not in a sexual relationship and her fertility has never been assessed.[20]

Interestingly, this 'willingness to sterilise' was less evident when the proposed sterilisation affected a young man rather than a woman. In *Re A (Medical Treatment: Male Sterilisation)*,[21] the man in question was a 28-year-old with Down's syndrome. He was assessed as being significantly impaired. At the behest of his mother, who was his primary carer, the court was asked to endorse his sterilisation. It was felt that, although he had sexual feelings, he would be unable to understand the link between sex and pregnancy, or to take his responsibilities for any child conceived. The judge made the point that there is a difference between men and women in these circumstances, as men would be likely to be less seriously affected should a pregnancy occur. However, the really important issue, which was picked up by only one judge, was that, '[i]n relation to whether the best interests of others may legitimately be regarded in the application of a best interest test, the point was not fully argued in the present appeal...'.[22]

In other words, unlike in the Canadian case, this court essentially set aside the question of respect for the individual, in the interests of making a purportedly best-interests decision. Much more could be said on this subject, but the point of this brief consideration of the respect accorded to, and the assumptions made about, the interests of people with impairment, is that negative attitudes to disability can pervade all areas of life. Assumptions about the respect due to the individuals concerned hinge on the beliefs and/or prejudices of the non-impaired about the best way to 'protect' people who have impairments; beliefs which are too often rooted in intuition rather than evidence. This permeates through to decisions at the end of life, which are the primary concern of this chapter. The large, and sometimes ferocious, debate about assisted dying will be dealt with in Chapter 6.

For the moment we will confine ourselves to addressing how, and on what basis, decisions are made that someone should not be assisted to continue living. For clarity, this chapter will be divided into two main parts. The first will deal with decisions about whether or not to offer medical treatment in the non-emergency situation. The second will discuss the highly contentious area of Do Not Resuscitate Orders (DNR). Each of these areas is, as we have suggested, of relevance to virtually everyone at the end of life, but there can be little doubt that they are of particular concern to people with pre-existing impairment or disability and those who advocate their rights. National law and a plethora of international statements mandate adherence to the principles of equality and

20 McLean, S.A.M., *Old Law, New Medicine*, London, Rivers Oram/Pandora, 1999 at p. 107.
21 53 BMLR 66 (1999).
22 Per Thorpe, LJ at p. 75.

non-discrimination and commit states to ensuring that disabled people are equally respected and equally treated.[23] Whether or not this is their effect in reality is, however, moot.

The provision or removal of therapy

We have already indicated that some of this discussion will be relevant to people who may have in the past been unimpaired, but by the nature of their clinical situation have become so towards the end of their lives. Therefore, people who are in a permanent vegetative state or temporarily unconscious or seriously ill, will count as 'impaired' for this part of our discussion. Unusually for them, but arguably not for people who have lived with impairment or disability, the primary emphasis which we have suggested is generally accorded to concepts such as respect and autonomy may, in these situations, give way to a 'best interests' or QoL agenda.

Persistent or permanent vegetative state (PVS)

It is now generally accepted that patients who are diagnosed as being in a persistent or permanent vegetative state are unlikely to recover. Since they can live in this condition for some considerable time, with appropriate care and treatment, their management has come to be of crucial importance in healthcare decision-making. Not only are there hard choices made about whether or not individuals should have their existence maintained, there are also real questions about the appropriate use of resources. Although life-and-death decisions should, so the mantra goes, never be based on resources[24] – emotional or financial – in fact, of course, they often are. Families, healthcare professionals and healthcare institutions may find the maintenance of existence, with no hope of recovery, to be both distressing and wasteful. Even although some, such as McCullagh, have argued that '[i]t is time for reappraisal of the subject of vegetative states...',[25] diagnosis of PVS generally triggers evaluation of treatment options. Should we continue to maintain life by, for example, providing assisted nutrition and hydration (ANH), or should we remove the essentials of life and await the inevitable death?

In PVS cases, there is arguably less need to consider the models of disability and impairment that we discussed in Chapter 2. The fact and impact of the impairment is clear, and the question really is whether mere existence should be maintained. On one view, the persons in PVS could be shown respect by allowing them to die. Once again, maintaining existence does not inevitably demonstrate respect for persons. However, as we have already suggested, medical diagnosis

23 For further discussion, see Chapter 1.
24 See, for example, *R v Cambridge Health Authority, ex parte B* [1995] 2 All ER 129.
25 McCullagh, P., *Conscious in a Vegetative State?*, Dordrecht, Kluwer Academic 2004 at p. 324.

and prognosis in this area are not value-free. The decision about the likely quality (or lack of it) of life for the individual patient may be rooted in clinical evidence, but the familial or societal consequences of diagnosis and prognosis will also be relevant. Patients in PVS may well be experiencing a 'living death', but, as we will see, given that the diagnosis itself means that the person cannot experience either pain or suffering, the reasons for not maintaining existence are arguably not rooted specifically in concern for the patient; rather, they relate to the needs and interests of others. When this is the case, it is likely that – as we will argue has already happened – these interests can predominate to the extent that the basic ethical principles which we have already discussed are seen as inapplicable or irrelevant.

In what follows, we will consider and critique the way in which such cases have been decided in courts of law, the final arbiter in many PVS cases. In the important case of *Airedale NHS Trust v Bland*,[26] a young man diagnosed as being in what was then called a persistent vegetative state, but would now be called PVS, was the subject of a case which ultimately reached the House of Lords. The doctors and family of Anthony Bland sought a declaration from the courts[27] that it would not be unlawful to remove nasogastric nutrition and hydration, with the intention that Anthony would die. As one of Their Lordships said, '... the whole purpose of stopping artificial feeding is to bring about the death of Anthony Bland'.[28] The ultimate decision of the House of Lords was to permit the removal, although Their Lordships were by no means unanimous in their reasoning as to why this was permissible. It is worth considering their reasoning in a little depth, as it clearly has resonance for all similar decisions.

A range of justifications was provided, of which arguably the most significant was the distinction drawn between acts and omissions. This is a device commonly used in criminal law to delineate the culpability of behaviour, even although it may on a common sense – even ethical – basis sometimes feel rather artificial. The doctrine holds that while we are responsible for the consequences of our acts – even if these are foreseeable rather than intended[29] – we are not legally held to account for the consequences of our omissions unless we have a pre-existing duty not to omit to do something. This was problematic in the *Bland* case for two main reasons. First, the doctors did indeed owe a duty of care to the patient in question because they had established a professional relationship with him. This difficulty was circumvented by the argument that the duty of care ceased to exist when the treatment became futile.[30] Second, discontinuing ANH

---

26 (1993) 12 BMLR 64.

27 This was necessary in part because of the removal of the *parens patriae* jurisdiction.

28 Per Lord Browne–Wilkinson, at p. 127.

29 *R v Woollin* [1998] 4 All ER 103.

30 Although in fact given that ANH would have kept Anthony Bland alive, it is not clear precisely how it could be classified as 'futile'; it certainly could achieve its intended aim.

could just as easily be categorised as an act or as an omission. In addition, although agreeing with the final decision of his fellow judges, Lord Mustill described the distinction between the two as 'intellectually dubious'.[31] Indeed, it has been said that '[e]ven if the treatment refusal is an omission, it is the cause of death where this is the known, inevitable consequence of the patient's decision.'[32]

Interestingly, a number of Their Lordships seem to have endorsed the application of the *Bolam Test* in reaching decisions in this area. This test, derived from the case of *Bolam v Friern Hospital Management Committee*,[33] is generally used in cases where doctors face an allegation of negligence. The test, which has now been slightly modified by the case of *Bolitho v City and Hackney Health Authority*,[34] essentially says that a doctor will not be held liable if s/he has acted in a manner regarded as reasonable by a responsible body of medical opinion. Indeed, although the rigour of this test has been subject to considerable challenge even in matters of operational negligence,[35] Lord Browne–Wilkinson said:

> ...on an application to the court for a declaration that the discontinuance of medical care will be lawful, the court's only concern will be to be satisfied that the doctor's decision to discontinue is in accordance with a respectable body of medical opinion and that it is reasonable...[36]

Lord Mustill, however, expressed:

> ...some reservations about the application of the principle of civil liability in negligence as laid down in *Bolam*...to decisions on 'best interests' in a field dominated by criminal law. I accept without difficulty that this principle applies to the ascertainment of the medical raw material such as diagnosis, prognosis and appraisal of the patient's cognitive functions. Beyond this point, however, it may be said that the decision is ethical, not medical, and that there is no reason in logic why on such a decision the opinion of doctors should be decisive.[37]

Certainly, there must be concern that a test set as low as the *Bolam Test* should be used in our courts to assist in making decisions which will result in death.

31 At p. 142.
32 Price, D.T., 'Assisted Suicide and Refusing Medical Treatment: Linguistics, Morals and Legal Contortions', *MLR*, 4, Autumn 1996, 270–299 at pp. 287–288.
33 (1957) 1 BMLR 1.
34 (1997) 39 BMLR 1.
35 Cf Mason, J.K. and Laurie, G.T., *Mason and McCall Smith's Law and Medical Ethics*, 7th edn, Oxford University Press, Oxford, 2006; McLean, S.A.M., *A Patient's Right to Know*, Aldershot, Dartmouth, 1989.
36 At p. 20.
37 At pp. 142–143.

Its inherent dependence on what doctors do, rather than what they *should* do, scarcely generates confidence about the law's willingness or ability to protect at this most crucial juncture in life. Despite this, it is clear from both the *Bland* judgement and from subsequent cases, that medical evidence as to the existence of the state of PVS, coupled with clinical recommendations as to purported best interests of the patient or the futility of providing treatment such as ANH, are essentially definitive for the courts. Since the *Bland* case, there have been a number of other cases heard in the courts of England.[38] In *Frenchay Healthcare NHS Trust v S*,[39] the patient, who was in PVS, was being fed by gastronomy. The tube had become detached, and the court held that the hospital could lawfully refrain from replacing it or providing any measures other than those which would allow him to die a peaceful death. In *Re C*,[40] the court again authorised withdrawal, in this case apparently because of their acceptance that this is what the patient would have wanted. *Re G*[41] held that – even where, as in this case, there was no unanimity as to the best way forward – the patient's best interests would not be served by continuing treatment. In *Swindon and Marlborough NHS Trust v S*,[42] the patient was being cared for at home, but given that the patient was certainly in PVS, the court held that it would be lawful to fail to clear a blocked gastronomy tube.

Furthermore, in what can perhaps be seen as the most legally significant of these cases, the High Court was asked to consider the proposed management of two patients in PVS against the backdrop of the Human Rights Act 1998, Art 2 of which guarantees a 'right to life'. In the case of *NHS Trust A v Mrs M, NHS Trust B v Mrs H*,[43] it was anticipated by some that the terms of the Human Rights Act would be used to cast doubt on the approach adopted in earlier cases. However, the court held that removal of nasogastric nutrition and hydration did not breach the right to life when treatment was not in the best interests of the patient. In addition, the court considered Art 8 of the Convention on Human Rights (the basis of the Human Rights Act 1998) which guarantees the right to respect for what might loosely be called personal autonomy. Rather than this Article providing protection, the court's view was that it would be a breach to *continue* invasive and unconsented-to treatment. The court also held that there was no breach of Art 3 (prohibition of torture and degrading and inhumane treatment) as people had to be aware of the degradation before it could breach their human rights.

38 The British Medical Association (BMA) notes that by the end of 1998, 18 PVS cases had been heard and approved in the Courts. BMA, *Withholding and Withdrawing Life-Prolonging Medical Treatment: Guidance for Decision-Making*, BMA Books, 1999.
39 [1994] 2 All ER 403.
40 'The Times', 18 November 1995.
41 [1995] 3 Med L Rev 80.
42 [1995] 3 Med LR 84.
43 (2001) 58 BMLR 87.

A different approach was taken in the case of *R (on the application of Burke) v General Medical Council*,[44] Mr Justice Munby argued that Art 3 of the Convention did indeed apply to those who are unaware of their circumstances. As he said:

> ...however unconscious or unaware of ill-treatment a particular incompetent adult or a baby may be, treatment which has the effect on those who witness it of degrading the individual may come within art 3. Otherwise...the Convention's emphasis on the protection of the vulnerable may be circumvented.[45]

Moreover, he continued:

> The dignity interests protected by the Convention include, under art 8, the preservation of mental stability and, under art 3, the right to die with dignity and the right to be protected from treatment, or from lack of treatment, which will result in one dying in avoidable distressing circumstances.[46]

It must be said that Munby's account of the protection offered by the Human Rights Convention is, we believe, to be preferred. As this is directly in point to the issue of third party decision-making, the *Burke* judgement will be considered in more depth later in this chapter.

The only additional protection offered (however marginal it may be) is that, in England and Wales, all such cases must be decided upon by a court of law.[47] In Scotland, the issue has been decided slightly differently. In the case of *Law Hospital NHS Trust v Lord Advocate*[48] The Court of Session (Scotland's most senior civil court) held that nasogastric feeding and hydration could be withdrawn from a patient in PVS where continuation would provide no benefit; arguably a more clearly clinical test than that of best interests, and therefore, also arguably, more susceptible of medical influence. The Court of Session did not require that all cases should be heard in court, but the Lord Advocate subsequently declared that he would only guarantee that no prosecution would follow any such decision where the authority of the Court of Session had been sought and granted.[49]

Finally, it is worth noting that the Official Solicitor's Practice Note of 2001[50] suggests that the application to the High Court for authority to withdraw feeding

44 (2004) 79 BMLR 126.
45 At p. 177.
46 At p. 169.
47 *Practice Note* [1996] 4 All ER 766.
48 1996 SLT 848, 869.
49 'The Scotsman', 12 April 1996, p. 1.
50 *Practice Note (Official Solicitor: Declaratory Proceedings: Medical and Welfare Decisions for Adults Who Lack Capacity)* [2001] 2 FLR 158.

and hydration is essentially an administrative exercise where the diagnosis of PVS has been competently made. In other words, the significance of the clinical input is paramount; the role of the law is merely to ensure the diagnosis has been correctly made – not to question whether or not ANH should be discontinued.

Laurie and Mason consider – and it is difficult to argue with them – that '[t]he courts have medicalised the problem of the patient in PVS and have, thus, handed over responsibility for its discharge to the medical profession.'[51] This seems to have been welcomed by the medical profession, and appears with approbation in the BMA's guidelines on withholding and withdrawing treatment.[52] Although agreeing that relatives should be consulted when decisions of this sort are being taken, the BMA concludes:

> . . . it is essential that those consulted are absolutely clear that, ultimately, the treatment decision is not their right or responsibility. Rather, the decision will be made by the clinician in charge of the patient's case on the basis of what he or she considers will benefit the patient.[53]

One further point is worth making. Although courts are reluctant ever to concede that their decisions are actually about bringing death for the patient, there are compelling reasons to doubt this. In fact as Price notes:

> It is noteworthy that in *Bland*, in the context of physicians deciding to withhold life-sustaining measures from an *incompetent* person, the House of Lords considered that the physicians involved *did* possess the requisite intention to kill. The view that death, and not just the withholding or withdrawal of food or other treatment, is intended in these treatment refusal cases seems compelling.[54]

Thus, although on the one hand the law wants to say that it upholds the value of all life – whatever its quality – this is not always the case. Indeed, the judgement in *Bland* has been criticised for the fact that it begs a number of questions, not least because the judges reached their conclusions using a variety of different routes. This makes it difficult to find any real coherence in the case, or to derive general principles from it, beyond the suspicion that removing nutrition and hydration was regarded as the 'right' thing to do, based on the anticipated quality of Anthony Bland's life, not on his right to life itself.[55] As we do not argue that

---

51 Laurie, G.T. and Mason, J.K., 'Negative Treatment of Vulnerable Patients: Euthanasia by Any Other Name?' [2000] *Juridical Review* 159 at p. 167.
52 BMA, *op. cit.*
53 P. 48, para 18.3.
54 Price, D.T., 'Assisted Suicide and Refusing Medical Treatment: Linguistics, Morals and Legal Contortions', Medical L Rev, 4, Autumn 1996, 270–299 at pp. 282–283.
55 See McLean, S.A.M., 'Is There a Legal Threat to Medicine?' *Journal of the Voluntary Euthanasia Society of Scotland*, Special Edition, September 1993.

life is always preferable to non-existence, our criticism of this case relates to the reasoning given by the courts, not with the final decision. However, some feared that the *Bland* judgement merely disguised unacceptable attitudes to people who were disabled by their condition. This suspicion is, if anything, reinforced when considering subsequent cases which seem to have 'moved the goalposts'.

'Not quite' in PVS

Following the *Bland* judgement a number of cases have arisen where the patient was insensate, but not in PVS. In *Re D*,[56] for example, the woman concerned had suffered severe brain damage and her gastronomy tube had become displaced. The President of the Family Division considered that it was in her best interests that the nasogastric nutrition and hydration be discontinued, even although she did not fall into the only category in which such decisions had been made before: that is, she was not in PVS. In *Re H*,[57] again a woman was agreed to be entirely insensate but not in PVS in terms of the guidelines laid down by the Royal College of Physicians.[58] However, the judge, Sir Stephen Brown, felt that she was in a vegetative state which was irreversible, even if she did not, strictly speaking, qualify as being in PVS as clinically defined.

What seems to have emerged is a shift based on assumptions about QoL, or the clinical judgement as to prognosis which has loosened the tight rein that originally was claimed to exist on decisions which bring about death. This has occurred despite the fact that the courts – in England and Wales at least – have indicated that their authority should be sought in virtually all cases where it is intended to remove feeding and hydration.[59] As was the case with patients in PVS, the courts were given the opportunity of testing these decisions against the backdrop of the Human Rights Act in the case of *Re G (adult incompetent: withdrawal of treatment)*.[60] In this case, the woman in question had suffered serious anoxic brain damage. The NHS Trust caring for her, with the support of her family, sought a declaration permitting the removal of artificial sustenance. The court was convinced that there was no prospect of recovery, and held that her human rights were not breached by deciding that treatment could be discontinued.

Not in PVS, not insensate

Decisions about whether or not to offer, or continue, treatment in respect of people with impairment or disability clearly play a vital role in their right to live.

56 (1997) 38 BMLR 1.
57 *Re H (adult: incompetent)* (1997) 38 BMLR 11.
58 'The Permanent Vegetative State – Review by a Working Group Convened by the Royal College of Physicians and Endorsed by the Conference of Medical Royal Colleges and their Faculties of the United Kingdom' *Journal of the Royal College of Physicians of London*, 30, 1996, 119.
59 *Practice Direction (Declaratory Proceedings: Incapacitated Adults)* (2002) 65 BMLR 72.
60 (2001) 65 BMLR 6.

In some cases, such as in the case of *Re D (medical treatment)*,[61] the nature of the impairment itself was central to the decision whether or not to continue treatment. In this case, it was held that haemodialysis could lawfully be discontinued on the basis that the man's long-standing mental impairment made it impossible for him to commit himself to the treatment.

More recently, Dame Elizabeth Butler-Sloss took what appears to have been a different approach in the case of *Hospital NHS Trust v (1) S (2) DG (3) SG*.[62] In this case, S had a severe developmental disorder and renal failure. He had been receiving dialysis when, in 2002, the catheter became infected by a bacterium which was highly resistant to antibiotics. Staff feared that no other entry points might be available if the catheter had to be removed. By the time of the court hearing the infection had been controlled and no decision was urgently needed. Butler-Sloss described the responsibility of the court in such cases in these terms:

> When considering the best interests of a patient it is...the duty of the court to assess the advantages and disadvantages of the various treatments and management options, the viability of each such option and the likely effect each would have on the patient's best interests and, I would add, his enjoyment of life.[63]

In other words, the evaluation of what, if any, treatment is to be offered hinged, in large part, on the question of QoL, in this case to be decided by a third party (here, the court). Indeed, the issue of QoL was specifically referred to in a later passage from this case, where Butler-Sloss continued: 'I consider that it is in S's best interests for him to continue to receive dialysis as long as some form of dialysis is working and is providing S with a reasonable quality of life.'[64] However, the court also recognised the difficulty of making such assessments, and in particular said:

> The hospital trust has, very properly, made it clear that it has always recognised the right of S to be treated as fairly as any other patient without his disabilities....But the approach of the medical and nursing team, both in the paediatric unit and in the adult unit, has been coloured by their real difficulties in the lack of verbal communication with S and their vivid recollections of how difficult he was to manage in the hospital after he was admitted for emergency life-saving treatment in May 2000. I have the feeling that those difficulties may have had a disproportionate effect upon their approach to future treatment for S.[65]

---

61 (1997) 41 BMLR 81.
62 *Hospital NHS Trust v (1) S (2) DG (3) SG*, [2003] Lloyd's Rep Med 137.
63 At p. 147.
64 At p. 148.
65 *Id.*

Although not overtly critical of the healthcare team, from Butler-Sloss's words we can see some concern that the extent of S's disability had led the staff to make assumptions about his abilities, and probably the quality of his life, without having considered alternatives. She said, for example:

> His lack of verbal communication skills does not appear to be a clear indicator of his overall cognitive ability...I gained the clear view that if S were able to be given specialist help and the appropriate aids he would have somewhat more ability to learn than the hospital trust has been able to accept. It is worth pointing out that none of the nursing staff or treating clinicians has tried to communicate with him other than by ordinary speech.[66]

Ultimately, the crux question in this case was whether or not, should it become necessary, it would be appropriate to provide S with a kidney transplant. The Trust sought a declaration that it would not be required to perform a transplant on S, even although his mother had volunteered to donate one of hers and it seemed likely to be compatible. Despite some counter-arguments Butler-Sloss was clear that:

> On balance...if the medical reasons for a kidney transplantation are in his favour, and alternative methods of dialysis are no longer viable, in my judgement a kidney transplantation ought not to be rejected on the grounds of his inability to understand the purpose and consequences of the operation or concerns about his management.[67]

In some ways, this is an interesting decision when read in conjunction with the judgements in *Bland*. That is, in the *Bland* case the fact that he was unable to offer a valid consent to treatment was used by some judges as a reason not to continue with it, whereas in this case the fact of likely inability to offer a (legally) valid consent to treatment was not, apparently, a barrier to its provision.

Naturally, it might be said that these two cases are different, justifying the dissimilar conclusions. In *Bland*, nutrition and hydration could never have restored health; in S's case, the treatment could achieve this. However, if the decisions were based purely on clinical indications as to the value of the treatment rather than the value of the life, then each case is essentially equivalent. Assisted nutrition and hydration is not – on at least one definition – futile in the case of a person in PVS. It does precisely what it is intended to do; namely it keeps the patient alive although it would not improve the underlying condition. In the case of S, the transplant also keeps him alive,

---

66 *Id.*
67 At p. 150.

without affecting his underlying impairment. The different decisions in these cases suggest that *in fact* what was critical was the projected quality of the person's life.

In summation, it must be noted that there has been a shift away from the (apparently) limited category of PVS in which it can be lawful to remove ANH into other cases where the diagnosis is different. Indeed, the view of the BMA is that, although in England and Wales it is necessary to obtain court authority for its removal in PVS cases, no such requirement exists in these other situations.[68] As Laurie and Mason say:

> ...the BMA begins to push the parameters with its suggestion that, when it comes to a medical assessment of the 'benefit' or otherwise of continuing artificial feeding and hydration, there should be no differentiation between PVS patients and other categories of patient such as those with severe dementia or who have suffered catastrophic strokes. While the Association acknowledged that no United Kingdom legal case has ever been ruled on this matter, it points out that a body of medical opinion has developed that holds that such action may be appropriate.[69]

However, there is no ethical coherence rendering equivalent PVS patients and others who are profoundly affected by, for example, dementia. The fact that doctors see such a link is irrelevant to the ethical evaluation which needs to be made. That the courts appear to go along with the medical evaluation points only to the truism that UK courts are notoriously reluctant to gainsay medical decisions, and to the pernicious influence of the *Bolam Test*.[70] Thus, it might be argued that the law's approach to clinical decision-making needs to be re-evaluated. For example, and we will return to this point, it has been argued that:

> ...over-deference to medicine (in particular to the scientific aspect of medicine) is dangerously rights-reducing. When coupled with a legal establishment reluctant to challenge medical decision-making – indeed, apparently oblivious to the question as to whether or not doctors' decisions are inevitably about medical matters – the individual's rights to self-determination and autonomy are eroded.[71]

In fact, the BMA itself is aware of the criticism that could be levelled at its approach; namely that it disguises 'quality of life' decisions under the mantle of

---

68 BMA, *op. cit.*, p. 56, para 21.4.
69 Laurie and Mason, *op. cit.*, pp. 170–171.
70 Derived from the case of *Bolam v Friern Hospital Management Committee* [1957] 2 All ER 118.
71 McLean, *op. cit.*, p. xiii.

making decisions about clinical futility or the appropriateness of treatment. It is worth bearing the following critique of this approach in mind.

> The BMA argues that doctors are concerned with the value of a particular *treatment* and not with the value of the *life* of the patient to whom the treatment might or might not be given. But the question concerns the value of the treatment *to* the patient, and, given that the patient cannot speak for him or herself, it is very difficult to understand how one can avoid conflating an assessment of '*treatment*' with an assessment of the *life* of the patient with or without the treatment. To many, such assessments are indistinguishable from euthanasia.[77]

The Burke case[73]

It is, of course, not only the patient in PVS who may require ANH, which has been described as 'relatively simple and straightforward and a routine staple of day-to-day medical practice in hospitals up and down the land...'.[74] This case involved a man with the degenerative condition known as cerebellar ataxia. The condition will inevitably lead to a situation in which he will be unable to do anything for himself although he will remain cognitively fully aware until the very final stages of his illness. He was concerned that the guidelines drawn up by the General Medical Council ((GMC)[75] would permit doctors when that time comes to remove ANH and that he would suffer the horror of dehydrating to death in full awareness of this. Specifically, he argued that a number of the guidelines were in breach of his human rights. One of the guidelines, for example, says:

> If you are the consultant or general practitioner in charge of a patient's care, it is your responsibility to make the decision about whether to withhold or withdraw a life-prolonging treatment, taking account of the views of the patient or those close to the patient as set out in paragraphs 41–48 and 53–57.[76]

Another indicates that:

> Where death is imminent, in judging the benefits, burdens or risks, it usually would not be appropriate to start either artificial hydration or nutrition, although artificial hydration provided by the less invasive measures may be appropriate where it is considered that this would be likely to provide symptom relief.

---

72 Laurie and Mason, *op. cit.*, pp. 159–178.
73 *R (on the application of Burke) v General Medical Council* (2004) 79 BMLR 126.
74 At p. 140.
75 *Withholding and Withdrawing Life-prolonging Treatments: Good Practice in Decision-making*, London, GMC, 2002.
76 Para 32.

Where death is imminent and artificial hydration and/or nutrition are already in use, it may be appropriate to withdraw them if it is considered that the burdens outweigh the possible benefits to the patient.[77]

At the first hearing of the case before Mr Justice Munby, the court's view on who should be responsible for making such decisions was robust: '... the decision as to what is in fact in the patient's best interests is not for the doctor: it is for the patient if competent or, if the patient is incompetent and the matter comes to court, for the judge'.[78] This approach endorses the position of Sir Thomas Bingham MR in the case of *Frenchay Healthcare NHS Trust v S*[79] where he said:

It is, I think, important that there should not be a belief that what the doctor says is in the patient's best interest is the patient's best interest. For my part I would certainly reserve to the court the ultimate power and duty to review the doctor's decision in the light of all the facts.[80]

Reflecting the concerns that we have already expressed about the best-interests concept, Munby further said:

Best interests may be the legal test but it is on its own a poor signpost to sound decision-making in an area as grave and difficult as this. In this and other areas of medical and non-medical decision-making the quality of the ultimate decision can only be enhanced by the adoption of a rigorously reasoned process of evaluation.[81]

His judgement that some of the guidelines on withdrawing treatment issued by the GMC were unlawful was, however, overturned on appeal.[82] The Court of Appeal was concerned about a number of matters, not least that Munby's judgement ranged very widely over matters which, the Court of Appeal felt, should not have been at issue. For example, the Court of Appeal said

The manner and circumstances in this these proceedings were commenced suggest that he was persuaded to advance a claim for judicial review by persons who wished to challenge aspects of the GMC Guidance which had no relevance to a man in Mr Burke's condition.[83]

77 Para 81.
78 At pp. 159–160.
79 (1994) 17 BMLR 156.
80 At p. 164.
81 At pp. 168–169.
82 *Burke v GMC* [2005] EWCA Civ 1003 (28 July 2005).
83 Para 14.

Specifically, it identified a number of matters considered in Munby's judgement which it felt to have been inappropriate:

> We have identified the following topics explored by Munby J in his judgment in passages which have given rise to concern because of apparent implications which extend beyond the predicament of Mr Burke:
>
> i) The right of a patient to select the treatment that he will receive;
> ii) The circumstances in which life-prolonging treatment can be withdrawn from a patient who is incompetent;
> iii) The duty to seek the approval of the court before withdrawing life-prolonging treatment.[84]

Against this critique of Munby's judgement, and arguably of Mr Burke having raised the case in the first place, the Court of Appeal could find no basis on which to hold the GMC's guidance to be unlawful. Indeed, the court said:

> No such difficulty arises, however, in the situation that has caused Mr Burke concern, that of the competent patient who, regardless of the pain, suffering or indignity of his condition, makes it plain that he wishes to be kept alive. No authority lends the slightest countenance to the suggestion that the duty on the doctors to take reasonable steps to keep the patient alive in such circumstances may not persist. Indeed, it seems to us that for a doctor deliberately to interrupt life-prolonging treatment in the face of a competent patient's expressed wish to be kept alive, with the intention of thereby terminating the patient's life, would leave the doctor with no answer to a charge of murder.[85]

The court therefore concluded that there was no basis to declare the guidance unlawful, so far as Mr Burke's situation was concerned.[86] The court further criticised the very basis of the action, saying:

> There are great dangers in a court grappling with issues such as those Munby J has addressed when these are divorced from a factual context that requires their determination. The court should not be used as a general advice centre. The danger is that the court will enunciate propositions of principle without full appreciation of the implications that these will have in practice. This danger is particularly acute where the issues raised involve ethical questions that any court should be reluctant to address, unless driven to do so by the need to resolve a practical problem that requires the court's intervention.[87]

---

84 Para 48.
85 Para 34.
86 Para 47.
87 Para 21.

In conclusion, the court was essentially satisfied that:

> Where life depends upon the continued provision of ANH there can be no question of the supply of ANH not being clinically indicated unless a clinical decision has been taken that the life in question should come to an end. That is not a question that can lawfully be taken in the case of a competent patient who expresses the wish to remain alive.[88]

The judgement of the Court of Appeal was greeted with enthusiasm by the GMC, but with more concern by the Disability Rights Commission (DRC). The President of the GMC stated:

> Patients should be reassured by this judgement which emphasises the partnership needed to resolve end of life issues. Our guidance makes it clear that patients should never be discriminated against on the grounds of disability. And we have always said that causing patients to die from starvation and dehydration is absolutely unacceptable practice and unlawful....[89]

The DRC on the other hand said:

> Many disabled people fear that some doctors make negative, stereotypical assumptions about their quality of life. This ruling will not allay many of their fears. If you become incompetent someone else can still decide what is burdensome and what is in your best interests.[90]

In fact, of course, there is room for some concern about the tenor of the appeal judgement in that it is confined to those who are competent at the stage when consideration of removal of ANH is undertaken. Even more importantly, the implication in the judgement that patients will not have ANH removed against their wishes is at odds with the simultaneous finding – echoed in the GMC guidance – that doctors cannot be forced to provide treatment against their clinical judgement about whether or not it is appropriate, or in the patient's interests, to provide it. Thus, even if the patient wishes treatment, doctors cannot be made to offer it. The Court of Appeal said that '[i]n truth the right to choose is no more than a reflection of the fact that it is the doctor's duty to provide a treatment that he considers to be in the interests of the patient and that the patient is prepared to accept.'[91] Best interests again become central. For Munby,

88 Para 53.
89 Available at http://www.gmcpressoffice.org.uk/apps/news/latest/print.php?key=181 (accessed on 8 August 2005).
90 Available at http://www.drc-gb.org/newsroom/newsdetails.asp?id=833&section=1 (accessed on 8 August 2005).
91 Para 51.

as we have seen, best interests is an inadequate basis from which to proceed, and certainly cannot be equiperated with the clinical view of what is best interests. He conceded that 'I am quite prepared to accept for present purposes that the court will not grant a mandatory order requiring an individual doctor to treat a patient'[92] but felt that this did not mean that 'a doctor can simply decline to go on treating his patient merely because his views as to what is in his patient's best interests differ from those of the patient or the court'.[93]

This approach is arguably in line with acceptance by other courts of the position that best interests are not necessarily the same as best *medical* interests. As was said in the case of *Re S (adult patient: sterilisation)*:

> In deciding what is best for the disabled patient the judge must have regard to the patient's welfare as the paramount consideration. That embraces issues far wider than the medical. Indeed it would be undesirable and probably impossible to set bounds to what is relevant to a welfare decision.[94]

The Court of Appeal in the *Burke* case, however, preferred a different approach, saying:

> The concept of 'best interests' depends very much on the context in which it is used, as indeed does the *Bolam* test, but neither is of much relevance when considering the situation with which we are concerned....It seems to us that it is best to confine the use of the phrase "best interests" to an objective test, which is of most use when considering the duty owed to a patient who is not competent and is easiest to apply when confined to a situation where the relevant interests are medical.[95]

It remains to be seen what will be the impact of the Court of Appeal's judgement, and it is possible that Mr Burke may appeal against it. What is clear, however, that from a seemingly narrowly drawn – and possibly unobjectionable – group of people for whom life seems plausibly to have no value (those in PVS) we have moved to making similar judgements about those who may still experience some value in continued existence. Where people are unable to offer their own opinions about this, it probably inevitably falls to the courts to decide. In our contention, such decisions should be based on respect, not on QoL judgements, and not on what doctors believe to be acceptable medical practice.

92 At p. 191.
93 *Id.*
94 [2001] Fam 15, per Thorpe, LJ at p. 30.
95 Para 29.

Do not resuscitate (DNR) orders

In some situations, the likely prognosis for a patient is sufficiently poor to lead healthcare professionals to believe that, in the event of specific circumstances arising, no attempt should be made to resuscitate the patient. The DNR Order – sometimes referred to as a Do Not Attempt Resuscitation Order (DNAR) – has an important role to play in the management of patients who need, or are likely to need, Cardiopulmonary Resuscitation (CPR). In 1995, Tassona claimed that, '[t]he use of "do not resuscitate" (DNR) orders without the knowledge of either the client or his relatives has become one of the more notorious scandals of the medical industry.'[96] Indeed, Montgomery notes that this 'scandal' 'led to the Government requiring (by a circular[97]) that NHS Trusts agreed and published policies on when resuscitation should be attempted'.[98] Battin, has also noted the trend to produce guidelines to avoid poor practice, but says that 'such directives are by no means always followed'.[99]

Guidelines – hopefully followed – produced by, amongst others, the Resuscitation Council (UK) have been in place since 2001,[100] and standards for clinical practice and training were promulgated in 2004.[101] These guidelines and standards are intended to provide for the appropriate management of DNAR decisions and to ensure that patients and relatives are satisfied that any decisions made will be based on best clinical evaluation as well as – where available – their own views.[102] They followed widespread concern about the possible misuse of such orders, acknowledging '...recent public concern about "do not resuscitate" (DNR) orders after several cases in which patients or their relatives have complained that resuscitation orders have been written in notes without their knowledge or consent'.[103] Oratz says, despite this, that:

> Decisions about cardiopulmonary resuscitation are not different in process from other health care decisions....They should be made by competent patients after disclosure of the pertinent medical facts and discussion of

96 Tassano, F., *The Power of Life or Death: A Critique of Medical Tyranny*, London, Duckworth, 1995 at p. 126.

97 *Resuscitation Policy* HSC 2000/028.

98 Montgomery, J., *Health Care Law and Ethics* (2nd Ed), Oxford University Press, 2003 at p. 474.

99 Battin, M.P., *The Least Worst Death*, Oxford University Press, 1994 at p. 117.

100 Available at http://www.resus.org.uk/pages/guide.htm (accessed on 30 August 2005).

101 *Cardiopulmonary Resuscitation: Standards for Clinical Practice and Training*, A Joint Statement from the Royal College of Anaesthetists, The Royal College of Physicians of London, The Intensive Care Society and the Resuscitation Council (UK), available at http://www.resus.org.uk (accessed on 30 August 2005), October 2004.

102 See 2004 recommendations, particularly at pp. 16–17.

103 Mayor, S., 'New UK Guidance on Resuscitation Calls for Open Decision Making', *BMJ* 2001, 322, 509.

relevant issues with health care providers, family members, and significant others. DNR status should reflect the patient's own preferences.[104]

According to the most recent guidelines:

> The overall responsibility for a DNAR decision rests with the most senior doctor in charge of the patient's care. The opinions of the members of the medical and nursing team (including the GP), the patient, and the patient's relatives, where appropriate, should be taken into account when forming the decision.[105]

Evidence suggests that DNAR Orders are increasingly used in hospitals throughout the world, and it is not unreasonable to assume that their use will be of special significance to certain groups, such as those referred to above. Given this, the ways in which decisions about such orders are made will be of considerable importance to this discussion. As Cherniak says:

> The use of do-not-resuscitate (DNR) orders, which preclude the use of cardiopulmonary resuscitation (CPR) has been increasing in all individuals, including the elderly, over the past several decades. Several surveys suggest that the majority of hospitalised and institutionalised patients in the United States, and many abroad, die with a DNR order in place, which was not true twenty years ago.[106]

In one case involving a person with impairment the court was clear that CPR should not be attempted because it was unlikely to be successful.[107] In this case, the patient in question was a young man of 23 years of age who was unable to perform elementary tasks. He was probably blind and deaf and had other physiological problems. The DNR order was signed by a consultant psychiatrist and was agreed to by the man's mother. Judicial review of the order was sought and a declaration was finally made that CPR should not be attempted. The Judge, Sir Stephen Brown, said:

> The extensive medical evidence in this case is unanimous in concluding that it would not be in the best interests of R to subject him to cardio-pulmonary resuscitation in the event of his suffering a cardiac arrest.... I agree that this declaration should be made.[108]

---

104 Oratz, R. 'Commentary', in Cohen, C.B. (ed) *Casebook on the Termination of Life-Sustaining Treatment and Care of the Dying*, Bloomington, Indiana University Press, 1988, pp. 39–41 at p. 39.
105 At p.17.
106 Cherniak, E.P., 'Increasing Use of DNR Orders in the Elderly Worldwide; Whose Choice Is It?', *JME* 28, 2002, 303 at p. 303.
107 *Re R (adult: medical treatment)* (1996) 31 BMLR 127.
108 At pp. 136–137.

Once again seeking to distance the courts' judgements in such cases from euthanasia, the judge also said, '[i]n this case there is no question of the court being asked to approve a course aimed at terminating life or accelerating death. The court is concerned with circumstances in which steps should not be taken to prolong life.'[109] However often this statement is made in the various decisions taken, it remains the case that 'best interests' is often uncritically evaluated when the patients concerned are impaired or disabled, and that the conclusion seldom works in their favour; their death is indeed accelerated. Moreover, the decision in this case seems yet again to place considerable authority in the medical profession. As Hendrick and Brennan suggest:

> Undoubtedly the decision in *Re R* was a comforting one for the medical profession in that it appeared to leave it firmly in control of DNR decision-making. Given the very limited analysis of the guidelines [BMA, etc.] which were only very briefly referred to, it also appeared to confirm their legality. Regrettably, however, far from clarifying the law, the latter remains as uncertain as before; in particular, the case (which gave an ideal opportunity for medical practice to be scrutinised by the courts) failed to provide any guidance on how such central concepts as 'futility' and 'quality of life' should be defined.[110]

It must, of course, be conceded that CPR is notoriously unsuccessful. This might be taken to suggest that the primary judgement of whether or not to impose a DNR order is purely clinical, and in many cases this will in fact be true. However, the real problem in respect of DNR orders may lie not in the clinical efficacy of CPR, but rather in the extent to which patients are involved in the decision as to its suitability. It is generally accepted that patients should be involved in decisions about their medical care,[111] but we have also suggested that this may be less commonly adhered to in respect of those who are seen in some way as not being 'normal'. This also seems to extend to those whose 'impairment' is simple physical ill-health. Manisty and Waxman, for example, have argued that:

> Patients increasingly want to participate in decisions about their medical treatment. Although this is appropriate in most circumstances, discussing cardiopulmonary resuscitation with terminally ill patients is not practical, sensible, or in the patient's best interests. In these special situations, patient involvement is tokenism and entirely of negative value.[112]

---

109 At p. 135.
110 Hendrick, J. and Brennan, C., 'Do Not Resuscitate Orders: Guidelines in Practice', *Nottingham Law Journal* 6, 24, 1997 at p. 37.
111 *Re C (adult: refusal of treatment)* (1994) 15 BMLR 77.
112 Manisty, C. and Waxman, J., *loc. cit.*, p. 614.

It has to be said that this argument is open to criticism, as it seems to overestimate the impact of illness on a person's ability to receive and use information;[113] indeed it effectively negates his or her right to be involved. It is nonetheless arguably characteristic of the paternalism which we are told no longer permeates medical practice.[114]

Hendrick and Brennan state that:

> A doctor's decision to make a DNR order is justified in one of two situations. First, in respect of a non-competent patient, when the doctor judges that resuscitation will not be in his best interests. Such a judgement will involve assessing the possible quality of the patient's life both before and following resuscitation and will thus involve consideration of subjective and non-medical factors. Alternatively, in respect of either a competent or non-competent patient, it may be estimated that the chances of a successful resuscitation are so low that such action can be termed futile. In this event the doctor has no obligation to provide CPR, regardless of the patient's views.[115]

Of course, the medical success of a given treatment is rightly considered as relevant to the decision whether or not to offer or provide it. In the case of CPR, the evidence in favour of its use (in any circumstances) is not unequivocal. There is a wealth of literature on the limited success of CPR,[116] with Doyal and Wilsher, for example, reporting only a 10–20 per cent survival to discharge in the elderly.[117] Thus, it cannot be assumed *simpliciter* that a failure to offer CPR is a discriminatory act; rather, it may be based on a genuine belief that CPR is likely to be futile in the situation of that particular patient. Nonetheless, the concept of futility is open to considerable interpretation and seems likely to be informed by the attitudes of individual healthcare providers.

Davey, for example, reports that in one study:

> The dominant paradigm on the surgical wards...seems to give primacy to one of several overlapping and sometimes incompatible 'moral imperatives'. The most clearly articulated was the nurses' desire to protect patients from the physical violence of a futile resuscitation attempt, and to defend the

113 See, Buchanan, A., 'Medical Paternalism', *Journal of Philosophy and Public Affairs* 7, 1978, 370–390.
114 For discussion see McLean, S.A.M., *A Patient's Right to Know: Information Disclosure, the Doctor and the Law*, Aldershot, Dartmouth, 1989.
115 Hendrick and Brennan, *op. cit.*, pp. 25–26.
116 Cf Tunstall-Pedoe, H., Bailey, L., Chamberlain, D.A., Marsden, A.K., Ward, M.E. and Zideman, D.A., 'Survey of 3765 cardiopulmonary resuscitations in British hospitals (the BRESUS study): methods and overall results', *BMJ*, 1993, 306, 1347.
117 Doyal, L. and Wilsher, D., 'Withholding Cardiopulmonary Resuscitation: Proposals for Formal Guidelines', *BMJ*, 1993, 306, 1593.

patient's right to a death that 'just needs to be allowed to happen' without the intrusion of needles, tubes, electric shocks and staff 'jumping up and down' on the patient's chest.[118]

Other studies suggest that end-of-life decisions 'involve major moral issues that impinge on hospital staff's personal and professional attitudes.... The data identify how differing perceptions exist regarding quality of life....'[119] Hinkka *et al.* also conclude that, 'experience and training, as well as personal life-values and attitudes to terminal care, markedly influence decision making in this situation.'[120] Most worryingly, in what was admittedly a small study, Perront, Morabia and de Torrente[121] present the following evidence:

> Our two main results were, first, that quality of life intervenes in more than 70% of the DNR decisions taken by medical staff. Thus, when implementing a DNR order, physicians are very often influenced by their perception of patients' quality of life. Second, physicians systematically underrate their DNR patients' quality of life components (including mental state, physical and social condition, degree of pain and depression).[122]

The authors concede that the sample is small, but note that it does seem to replicate the findings of other more substantial studies, such as those conducted by Pearlman *et al.*[123] Indeed, despite the sample size, the overall weight of evidence led Perront *et al.* to conclude that:

> Despite [the] limitations on the interpretations of the results, the poor correlation between physicians and DNR patients about quality of life shown in this study strongly suggests that physicians in training are not good in assessing their patients' quality of life.... In practice, physicians

118 Davey, B., 'Do-Not-Resuscitate Decisions: Too Many, Too Few, Too Late?', *Mortality*, 6, 3, 2001, 247.

119 Costello, J., 'Do Not Resuscitate Orders and Older Patients: Findings from an Ethnographic Study of Hospital Wards for Older People', *Journal of Advanced Nursing*, 39, 5, 2002, 491–499 at p. 497.

120 Hinkka, H. *et al.*, 'Factors Affecting Physicians' Decisions to Forgo Life-Sustaining Treatments in Terminal Care', *JME*, 28, 2002, 28(2), 109–114.

121 Perront, N.J., Morabia, A. and de Torrente, A., 'Quality of Life and Do-Not-Resuscitate (DNR) Patients: How Good are Physicians in Assessing DNR Patients' Quality of Life?', *Swiss Medical Weekly*, 2002, 132, 562–565.

122 At p. 564.

123 Cf Pearlman, R.A. and Uhlmann, RF, 'Quality of Life and Resuscitation Decisions in Elderly Patients', *J Gen Intern Med*, 1986, 43, M25–30; Starr, T.J., Pearlman, R.A. and Uhlmann, R.F., 'Quality of Life and Resuscitation Decisions in Elderly Patients', *J Gen Intern Med* 1986, 1, 373–379; Uhlmann, R.F. and Pearlman, R.A. 'Perceived Quality of Life and Preferences for Life-sustaining Treatment in Older Adults', *Arch Intern Med* 1991, 151, 495–497.

should not base decisions on their perception of patients' quality of life, especially in those involving life-and-death issues.[124]

As an attempt to allay concerns of this sort, a joint statement was issued by the BMA, the Resuscitation Council (UK) and the Royal College of Nursing.[125] Coming from such authoritative sources, this statement is likely to be highly influential and is therefore worth considering in some detail. First, it must be noted that the guidelines are underpinned by some important principles, namely:

- Timely support for patients and people close to them, and effective sensitive communication are essential.
- Decisions must be based on the individual patient's circumstances and reviewed regularly.
- Sensitive advance discussion should always be encouraged, but not forced.
- Information about CPR and the chances of a successful outcome needs to be realistic.

Additionally, the statement makes it clear as to what the limitations of a DNR Order are:

A decision not to attempt resuscitation applies only to CPR. It should be made clear to the patient, people close to the patient and members of the health care team that it does not imply 'non-treatment' and that all other treatment and care that are appropriate for the patient will continue to be considered and offered.[126]

The statement clarifies those situations in which it is appropriate to consider making a DNR order.[127] These are as follows: '[w]here attempting CPR will not restart the patient's heart and breathing';[128] '[w]here there is no benefit in restarting the patient's heart and breathing. Although in most cases there is a benefit when a patient's heart and breathing are successfully restarted following cardiopulmonary arrest, this is not true in all cases. No benefit is gained if only a brief extension of life can be achieved and the patient's co-morbidity is such that imminent death cannot be averted. Similarly no benefit is gained by the patient if he or she will never have awareness or the ability to interact and is therefore unable to experience benefit';[129] and '[w]here the expected benefit is

124 At p. 565.
125 *Decisions Relating to Cardiopulmonary Resuscitation* 2001. Available at www.resus.org.uk (accessed on 19 September 2003).
126 Para 15.
127 Para 10.
128 Para 10.1.
129 Para 10.2.

outweighed by the burdens....Where the patient is not competent, any previously expressed wishes should form a core part of assessing the benefit to that person...The courts have confirmed it is lawful to withhold CPR on the basis that it would not confer a benefit upon the patient where consideration has been given to the relevant medical factors and to whether the treatment may provide a reasonable quality of life for the patient.'[130]

In *Mason and McCall Smith's Law and Medical Ethics*, the authors describe these guidelines as 'well meaning',[131] but conclude that 'they conceal a hornet's nest of moral dilemmas.'[132] Not least, although they note that evidence suggests most people welcome being involved in DNR decisions,[133] they also say that, '[d]espite the...guidance that the patient's consent is highly desirable, one would have thought that obtaining such consent would raise intractable practical difficulties'.[134]

In other words, as in *Re R*, it may be difficult to subscribe to the importance of autonomy where, for example, the individual concerned is extremely impaired or seriously ill. How precisely the patient in these circumstances can be involved is a matter of ethical and practical concern. This raises specific questions, particularly if it is indeed the case that:

> ...people with disabilities have already been endangered by relaxation of laws and policies protecting their lives. Medical rehabilitation specialists report that quadriplegics and other significantly disabled people are dying wrongfully in increasing numbers because emergency room physicians judge their quality of life as low and, therefore, withhold aggressive treatment.[135]

Finally, it is worth heeding the voice of the DRC, which claims that '[e]ven today, in the UK, disabled and older people are reporting that, when they are receiving treatment in hospital, Do Not Resuscitate (DNR) notices are being put on their notes by medical professionals, without their consent, contrary to regulatory guidance.'[136]

Although it is not clear on what evidence the DRC bases this assertion, there is at least one recent case where we know that problems did arise; the case of

---

130 Para 10.3.

131 Mason, J.K. and Laurie, G.T., *Mason and McCall Smith's Law and Medical Ethics* (7th Ed), Oxford, Oxford University Press, 2006 at p. 636, para 17.94.

132 *Id.*

133 Cf Hill, M.E., MacQuillan, G., Forsyth, M. and Heath, D.A., 'Cardiopulmonary Resuscitation: Who Makes the Decision?', *BMJ*, 308, 1994, 1677.

134 Mason and Laurie, *op. cit.*, pp. 636–637, para 17.94.

135 Not Dead Yet 'Testimony of Diane Coleman, J.D. and Carol Gill Ph.D., Before the Constitution Sub-committee of the Judiciary Committee of the United States House of Representatives', available at http://www.notdeadyet.org (accessed on 18 June 2003).

136 Disability Rights Commission, Briefings and Reports, available at http://www.drc-gb.org (accessed on 24 June 2003), para 3.1.

David Glass v The United Kingdom.[137] This case concerned a disabled child who had been admitted to hospital in July 1998 and had undergone surgery. He subsequently suffered complications and infections, making him critically ill. The medical notes from 9 September 1998 indicated that an agreement had been reached between doctors and his mother that morphine would be given for pain if necessary, but that resuscitation measures would not extend to full intubation and treatment in an intensive care unit.

David was re-admitted to hospital in October 1998 following respiratory failure. By 20 October his doctors concluded that he was dying and advised that diamorphine should be given. David's family, however, disagreed with the doctors' view and objected to the diamorphine because they thought it would compromise his chances of recovery. A meeting with the CEO of the hospital failed to resolve the situation, but on the evening of 20 October diamorphine infusion was begun against the wishes of the mother. Also, and without her knowledge, at some stage a DNR order was placed in his medical notes.

On 21 October, a fight broke out between members of the family (who were subsequently convicted of assault) and the medical staff. David's mother successfully resuscitated her son while the fight was going on. His condition improved and he was discharged on that day. In a letter dated 5 November the hospital suggested that any further treatment should be offered by a hospital 25 miles away. An application for Judicial Review was refused, as was an application to the Court of Appeal in 1999 for permission to appeal. The family complained both to the police and the GMC, but no charges were brought.

Mrs Glass took her case to the Court of Human Rights, relying on the following articles of the European Convention on Human Rights, incorporated into UK law by the Human Rights Act 1998.

Article 2 – the right to life: it was alleged that the doctors had put David's life at risk of premature termination.

Article 6 – the right to a fair trial: it was argued that the giving of treatment without court authorisation and thereafter the refusal of the courts to adjudicate both on the treatment given and the refusal to treat in the future breached David's rights under this Article.

Article 8 – the right to private and family life: it was argued that the doctors' conduct interfered with David's right to physical and moral integrity and was done in the absence of consent from his mother and without the involvement of the courts.

Article 13 – it was argued that there had been a denial of an effective domestic remedy.

Article 14 – the non-discrimination provision: it was argued that David had been discriminated against on the grounds of his disabilities.

137 [2004] Lloyd's Rep Med 76 (ECHR).

The Court held that the complaint under Art 8 stood, but that the complaints under the other Articles were unfounded and were therefore declared inadmissible. It is worth briefly considering the bases on which the claims based on the other Articles were dismissed. In respect of Art 2, the court said:

> In the court's opinion, the applicants' complaints under Article 2 amount in effect to a criticism of the doctors' clinical judgment in the situation which arose, a situation which, in the applicants' view, could not be considered an emergency. However, it is not its function under Article 2 to gainsay the doctors' assessment of the first applicant's condition at the time, nor their decision to forego suction treatment in favour of the administration of diamorphine nor their view on the appropriate dose of diamorphine to be administered. These assessments and decisions were made against the backdrop of the first applicant's state of health at the time, his recent case history and their perception that he was distressed and in pain and that steps needed to be taken to alleviate his respiratory difficulties.[138]

The Art 6 claim, which was also rejected, was considered from two distinct perspectives. First, even if it could be said that a right of access to a court did arise in this case, it was better considered under Art 8.[139] Second:

> ...the court accepts the concern of the second applicant that the domestic courts in the judicial review proceedings did not pronounce on the unlawfulness of the Trust's decision to administer diamorphine to her son against her wishes or to refuse to treat him in the future. However, it considers that the domestic courts' unwillingness to be drawn on this question is understandable in the circumstances, having regard to the nature of the proceedings and to the factual dispute and to the factual dispute between the second applicant and the Trust over the first applicant's precise condition at the time and the correct manner of treating him. Although Article 6 guarantees an applicant a right to have a ruling on matters involving his civil rights which he submits to a domestic court, it must be accepted that domestic courts must have some degree of flexibility in framing their response to the issues put to them, provided of course that they do not abdicate the essence of their adjudicative function.[140]

Since the domestic courts had told the mother of her right to seek the intervention of the High Court if she had future disputes about treatment, '[t]he approach taken cannot be considered a denial of the applicants' right of access to

---

138 At p. 85.
139 At p. 87.
140 *Id.*

a court; nor can the domestic court's failure to pronounce on the Trust's refusal to treat the first applicant in the future be so considered'.[141]

Article 13 was held to be inapplicable because there was no arguable claim. Finally, the court addressed the complaint under Art 14. For our purposes this was the most significant aspect of the case, and it too was rejected:

> The court finds that there is no evidence whatsoever on which to base an arguable complaint that the first applicant was the victim of discrimination on account of the fact that he was severely handicapped. [His]...disability was undoubtedly a relevant factor in assessing clinically his chances of survival and determining the treatment which was considered the most appropriate in the circumstances. However, it cannot be maintained that the doctors allowed themselves to be influenced by considerations based on his quality of life compared with that of able-bodied patients. There is no indication either that such considerations played a part in either the Trust's decision not to seek the advance approval of the High Court for the treatment administered to the first applicant or in the domestic court's reluctance to address specifically the issues put to it by the applicants in the judicial review proceedings.[142]

Interestingly, the UK Government was compelled to respond to the assertion that we have already mentioned; namely that ' "Do Not Resuscitate" notices are used as a means of rationing the provision of healthcare to vulnerable groups of patients.'[143] Despite the allegations that we referred to, the UK Government argued that '[o]n the contrary, the policy of the authorities is to ensure that hospitals have in place appropriate resuscitation practices which respect the rights of patients.'[144] In light of the very real concerns expressed, for example, by the DRC it remains moot whether such 'appropriate policies' are in fact protective of the rights of people with disabilities. Ultimately, therefore, the *Glass* case did uphold the child's right to have his family involved in decisions about his health, but takes us no further forward in terms of allegations that people with disabilities are the victims of discrimination in such treatment decisions, although it decided that *in this case* no such discrimination existed. However, if we recall the case of Jill Baker, a competent cancer patient who only discovered that a 'Do Not Resuscitate' order had been placed on her notes after she discharged herself from hospital, it is clear that in some cases vulnerable people may well be judged without having the opportunity to have their voice heard.[145]

141 *Id.*
142 At p. 88.
143 At p. 86.
144 *Id.*
145 Available at http://news.bbc.co.uk/1/hi/health/711117.stm (accessed on 3 June 2006).

Conclusion

Life must clearly end, and there will be situations when decisions must be taken on our behalf by those healthcare professionals caring for us at that time. The fact that these decisions can – probably will – affect many if not most of the population adds to the strength of our expectation that they are made with care and without discrimination. The problem, however, is twofold. First, as we have seen from our discussion of patients in PVS, the apparent care which characterised the early decisions in *Bland* and *Law Hospital*, has slipped somewhat, permitting patients who do not qualify for that diagnosis to be 'allowed to die'. Thus, issues about QoL have come to take an important place in life-and-death decisions, quality being judged by doctors and/or courts. This may be inevitable, even if problematic, but the basis on which others judge the QoL of any patient is shrouded in mystery. Most likely, personal assumptions about the kind of life the decision maker would want to live will directly affect the decisions he or she makes for others. Indeed, in the *Bland* case, Lord Browne-Wilkinson made precisely this point, saying that, 'if the judges seek to develop new law to regulate...new circumstances, the law so laid down will of necessity reflect judges' views on the underlying ethical questions...'.[146]

Second, quality-of-life decisions are also apparently common when the question of to whether or not to withhold or withdraw treatment is raised. In general, there may be nothing inherently wrong in this; people who are in fact able to make such decisions have the right to reject treatment, even if it is life-saving, and, as was said in the US case of *Belchertown State School Superintendent v Saikewicz*:

> To presume that the incompetent person must always be subjected to what many rational and intelligent persons may decline is to downgrade the status of the incompetent person by placing a lesser value on his intrinsic human worth and vitality.[147]

It would be equally inappropriate to presume that someone who is impaired or incompetent would inevitably not want to be treated.

No matter in which form decisions at the end of life appear, there is reason to be concerned that the assumptions made by those caring for them will tend to be autonomy reducing rather than enhancing; that respect for persons will not be the dominant principle. If, as we have suggested, decisions about people where judgements have been made about their capacity to make their own choices can be based on flawed presuppositions, this has the potential to result in people with impairments or disabilities being treated as second-rate citizens. Much, therefore, depends on a number of factors. We have suggested that when the

146 At p. 126.
147 (1977) 373 Mass 728 at p. 747.

issues concern the beginning of life, the medical model seems to predominate both clinical and judicial thinking. At the end of life, it would also appear that the medical model is dominant. This arises in two ways. First, the fact of impairment may be taken to minimise the input that people who are impaired are entitled to have in decisions about their lives and their futures; authority goes by default to the medical profession (or in some cases, the courts). Second, assumptions about the QoL of people with pre-existing impairments (disabilities) may render them more than usually vulnerable to treatment withdrawal, or even to the non-initiation of therapy. However, as we have seen throughout our examinations to date, reliance on the medical model can inadvertently conceal the role of negative stereotypes and social prejudice in what are reputedly value-free medico-legal judgements. In this respect, we have repeatedly discovered that the social model has much to teach us regarding the prejudices that influence decisions regarding impaired (disabled) lives. However, we have also argued that it has inherent shortcomings, which apply in this situation also.

As Shakespeare has said, '[i]mpairment and disability are part of the human condition, and society needs to come to terms with disability, not encourage people to think that disabled lives are not worth living.'[148] To do this it is necessary that we have at our disposal much more robust and self-critically aware ethico-legal resources. Currently the over-emphasis on clinical judgement may in this area result in the prejudices of the 'abled' becoming critical in the right of the 'dis-abled' to continue living or to be given otherwise indicated treatment. The DRC, for example, says that:

> The language used in legal decisions to describe impairment and life with a disability reveals an institutional discomfort with disability. There is a very strong presumption that life with a disability is a lesser life that, even when tolerable, is tragic or regrettable. Legal decisions reinforce the notion that some people are too disabled to merit treatment, or sustain life and rely on explicit 'quality of life' assessments, largely by medical professionals, to determine what that is.[149]

It further notes that:

> It is impossible at present to quantify how widespread discrimination is, in relation to disability, in withholding or withdrawing treatment cases. The cases that have come to light have been through, for example, an individual or his or her family asking to see the patient's notes. There has been no national

---

148 Submission to Select Committee, para 3.4.
149 Disability Rights Commission, Policy statement on voluntary euthanasia and assisted suicide, available at http://www.drc-gb.org/library/policy/health_and_independent_living/disability_rights_commission_.aspx, p. 22, para 3.33 (accessed on 4 July 2006).

mechanism for systematically monitoring policy and practice in relation to disabled people.[150]

If so, this must surely be a matter of concern. What seems clear to us, however, is that in these cases there is no single source for the decision that a person's life is not worth living. Although it is clear that clinical indications are taken most seriously, including by the courts, it is not obvious that this means that the medical model is being applied *simpliciter*. Presumably, the ability to function socially is also a feature of such decisions, and it is unclear how the application of the social model to, for example, decisions about people in PVS would significantly moderate the decisions being taken. Arguably, in less clear-cut cases, the contribution of the social model cannot be dismissed as irrelevant. However, as Shakespeare has said, concentration on impairment or disability as a purely social phenomenon has left the disability rights movement having difficulty engaging with 'debates about illness, impairment and end of life. It could be argued that a social model philosophy enables some to disengage from troubling questions about bodies and mortality.'[151]

These are complex and sensitive situations which require complex and sensitive solutions. At the very least, when lives could be maintained, evaluation of quality or 'best interests' needs to be transparent, accountable and non-discriminatory. Although evidence that people with pre-existing impairment, as opposed to those who become impaired only at the end of their lives, are routinely discriminated against may be anecdotal, it is implausible that the assumptions we have argued underpin other decisions taken on their behalf would not endure to end-of-life situations. This, we believe makes it even more necessary that the voices of those with impairment or disability are heard at this critical stage. This is not because it is anticipated that they will speak with one voice but rather because, if the rationale for decisions is unclear, their personal contributions can potentially assist in focussing on the principles which should be given primacy. As has been said:

> Given that persons suffering from terminal illnesses and those experiencing severe pain almost always meet the definition of individuals with disabilities, and that people with disabilities run the risk of being subject to life-shortening measures even when they may not in fact have life-threatening conditions, the views and insights of people with disabilities would seem to be very significant to the debate on this issue. And yet the viewpoints of individuals with disabilities have been, if not ignored, at least not a major piece of the public and judicial debate on this issue.[152]

150 Disability Rights Commission, Policy statement on voluntary euthanasia and assisted suicide, available at http://www.drc-gb.org/library/policy/health_and_independent_living/disability_rights_commission_.aspx, p. 21, para 3.29 (accessed on 4 July 2006).
151 Para 2.7.
152 National Council on Disability (US), Assisted Suicide: A Disability Perspective, available at http://www.ncd.gov/newsroom/publisations/1997/suicide.htm (accessed on 16 June 2005) at p. 5.

Of course, it is clear that in seeking to unravel the principles which should be applied there are problems in at least some of the situations we have described. Commitment, for example, to autonomy becomes of little relevance where the person concerned is unable to exercise it. However, we continue to maintain that respect for persons is a fundamental principle which can and should have relevance at this time. Respect may of course require consideration of the individual's best interests, and even perhaps of the likely quality of his or her life, but the use of these considerations needs to be set against the backdrop of respect. It is insufficient to rely solely or exclusively on the views of those with clinical expertise, or indeed of courts. Meat needs to be placed on the bones of these tests, based on underpinning concerns for the foundational ethical principle we have adopted.[153] Even although in the cases we have discussed the facilitating principles of consent and autonomy may not be relevant, respect is bolstered by the principle of respect for human rights.

153 See Chapter 3.

Chapter 6

Seeking assistance in dying

Introduction

For people with impairment or disability, one final – and major – area of concern remains, namely, that the increasing pressure in many countries to legalise assisted suicide and voluntary euthanasia will add yet one more threat to their very right to exist. Before exploring these concerns, one fundamental point needs to be made. In what follows, we will not use the language of the 'right' to die. We have a *certainty* to die, we might have rights in respect of *choosing* to die, but we do not have a right to die. In other words, we believe that it is a mistake to couch the debate in terms of a right to *die*. Rather, the important issue is the right to *choose*. This has particular resonance, as choice is traditionally what is said to protect people from the unwarranted assumption of authority over their body. The ability to make choices, and to have those choices respected, is of fundamental importance to ensuring that we can live self-directing lives. That some people also wish to experience self-directed deaths is a matter of concern for many people both within and outwith the disability rights lobby. However, it is probably true to say that for the former group the concerns are both more urgent and more difficult to resolve.

The individual's choice for assistance in dying may arise in two distinct situations; first, where people reject treatment which could be life-saving and second, where they actively seek help from their physicians – or other persons – to end their life. In light of the primarily legal emphasis in this section of the book, we will be considering two recent, and highly relevant, legal judgements, namely, *Ms B v an NHS Hospital Trust* and *Pretty v United Kingdom*. In the first case to be considered, we see that for some people the ability to choose not to be kept alive, even if continued life is possible, is highly prized. As a result they reject all life-sustaining treatment. In the second case we will investigate circumstances in which individuals experience such deterioration in their well-being that they seek active assistance to end their lives.

Decisions in such cases are generally based on quality of life indications, just as are the decisions we discussed in the last chapter. There is, however, one important difference: in this case, the quality-of-life judgement is made *by the individual* whose life it is, rather than by third parties. It is, therefore, more likely accurately to reflect the reality of the person's wishes and perceptions of his or her current condition and to mirror his or her own intentions. In this context, while medical status is likely to be important, people's decisions can also incorporate the social consequences of continued existence. Proponents of the social model of disability may object to some of the decisions taken because they seem exactly to support their argument. When people choose death over life with disability, they might argue, society's failure to offer the ambience which would make that choice unnecessary is a direct cause of their death. In the first case to be considered, however, the patient specifically rejected a route which would have ameliorated the effects of her impairment on the simple basis that she did not wish to live on in the condition in which she found herself.

Rejecting life-sustaining treatment

In the case of *Ms B v an NHS Hospital Trust*[1] the question of whether or not a patient was able competently and lawfully to refuse life-sustaining treatment was considered. This was, of course, not the first case of this sort to reach a court. Perhaps the most significant of the earlier cases was *Re C*,[2] in which a man suffering from paranoid schizophrenia was allowed to refuse potentially life-saving surgery both then and in the future. That Ms B's case reached the courts at all came as something of a surprise, given that most academic commentators had firmly believed the law to be absolutely settled on this matter. The legal consensus had been that a competent adult person was permitted to refuse life-sustaining treatment for any reason whatsoever and that for healthcare providers to impose refused treatment would amount to an assault.[3]

Briefly the facts of the case were as follows: the applicant was a 43-year-old woman who had initially suffered a haemorrhage in her spinal column. She was informed that there was a small possibility that a further bleed might happen and at that stage (in 1999) she drafted a living will (or advance directive) indicating the circumstances in which she would not wish treatment to be continued. Some 18 months later, she was readmitted to hospital having suffered a deterioration in her condition and after becoming tetraplegic. Survival depended on ventilation, and although hospital staff were aware of the existence of her advance directive, they declined to act on it, believing that it did not specifically meet the particular circumstances in which Ms B now found herself. A number of psychiatric assessments were carried out on Ms B, who repeated her desire that the ventilation should be discontinued. Although some psychiatric opinion held that she was not competent, it was ultimately concluded that she was indeed

---

1 [2002] Lloyd's Rep Med 265.
2 [1994] 1 ALL ER 819.
3 See, for example, *Re MB (an adult: medical treatment)* (1997) 38 BMLR 175.

competent to make a contemporaneous decision which would, in any event, override the terms of her previous advance directive.

Ms B subsequently executed a second living will in which she restated her desire not to be ventilated. The hospital's perspective was that there was treatment available which might allow Ms B to continue surviving ventilator free. This would require weaning her off the ventilator gradually with the aid of sedation. Ms B indicated that she was unwilling to undertake such a programme and repeated her request for discontinuation of ventilation.

As we have already indicated, courts in this country and elsewhere have repeatedly stressed the importance of facilitating the autonomous decisions of individuals. For example, in the case of *S v McPhee: W v W*, Lord Reid said:

> ...English law goes to great lengths to protect a person of full age and capacity from interference with his personal liberty. We have too often seen freedom disappear in other countries not only by coups d'etat but by gradual erosion; and often it is the first step that counts. So it would be unwise to make even minor concessions.[4]

Two issues arise from Ms B's case. The first relates to whether individuals can legitimately refuse life-sustaining treatment and if so in what circumstances.

Refusal of treatment

In the United Kingdom, the case of *Re MB (Medical Treatment)*[5] made it clear that a competent adult can reject even life-saving treatment. In the United States, in the case of *Cruzan v Director, Missouri Department of Health*,[6] the United States Supreme Court also held to this position, endorsing the words of Mr Justice Cardozo in *Schloendorff v Society of New York Hospital*[7] which iterated the absolute right of an individual to make his or her own decisions about what can or cannot be done to his or her own body.

In Ms B's case, although continued existence was possible, the quality of that life with or without ventilation was inadequate *from her own perspective*. Even were she able to be weaned off the ventilator, life as a tetraplegic held no interest for her; it seems that both the impairment and the consequent disability were unacceptable to her. The critical point here is that although some other people suffering from the same condition might well regard their life as being worth living, the decision as to whether or not it *is* worth living is one that can

4 [1972] AC 25 at p. 43.
5 Cited earlier.
6 110 S Ct 2841 (1990).
7 211 NY 125 (1914).

accurately be made only by the individual him/herself. In this case, Butler-Sloss made the following important point in endorsing Ms B's decision. She said:

> The treating clinicians and the hospital should always have in mind that a seriously physically disabled patient who is mentally competent has the same right to personal autonomy and to make decisions as any other person with mental capacity.[8]

In the context of this discussion, this statement is of critical importance, especially when coupled with Butler-Sloss's reminder that competence should be presumed and that only compelling evidence would be sufficient to overturn that assumption.[9] The mere presence of disability or impairment is not sufficient to overturn it: indeed the case of *Re C*, which has already been referred to, shows that not even the presence of mental illness is necessarily sufficient to overturn it.

From the perspective of some disability theorists, however, this judgement might be seen as less than reassuring. Although the decision seems like a triumphant restatement of respect for the autonomy rights of individuals, and rejects the paternalism of medicine, it also cannot be taken out of context. Ms B was offered alternative regimes in order to convince her that she could have a life which – for her – was indeed worth living. That she rejected the alternative is less significant than the fact that an alternative was offered, because the offer recognised that her decisions depended on real choice between available options. However, it has been said in respect of disabled people generally that:

> Many cases in which state courts have expanded the right to refuse treatment demonstrate that prejudice, stereotypes and devaluation of people with disabilities have already had a substantial adverse impact on members of this minority group. Flagrant prejudice against people with disabilities pervades each decision.[10]

Doubting the reality of choice, and noting the general lack of support for disabled people it is sometimes argued that:

> Without access to competent medical care, options and information about disability, people with severe disabilities are not able to make informed decisions. Without the professional commitment to help make living

---

8 At p. 281.

9 *Id.*

10 Amici Curiae Brief of Not Dead Yet and American Disabled for Attendant Programs Today in Support of Petitioners, in the case of *Vac, et al. v Quill, et al.*, No 95–1858, Supreme Court of the United States, October Term 1995, available at http://www.notdeadyet.org (accessed on 18 June 2003).

worthwhile for people with disabilities, which is the core of suicide prevention, people with disabilities will not receive the support necessary for informed and voluntary decisions.[11]

There is a tension between, on the one hand, wishing to ascribe to people with impairment the same rights as those which extend to everyone else, and on the other, recognising the very real possibility that the negative perceptions of disability that pervade society together with lack of social and other support mechanisms might influence their decision. Thus, it could be argued, an apparently autonomous decision is in reality a pressurised or coerced one. By implication, therefore, such decisions should not be taken at face value. The Disability Rights Commission (DRC), for example, argues that:

> If a disabled person expresses the wish to die the first task must be to try to enable them to make the choice to live. Until disabled people are treated equally – their lives accorded the same value as the lives of non-disabled people, their access to necessary services guaranteed, their social and economic opportunities equal to those of non-disabled people – the 'right to die' may jeopardise people's right to live.[12]

Of course, it could be argued – as we discussed in Chapter 3 – that everyone is pressurised or influenced by some factors in their lives, and that impaired or disabled people are in no different a position than any other person making a decision to refuse treatment It is obviously the case that we must accept that resources to enable disabled people to fulfil their lives to the fullest extent are sadly often lacking. However, the same is true of those in restricted financial circumstances, for example. Arguably, if we walk down that path, we will disvalue every competent decision made in virtually any circumstance, because we are never free to make totally unpressurised decisions. This, however, does not mean that we should not be concerned, rather, the choice is between paternalism in the short term and liberation in the long term. It is a matter of judgement whether the decisions of disabled people that their own lives are not worth living should be taken as being unusually coerced, so as to deny them the same decision-making rights to which others (who are also apparently pressurised, albeit by other concerns) would be entitled. The DRC's statement also arguably ignores the reality of life with impairment or disability for some people. As we have seen in Chapter 2, disability theorists such as Crow and Swain and French have raised concerns that the social model of disability has

11 *Ibid.*
12 Disability Rights Commission, para 2.2.

a tendency to overlook the negative experiences that can be associated with impairment.[13] As Shakespeare summarises:

> The disability rights movement has developed a social model understanding of disability, in which people are disabled by society, not by their bodies. This has made it harder for the disability rights community to engage with debates about illness, impairment and end of life. It could be argued that a social model philosophy enables some to disengage from troubling questions about bodies and mortality.[14]

Indeed, he also argues that it is 'inconsistent to support autonomy for disabled people in all matters except at the end of life'.[15] The tension between the two primary models of disability is never more clear than where decisions may result in death.

The second main issue to arise from Ms B's case relates to the question of whether or not people can make decisions about treatment which will be binding on their doctors in the future.

Advance directives

In Canada, the case of *Malette v Schulman*[16] upheld the validity of a living will or advance directive. In this case, a woman who carried a 'no blood' card was given a blood transfusion even though the doctor was aware of the existence of the card. She sued the doctor successfully, as the court recognised her right to make such preemptive choices. In the United Kingdom, the first case to consider this was probably that of *Re C* mentioned above, where the court not only endorsed C's contemporaneous refusal of treatment but also made a ruling which prevented treatment being provided in the future should he become incompetent. Indeed, the fact that Anthony Bland had not made such a directive was regretted by some of the judges in his case,[17] as it would – in their opinion – have settled the matter, adding additional support to the view that advance directives have considerable legal force.

---

13 Crow, L., 'Including all of our Lives: Renewing the Social Model of Disability', in Barnes, C. and Mercer, G. (eds), *Exploring the Divide*, Leeds, The Disability Press, 1996 55–72. This document is available at http://www.leeds.ac.uk/disability-studies/archiveuk but the edition has no page numbers; Swain, J. and French, S. 'Towards an Affirmative Model of Disability', *Disability and Society*, 15, 4, 2000, 569–582; Shakespeare, T. and Watson, N., 'Defending the Social Model of Disability', *Disability and Society*, 12, 2, 1997, 293–300.

14 Submission to the House of Lords Select Committee on the Assisted Dying for the Terminally Ill Bill at para 2.7, (personal communication); available at Volume II of the Report, 254 (with Ms Alison Davies).

15 *Ibid.*, para 1.4.

16 (1990) 67 DLR (4th) 321.

17 *Airedale NHS Trust v Bland* (1993) 12 BMLR 64.

This was further endorsed by a practice note issued in 1994,[18] and by the publication by the British Medical Association (BMA) of their guidance, *Advance Statements About Medical Treatment*.[19] Although concluding that advance directives or statements are not binding on medical practitioners, '[w]here valid and applicable, advance directives (refusals) must be followed.'[20] This wording has generally been accepted in law since the BMA's guidance was issued. In the recent case of *AK (adult patient) (medical treatment: consent)*[21] a court agreed that a young man who was in the final stages of motor neurone disease could – as he requested – have life-sustaining treatment discontinued two weeks after he was no longer able to communicate. In England and Wales the authority of the advance directive has now been placed on a statutory footing by the terms of the Mental Capacity Act 2005. In terms of this legislation, a legally competent person over eighteen years of age can make an advance decision about specific treatments which may become indicated when he is no longer competent.[22] Furthermore, as the Act says:

(1) An advance decision does not affect the liability which a person may incur for carrying out or continuing a treatment in relation to P unless the decision is at the material time –

    (a) valid, and

    (b) applicable to the treatment.

(2) An advance decision is not valid if P –

    (a) has withdrawn the decision at a time when he had capacity to do so,

    (b) has, under a lasting power of attorney created after the advance decision was made, conferred authority on the donee (or, if more than one, any of them) to give or refuse consent to the treatment to which the advance decision relates, or

    (c) has done anything else clearly inconsistent with the advance decision remaining his fixed decision.[23]

The statement must be in writing, signed by the person concerned and witnessed.[24] As we have already indicated, the statement must be valid and applicable to the treatment in question.[25] In Scotland, the equivalent legislation, the Adults with Incapacity (Scotland) Act 2000, did not specifically refer to

18 *Practice Note* [1994] 2 All ER 413.
19 London, BMJ Publishing Group, 1995.
20 Para 14.2, p. 37.
21 (2001) 58 BMLR 151.
22 s 24 (1).
23 s 25.
24 s 25 (6).
25 s 26 (1).

advance directives. The situation will, therefore, continue to be dealt with at common law.

Although the law appears relatively settled, the debate about advance directives is by no means over. Some, for example, question whether or not decisions made at a time when life with impairment might seem to be intolerable should be given weight when the impairment actually arises and the person seems unaware of the 'intolerability' of his or her condition. For example, A might decide that it would be intolerable to live with advanced Alzheimer's Disease, and draft an advance directive stating that in the event of that condition arising s/he should not be treated for infections, that is, s/he should be allowed to die. However, once incapacitated by Alzheimer's, A appears happy and content. What, it is asked, should those caring for A do? On the one hand, they are aware that this is a condition in which A – when competent – did not wish to live, on the other, A is no longer aware of this and seems happy enough. Should the healthcare professionals follow the directive or not? This is a hotly debated topic with some believing that the directive is no longer applicable because the person who made it is no longer the same person. Others argue that it is essential to respect the views of the person who made the directive as s/he was just part of the continuum that includes the person with Alzheimer's. Judging what weight should be given to these contrasting views is clearly not easy, and may depend on the attitude taken towards the particular impairment under consideration.

Seeking assistance in dying: the case of assisted suicide/voluntary euthanasia

The second main consideration in this part of our discussion arose most recently and most topically in the case of Diane Pretty.[26] Mrs Pretty suffered from motor neurone disease, a progressive condition which had left her wheelchair-bound and unable to do most things unaided. The condition has a particularly unpleasant progression and Mrs Pretty was aware that in its final stages, although she would remain intellectually unimpaired, she would be unable to do anything for herself. As in the Canadian case of *Rodriguez v A-G of British Columbia*,[27] Mrs Pretty wanted to be assisted in her dying at a time of her own choice. Unlike the *Rodriguez* case, however, Mrs Pretty wanted the final assistance to be provided by her husband rather than by a doctor. The Suicide Act 1961 specifically precludes an individual from assisting in the death of another.[28] As a matter of interest, there is no such specific statutory crime in Scotland, although there is little doubt that a prosecution would follow any such

---

26 Cited earlier.
27 107 DLR (4th) 342 (1993).
28 s 2 (1).

assistance.[29] Doctors too are, of course, precluded by law from participation in assisted suicide, even although there is some evidence that a number of doctors already do so.[30] Indeed, some healthcare professionals would prefer to see the law changed to permit such involvement – as has already been done in a number of other countries[31] – although this still remains a matter of considerable contention.[32] In 2005, the Royal College of Nursing (RCN) held a debate at its annual conference in which '…at least half of those who spoke called for a change in RCN policy'.[33] Moreover, in a remarkable change from tradition, the BMA voted at its conference in 2005 to drop its opposition to the legalisation of assisted suicide, backing a motion which stated:

> The BMA should not oppose legislation which alters the criminal law, but should press for robust safeguards both for patients and for doctors who do not wish to be involved in such procedures.[34]

This was, however, rapidly overturned at its 2006 meeting.[35]

In the *Pretty* case, the Director of Public Prosecutions was unwilling – arguably unable – to make such a declaration, and Mrs Pretty ultimately had her case heard by the European Court of Human Rights. She alleged that her situation engaged a number of her fundamental rights, and indeed that s 2(1) of the Suicide Act 1961 was in direct breach of the European Convention on Human Rights, which was incorporated into UK law by the Human Rights Act 1998. The Articles on which Mrs Pretty based her case were Articles 2, 3, 8, 9 and 14. As this is a very important case, and will shape UK law for the future unless overturned by statute, it is worth considering the arguments in some detail. Article 2 of the Convention on Human Rights is the fundamental expression of the right to life. Clearly, it is absolutely central to the Convention, as without the right to life the other rights become meaningless. In terms of Art 2, the State is obliged to refrain from the intentional and unlawful taking of life, as well as being required to take positive steps to safeguard the lives of those within its jurisdiction. The Court of Human Rights was, however, unimpressed by Mrs Pretty's assertion that Art 2 also must be read as containing the negative. In other words, she contended that the right to life guaranteed in Art 2 could also be

---

29 See for example, the prosecution of Mr Brady who assisted his brother, who was suffering from Huntington's Disease, to die; *The Herald*, 15 October 1996.

30 McLean, S.A.M. and Britton, A., *Sometimes a Small Victory*, Institute of Law and Ethics in Medicine, Glasgow, 1996.

31 *Ibid.*; Knox, R.A., 'One in Five US Physicians Say They Have Deliberately Taken Action to Cause a Patient's Death', *The Boston Globe*, 28 February 1992.

32 See, for example, Hawkes, N., 'Nurses split over stance on euthanasia', 26 April 2005, available at http://www.tiesonline.co.uk/article/0,,8122-1586065,00.hrml (accessed on 19 May 2005).

33 *Ibid.*

34 http://news.bbc.co.uk/1/hi/health/4637835.stm (accessed on 06 July 2005).

35 See http://news.bbc.co.uk/1/hi/health/5123974.stm (accessed on 07 July 2006).

interpreted as implying a right to die (terminology which we have already rejected). However, even although in other jurisdictions the right to assistance in dying is permitted, this, in the view of the Court, did not mean that the provisions of the 1961 Act contravened the terms of the Convention. As the Court said:

> It is not enough for Mrs Pretty to show that the United Kingdom would not be acting inconsistently with the Convention if it were to permit assisted suicide; she must go further and establish that the United Kingdom is in breach of the Convention by failing to permit it or would be in breach of the Convention if it did not permit it.[36]

Article 3 of the Convention is an absolute guarantee against inhuman or degrading treatment. Unlike many of the other articles of the Convention, no derogation is permitted from this Article. Mrs Pretty argued her case in three steps. First that member states, as a consequence of Art 3, had an absolute obligation not to inflict inhuman or degrading treatment on a citizen and by implication that they also had a positive responsibility to prevent individuals being subjected to such treatment. She then argued that suffering consequent on a disease could amount to such treatment if the State was in a position where it could in fact prevent the suffering and does not do so. Third, she argued that, in denying the opportunity to bring her suffering to an end, the State effectively was requiring her to undergo proscribed treatment. She also argued that, since the United Kingdom could remove its prohibition on assisted suicide without breaching the terms of the Convention, the Director of Public Prosecutions could give the undertaking that she sought, and further that if the Director of Public Prosecutions could not give such an undertaking then Section 2 of the legislation was incompatible with the terms of the Convention on Human Rights. In the event, the Court was not convinced that a positive obligation to permit assistance in dying could be inferred from the terms in Art 3, even it if were accepted that the progression of a disease could amount to inhuman or degrading treatment, holding that:

> ... it could not ... be said that the United Kingdom is under a positive obligation to ensure that a competent, terminally ill, person who wishes but is unable to take his or her own life should be entitled to seek the assistance of another without that other being exposed to the risk of prosecution.[37]

Article 8 of the Convention protects the right to private and family life, and has been widely interpreted as revalidating and restating the common law right of autonomy or self-determination. In Mrs Pretty's argument, her right to choose to

36 At p. 159.
37 At p. 162.

die rather than live with her disability followed intimately on her right to self-determination. The Court, in considering the Art 8 arguments, indicated that its obligation was to decide whether or not it was disproportionate for the Director of Public Prosecutions to refuse to give the undertaking which Mrs Pretty sought. In addition, it was obliged to consider whether the interference with Mrs Pretty's autonomy rights would be proportionate to the legitimate aims which are encapsulated in the prohibition of assisted suicide.

In an earlier decision, based on slightly different considerations, the Commission had considered the possibility that Art 8 rights might be engaged in these circumstances. In the case of *R v UK*,[38] the applicant challenged his conviction for aiding and abetting a suicide, on the basis that it violated his rights under Arts 8 and 10. The Commission said:

> The Commission does not consider that the activity for which the applicant was convicted, namely aiding and abetting suicide, can be described as falling into the sphere of his private life...*While it might be thought to touch directly on the private lives of those who sought to commit suicide*, it does not follow that the applicant's rights to privacy are involved. On the contrary, the Commission is of the opinion that the acts [of] aiding, abetting, counselling or procuring suicide are excluded from the concept of privacy by virtue of their trespass on the public interest of protecting life, as reflected in the criminal provisions of the 1961 Act.[39] (emphasis added)

It was also argued for Mrs Pretty that the imposition of a blanket ban on assisted suicide was disproportionate because it was unable to take account of individual circumstances. The court, like many courts before it, expressed its concern about the possibility that reform in the law might encourage, for example, elderly people to opt for a premature end to life if it was available.[40] Moreover, in line with the House of Lords Select Committee on Medical Ethics[41] recommendations, the court was reluctant to move down the path towards appearing to endorse assisted dying. The court seemed to share the concerns of the House of Lords Select Committee on the Assisted Dying for the Terminally Ill Bill,[42] which restated concerns about the so-called slippery slope argument; or what they referred to as the 'paradigm shift' argument.

> The essence of the concern here is that, if assisted suicide and voluntary euthanasia should be legalised and if implementation of the law were to be carried out within the health care system, these procedures will of necessity

---

38 (1983) 6 EHRR 140.
39 At pp. 166–167.
40 At p. 169.
41 HL Paper (1993–1994, 21-1)
42 Cited earlier.

become a therapeutic option; that over time there will be drift from regarding the death of a patient as an unavoidable necessity to regarding it as a morally acceptable form of therapy; and that pressure will grow as a result for euthanasia to be applied more widely – for example, to incompetent people or to minors – as a morally acceptable form of medical therapy which is considered to be in the patient's best interests.[43]

In the long run, it was the view of the European Court of Human Rights that the Secretary of State had provided sufficient grounds to justify the existing law and its application. As the Court said, '[t]hat is not to say that no other law or application would be consistent with the Convention, it is simply to say that the present legislative and practical regime do not offend this Convention'.[44]

Article 9 of the Convention protects freedom of thought, conscience and religion and the appropriate manifestation of that freedom. This Article was not a primary plank of Mrs Pretty's case and was dealt with in a relatively cursory manner by the court. Although accepting that Mrs Pretty genuinely believed in the virtue of assisted suicide, and indicating that she was free both to feel that and to express the belief, it nonetheless also found that the expression of that belief could not render her husband free from guilt if he were to carry out an act proscribed by the criminal law in the United Kingdom. It further concluded that even if 'she were able to establish an infringement of her right, the justification shown by the state in relation to Art 8 would still defeat it.'[45]

Finally, the court considered Art 14 of the Convention, which is the Article prohibiting discrimination. This Article does not contain a stand-alone right and can only be used in combination with other Articles of the Convention. Since the court had concluded that none of the Convention Rights had in fact been engaged by Mrs Pretty's action, it was clear that it did not need to consider the implications of Art 14. As she had done throughout the various hearings of her claim, Mrs Pretty lost her fight in the Court of Human Rights.

A right to assisted dying?

Unsurprisingly, there is a considerable body of literature emanating from commentators on disability concerning whether or not there should be a right for disabled people to receive assistance in dying at a time of their own choice. Equally unsurprising, much of it takes as its starting point the very real fear that people with disabilities would be additionally disadvantaged and increasingly at risk were assisted suicide or voluntary euthanasia to be legalised. We will

---

43 *Op. cit.*, p. 40, para 102.
44 At p. 169.
45 *Id.*

discuss the regimes in other countries later but for the moment it is instructive to consider the concerns that have been repeatedly expressed.

Hershey states the position as follows:

> Over the past decade disability-rights groups, particularly in North America, have begun campaigning against assisted suicide and euthanasia. Many activists see these practices as dangerous to people with disabilities, because they may create a double standard in which healthy nondisabled people seeking suicide are offered support and counseling, while people with disabilities and health problems are seen as 'better off dead'. Also, many disability-rights advocates argue that it is wrong to offer death as a solution to people whose problems stem largely from an unsupportive, inaccessible society. As long as support services and other necessary resources are still unavailable to many disabled people, these activists say, euthanasia should not be an option.[46]

In evidence given to the House of Lords Select Committee on the Assisted Dying for the Terminally Ill Bill,[47] it became clear that there is, however, no unanimity among those who speak for those with disabilities or impairments. The Committee acknowledged an important difference in the evidence it received from some of those with particular expertise in this area. For example, the DRC was concerned that:

> ... the Bill, if enacted, might reinforce existing public prejudices, including those of doctors, with regard to disabled people and that, if assisted suicide and voluntary euthanasia were to be on offer, disabled people might experience subtle pressures to avail themselves of these options and that support for independent living might become harder to obtain. They did not believe that the Bill offered disabled people real choice or autonomy in the same way that it might do so for those who were not disabled.[48]

On the other hand, the respected disability rights scholar, Dr Tom Shakespeare, has said: 'I think it is sad that some disability movements think of doctors as the enemy, whereas for the vast majority of disabled people doctors do not always get communication right but they are basically on their side.'[49]

Assisted suicide has also been described as the 'most lethal form'[50] of discrimination against disabled people, and as being the 'ultimate expression of

46 Hershey, L., 'Euthanasia Opponents React to Holland's New Law', Disability World, Issue No. 8, May–June 2001, available at http://www.disabilityworld.org (accessed on 18 June 2003).
47 HL Paper 86-I (April 2005).
48 At para 135, pp. 50–51.
49 Reported at para 137, p. 51.
50 Amici Curiae Brief of Not Dead Yet and American Disabled for Attendant Programs Today in Support of Petitioners, in the case of Vacco, et al. v Quill, et al., No. 95–1858, Supreme Court of the United States, October Term 1995, available at http://www.notdeadyet.org (accessed on 18 June 2003).

society's fear and revulsion regarding disability'.[51] Such commentaries are based on several important considerations; first, is the negative attitude that non-disabled people have to disability, and therefore to disabled people. Difficulty in understanding life with impairment or disability, coupled with a preference for life without impairment, can incline non-disabled people to make negative assumptions about the quality of life of disabled people, as we have already seen in previous chapters. This argument, however, is often used in a confusing manner. It is certainly the case that such negative assumptions are made, but they are arguably not directly relevant when the individual makes his or her *own* choice about the quality of his or her *own* life. To be sure, such decisions in context may reflect despair about the lack of support, but they are nonetheless individual decisions, even if they are influenced by factors which some argue should be irrelevant to continued existence. In any case, we should be cautious about challenging or second-guessing competent decisions made by people about their own lives.

Further, advocates of legalisation of assisted suicide do not primarily base their support on negative views of disability. Rather, they see the right to choose death as being one to which *everyone* should have access. Indeed, these advocates are often criticised for the fact that they do *not* confine themselves to people who are suffering from, for example, a terminal illness; great outcry results, for example, from decisions to permit assisted suicide for those who are *not* disabled, as we shall see later. Thus, it could be said that the perceptions of others about disabled people are not in reality central to the debate.

A second concern, which has already been touched on, relates to the much more difficult question of choice. An act is not autonomous if it has not been chosen, and even although we have suggested that no one acts entirely in a free willed manner, the pressures on disabled people are seen by many as being infinitely more significant, rendering their apparent choices even less free than those of others. It has, for example, been said that:

> As long as society, including the medical profession, demonstrates ignorance and prejudice regarding the lives of people with disabilities, no safeguards can be trusted to contain the torrent of discrimination that will be unleashed by lifting the ban on assisted suicide. As long as people with disabilities are treated as unwelcome and costly burdens on society, assisted suicide is not voluntary but is a forced 'choice'. Amici are profoundly disturbed by the finding of a constitutional right for assisted suicide in a society which refuses to find a right to adequate and appropriate health care to stay alive. Until society is committed to providing life supports, including in-home personal assistance services, health care, and technological supports, then there is not voluntary choice.[52]

51 Amici Curiae Brief of Not Dead Yet and American Disabled for Attendant Programs Today in Support of Petitioners, in the case of *Vacco, et al. v Quill, et al.*, No. 95–1858, Supreme Court of the United States, October Term 1995, available at http://www.notdeadyet.org (accessed on 18 June 2003).
52 *Id.*

Third, there is the question of safeguards. It might be argued that – if we concede that non-disabled people should have the right to assisted suicide – then so too should disabled people. In this way, the goal of equality is prima facie attained. However, many arguments against assisted suicide in general focus on the extent to which a 'slippery slope' could all too easily develop. That is, by permitting A (which is not bad) we inevitably will end up permitting B (which is bad). This is a problematic argument, and one which is roundly critiqued by many distinguished commentators. Beauchamp and Childress, for example, say:

> The ultimate success or failure of these slippery slope arguments depends on speculative predictions of a progressive erosion of moral restraints. If dire consequences will in fact flow from the legal legitimation of assisted suicide or voluntary active euthanasia, then the argument is cogent, and such practices are justifiably prohibited. But how good is the evidence that dire consequences will occur? Does the evidence indicate that we cannot maintain firm distinctions in public policies between patient-requested death and involuntary euthanasia? Scant evidence supports any of the answers that have been given to these questions, so far as we can see.[53]

Similarly Ronald Dworkin has stated '...slippery slope arguments...are very weak ones. They seem only disguises for deeper convictions that actually move most opponents of euthanasia.'[54] On the other hand, Miller talks of society's 'double standards' based on its 'prejudices against persons with disabilities'.[55]

Whether real or only feared, the question of how to regulate assisted suicide occupies much of the literature in this area. The brief of Not Dead Yet and American Disabled for Attendant Programs Today,[56] maintains that:

> ...no system of safeguards can control conduct which results in the death of the primary witness to any wrongdoing or duress. The only 'safeguard' that offers some protection against abuse is that assisted suicide remain illegal and socially condemned for all citizens equally.[57]

The question of safeguards is clearly, therefore, an important one, but it too must be placed in context. Many of the arguments canvassed against legalising assisted dying presume that euthanasia and assisted suicide would be carried out

53 Beauchamp, T.L. and Childress, J.S., *Principles of Biomedical Ethics* (4th Ed), Oxford, Oxford University Press, 1994 at p. 23.
54 Dworkin, R., 'When is it Right to Die?', *New York Times*, May 5, 1994.
55 Miller, P.S., 'The Impact of Assisted Suicide on Persons with Disabilities – Is It a Right Without Freedom?', *Issues in Law and Medicine*, 9, 1, Summer 1993, 47 at p. 48.
56 Refer note 50.
57 *Id.*

on a non-voluntary or even involuntary basis. Yet what proponents of legislative change are arguing for is only that such choices should be available on a voluntary basis. This confusion can be seen in the following example.

The DRC discusses the cases of Ms B and Diane Pretty to which we have just referred. It will be recalled that in each of these cases there was a sustained, overwhelming and competent request for death. However, the DRC follows its discussion of these cases with the following comment:

> The way in which the debate on these cases was reported in much of the media questioned the value of disabled people and their lives. It raised once again concerns among disabled people that *decisions by medical professionals on whether they lived or died, were being made against a backdrop of negative images and poorly informed assumptions of intolerable suffering and unacceptable dependence on others*.[58] (emphasis added)

This may be a valid concern, but it does not obviously flow from the two cases referred to. There is no suggestion in either of these cases that third parties were making decisions on behalf of the women concerned, rather, they were trying to obtain primacy for their *own* decisions. Also, somewhat paradoxically, the brief from Not Dead Yet referred to earlier appears to renege on its opposition to assisted suicide, concluding:

> ...if, in the prevailing confusion and despair of our culture, physician-assisted suicide will become a constitutional right for some, then it must be a constitutional right for all, nondisabled as well as disabled. The same safeguards, or lack of safeguards, that apply to some must apply to all.[59]

The question of actual voluntariness, however, and the effect of social and other pressures is placed in context by a report from Disabled Peoples International (DPI)[60] where it is said:

> Supporters of euthanasia argue that voluntary euthanasia is a matter of personal choice without recognising the sometimes very persuasive powers of doctors and relatives who may have subjective reasons for hastening the death of an individual, and the lack of palliative care and support services available to ensure a better quality of life.

58 Para 1.2.
59 Refer note 50.
60 Disabled Peoples International (DPI) 'Disabled People Speak on the New Genetics', DPI Europe Position Statement on Bioethics and Human Rights, http://www.dpieurope.org/htm (accessed on 1 June 2003).

The Coalition of Provincial Organisations of the Handicapped (COPOH) in its intervention in the case of *Rodriguez v Attorney General of Canada*[61] argued that:

> Both historically and to the present day the lives and freedoms of persons with disabilities have been threatened and, in some case, eliminated by the insensitivity, ignorance and hostility of those who believe that the lives of disabled people are somehow of less value or quality than those of other people...[62]

They also noted that 'safeguards should enhance rather than displace the decision made by a person who might require assistance to commit suicide. *Substitute decision-making in this context would violate the principles of personal autonomy and freedom of choice.*'[63] (emphasis added) This comment seems to admit the possibility that disabled people could make independent choices, but is coupled with the caution that:

> A person who depends upon another for assistance in committing suicide can be assumed to be dependent upon others for many essential services. How these services are performed (or not performed) could profoundly influence a person's decisions about living or dying. For this reason a person with a disability in such a position of extreme dependence is particularly vulnerable to external influence. Whether or not such people are entitled to all the services they require, COPOH submits that they should know about each and every service to which they are entitled and be provided with the means of accessing them.[64]

So far, it appears that the arguments against legalisation are powerful, especially in the case of people with impairment. However, it is necessary to note that there are also arguments that counteract them. Leaving aside the extent to which *anyone* can be said to act wholly free from external influences, the thrust of what has been said points to the very real fear that disabled people are likely to be more vulnerable to pressure from others, or society's shortcomings, into seeing death as the only (or most appropriate) choice. However, Mayo and Gunderson[65] argue that:

> These arguments [disability activists' against physician assisted death (PAD)] fail... *as a case against the legalization of PAD.* They fail because all of the risks of premature death they enumerate are already risks of current policy,

61 107 DLR (4th) 342 (1993).
62 Court File No. 23476, para 5.
63 *Ibid.*, para 33.
64 para 38.
65 Mayo, D. and Gunderson, M., 'Vitalism Revitalized: Vulnerable Populations, Prejudice, and Physician-Assisted Death', *Hastings Center Report*, July–August 2002, 32(4), 14–21.

as articulated by the President's Commission's endorsement of the doctrine of informed consent, even in connection with end of life decisions (by advance directive if necessary).[66]

They further claim that:

> The arguments advanced by disability critics of PAD make a compelling case for strengthening...safeguards, particularly for patients with disabilities. They have failed to show any *additional* risks to patients who may already opt to cut short a fate they view as worse than death. Indeed, the safeguards that accompany Oregon's 'right-to-die' law are clearly *more stringent* than those that apply to cases in which terminal patients routinely elect to forgo life-prolonging therapies, often in the context of electing hospice care.[67]

The value of building safeguards is not, however, universally accepted. For example, a statement from the National Council on Disability (US)[68] suggests that '...the more stringent and encompassing one seeks to make procedural safeguards in this context, the more intrusive they become, and the greater the extent to which doctors and psychiatrists become the gatekeepers.'[69] Moreover, it claims that:

> As the procedural noose tightens to prevent erroneous and inappropriate assisted suicides, the individual's privacy and control of the situation fly out the window, and the medical model runs rampant. Ironically, the pursuit of assisted suicide in the name of individual liberty would wind up necessitating egregious restrictions and highly invasive participation by members of the medical and legal professions.[70]

It would appear that there is no solution if this view is to be taken seriously. On the one hand, it is argued that we need stringent safeguards to ensure that people with disability are not vulnerable to the pressures arising from their impairment or pressure from others. On the other, these same safeguards are said to restrict their liberties unreasonably and in a discriminatory manner.

---

66 At p. 18.
67 *Id.*; the Oregon legislation will be considered in more depth later.
68 *Assisted Suicide: A Disability Perspective*, http://www.ncd.gov/newsroom/publisations/1997/suicide.htm (accessed on 16 June 2005).
69 At p. 13.
70 *Id.*

However, there are other reasons to scrutinise the apparent need to erect ever-difficult hurdles in the way of apparently freely taken decisions. Silvers, for example, claims that:

> Characterizing people with disabilities as incompetent, easily coerced, and inclined to end their lives places them in the roles to which they have been confined by disability discrimination. Doing so emphasizes their supposed fragility, which becomes a reason to deny that they are capable, and therefore deserving, of full social participation.[71]

Finally, Mayo and Gunderson conclude that:

> Arguing in favor of PAD as an implication of respect for the self-determination of persons with disabilities would in no way discount the legitimate concerns about the abuse of persons with severe disabilities at the hands of their caregivers. But it would redirect the response toward finding better safeguards, in connection with medical decisionmaking for vulnerable populations generally.[72]

Opinion poll evidence routinely suggests that a majority of the population in the countries in which they have been conducted would like to see assisted suicide legalised. Typically, about 70 per cent or so of those asked would support legalisation. Interestingly, one Harris Poll carried out in 2001 found that '68 per cent of people with disabilities polled nationwide [in the US] favored PAD'.[73] Moreover, as Shakespeare notes:

> In practice, disabled people themselves have often requested the right to assisted suicide, to withdrawal of treatment or other ways of ending life. When the Disability Rights Commission conducted an online survey in 2003, 63% supported new laws on end of life.[74]

In November 2004, a modest poll commissioned by the Voluntary Euthanasia Society also showed that the majority of disabled people supported the Assisted Dying for the Terminally Ill Bill, and indicated that, were euthanasia to be

71 Silvers, A., 'Protecting the Innocents from Physician-assisted Suicide: Disability Discrimination and the Duty to Protect Otherwise Vulnerable groups', in Battin, M.P., Rhodes, R. and Silvers, A. (eds), *Physician Assisted Suicide: Expanding the Debate*, New York, Routledge, 1998, 132 at p. 132.
72 Mayo and Gunderson, *op. cit.*, p. 20.
73 Corbet, B., 'Physician Assisted Death: Are We Asking the Right Questions?', http://notdeadyet.org (accessed on 18 June 2003).
74 Shakespeare, *op. cit.*, para 4.4 (refer note 14).

legalised, they would continue to trust their doctors.[75] As the Report of the House of Lords Select Committee on the Assisted Dying for the Terminally Ill Bill notes, '[d]isabled people also appear to believe slightly more strongly than others that the law currently discriminates against terminally ill disabled people who wish to commit suicide but need assistance to do so.'[76] Although it is important to note that the Select Committee urges caution in the use and evaluation of the range of opinion poll evidence that exists in this area[77] – and certainly we concede that it is essentially anecdotal evidence – the strength and consistency of support for legalisation of assisted dying merits serious consideration.

The UK debate

Interest in assisted suicide and end-of-life decision-making was reignited in the United Kingdom by the cases of *Ms B v An NHS Hospital Trust*[78] and Diane Pretty,[79] to which we have already referred. The introduction in the House of Lords of The Assisted Dying for the Terminally Ill Bill[80] has brought the debate about assisted dying into sharp focus in the United Kingdom. Its progress through Parliament was put on hold because of shortage of parliamentary time, so the Bill was reintroduced, given a formal Second Reading and the House of Lords Select Committee established to consider the Bill was able to complete its business. This Committee reported in 2005, and made a number of recommendations. Like its predecessor, the House of Lords Select Committee on Medical Ethics,[81] the recent Select Committee report can be described as essentially cautious. We will briefly consider each report in turn.

The Select Committee on Medical Ethics

The Select Committee on Medical Ethics declined to support legalisation of assisted suicide and euthanasia, basing its approach on respect for the sanctity of all human life, which it said was 'at the heart of civilised society....'[82] The Committee concluded that prohibition of the deliberate taking of life 'is the cornerstone of law and of social relationships'.[83] The Select Committee argued

---

75 YouGov Poll, 2004.
76 HL Paper 86-I (2005) at p. 130.
77 See Appendix 7.
78 [2002] Lloyd's Rep Med 265.
79 *Pretty v United Kingdom* (2002) 66 BMLR 147.
80 Not its original title.
81 HL Paper 21-1, 1994.
82 P. 13, para 34.
83 P. 48, para 237.

that 'the issue of euthanasia is one in which the interest of the individual cannot be separated from the interests of society as a whole.'[84]

Few would disagree with this assertion. However, the Select Committee then seems to place considerable, some might say excessive, confidence in the evidence from the medical profession, which was against legalisation. The Report itself says:

> Some people may consider that our conclusions overall give too much weight to the role of accepted medical practice, and that we advocate leaving too much responsibility in the hands of doctors and other members of the health-care team They may argue that doctors and their colleagues as no better qualified than any other group of people to take ethical decisions about life and death which ultimately have a bearing not only on individual patients but on society as a whole. But no other group of people is better qualified to do so...By virtue of their vocation, training and professional integrity they may be expected to act with rectitude and compassion.[85]

Select Committee on the Assisted Dying for the Terminally Ill Bill

As we have seen, this Select Committee was formed to consider the terms of a Bill introduced into the House of Lords by Lord Joffe. The Committee describes Lord Joffe's Bill thus:

> Briefly the Bill provides for a competent and terminally-ill person who has reached the age of majority and who is suffering unbearably to request either assisted suicide or voluntary euthanasia...the Bill provides for the requesting patient to sign a written declaration of intent and, if this has not been revoked within 14 days of the date on which the request was first made, to receive either the means to take his or her own life or, if the patient is physically unable to do that, to have his or her life ended through voluntary euthanasia.[86]

The Report took a cautious approach to legalisation and heard evidence over many months. In addition, members of the Committee visited The Netherlands and Oregon to witness first hand what was happening there. As we will see, Oregon only authorises assisted suicide, whereas both that and voluntary euthanasia are legal in the Netherlands. Unsurprisingly, therefore, the Select Committee found the incidence of assisted dying to be greater in the Netherlands,

---

84 P. 48, para 237.
85 P. 56, para 272.
86 At p. 15.

reporting that in 2003 'one in 38 of those who died did so via either assisted suicide or euthanasia, mainly the latter (the figure is 1 in 32 if cases of euthanasia without explicit request are included).'[87] On the other hand, in Oregon in the same year only 'one in 714 deaths resulted from assisted suicide'.[88]

In a careful consideration of the arguments for and against legalisation, the Select Committee pointed to a number of matters which it believed should form the basis of further Parliamentary debate. The Bill was reintroduced, and debated in October 2005. At that time, no vote was necessary, nor held. Lord Joffe then reintroduced an amended version of the Bill, this debate taking place in May 2006. At that stage, 148 Peers voted to delay the Bill for six months while 100 voted to allow it to proceed to the Committee. Thus, the Second reading cannot take place in this Parliamentary Session, and Lord Joffe has declared his intention to reintroduce it in the next Session of Parliament.

Interestingly, it was the safeguards which were built into the Joffe Bill that formed a major part of the matters which the Committee felt required consideration. For example, although the Joffe Bill sought to restrict its terms only to those who were terminally ill, the Select Committee heard evidence that 'the prognosis of a terminal illness is far from being an exact science.'[89] Moreover, like its predecessor, the Committee was impressed by medical evidence as to how professionals would feel about changes in the law. The Committee noted, for example, that:

> We were...given the results of a survey carried out by the Association of Palliative Medicine (APM). We were told that in the APM survey of its members, which attracted an 84% response rate, 72%...of respondents had said that they would not be prepared to participate in a process of patient assessment which formed part of an application for assisted suicide or voluntary euthanasia.[90]

With respect, this outcome is both predictable and arguably irrelevant. It is only to be expected that those working in palliative medicine would believe that there is always something they can do short of assisting their patients to die. However, it is unclear why the views of this group of doctors – or indeed any others – should carry such weight in a debate which goes far beyond the boundaries of medical ethics. It equally – arguably – tells an interesting story about the respect (or lack of it) that such doctors have for the choices of their patients. The Select Committee also heard evidence from expert witnesses that 'the attending and consulting physicians who are envisaged as being effectively the "gatekeepers"

---

87 P. 49, para 131.
88 *Id.*
89 P. 44, para 118.
90 P. 44, para 116.

in regard to applications for assisted dying could not be expected to spot impairment of judgement in all cases.'[91] Thus, what at first sight looks like lack of respect for patients' competent decisions might actually be more akin to doubts about their competence itself. However, unless we can hand-on-heart know that patients never make competent, reasoned decisions for death this is a dubious basis for precluding such choices. In fact, arguably, both Ms B's case and that of Diane Pretty (and others) show that competent people both can and do make real, informed and sustained claims for the right to have assistance in dying, however that is carried out.

International perspectives

It is not just in the United Kingdom that nation-states are re-evaluating their approach to assistance at the end of life. Throughout the world both voluntary euthanasia and assisted suicide are being increasingly tolerated, even legalised. In this section we will examine recent developments in the Netherlands, Oregon, Belgium and Switzerland.

Despite the fact that a number of countries and states have moved to legalise assisted suicide and/or voluntary euthanasia, as we have already seen, concern remains both within and beyond disability rights organisations about the extent to which legalisation would pose a threat to disabled people. Moreover, there is also concern over whether or not regulation would be able to prevent discrimination against them. For example, in its Briefing on the Assisted Dying for the Terminally Ill Bill[92] the DRC states that:

> The DRC is not aware of any country that has managed to frame a law that allows assisted suicide or voluntary euthanasia, for people with terminal illness, as in the cases of Mr Crew and Mrs Pretty, whilst ensuring that disabled people are protected from coercion, pressure, and involuntary euthanasia.[93]

In this respect, analysis of the situation in the Netherlands, where both voluntary euthanasia and assisted suicide are now legalised, is useful, as it can provide information on the ramifications of a State allowing euthanasia.

The Netherlands

In 1984, the Dutch Supreme Court found that a doctor who ended the life of his patient – under certain circumstances – could legitimately invoke the defence

91 P. 47, para 126.
92 The full text of the 2005 Bill can be found at http://www.publications.parliament.uk/pa/ld200506/ldbills/036/06036.i.html (accessed on 10 October 2006).
93 Disability Rights Commission, Briefing and Reports, available at http://www.drc-gb.org at para. 2.3 (accessed on 11 December 2004).

of necessity.[94] Since that time, doctors have often carried out euthanasia without being prosecuted. In addition, the Dutch Parliament passed a Bill to decriminalise euthanasia in April 2001 providing that certain conditions and reporting procedures are fulfilled. The Bill came into force in 2002.[95] In terms of the law, due care requires that the physician:

a.   holds the conviction that the request by the patient was voluntary and well considered,

b.   holds the conviction that the patient's suffering was lasting and unbearable,

c.   has informed the patient about the situation he was in and about his prospects,

d.   and the patient holds the conviction that there was no other reasonable solution for the situation he is in,

e.   has consulted at least one other, independent physician who has seen the patient and has given his written opinion on the requirements of due care, referred to in parts a–d, and

f.   has terminated a life or assisted in a suicide with due care.[96]

Since 1990, the Dutch Government has commissioned a number of studies to record how the practice of euthanasia and assisted suicide has developed in Holland. These surveys are intended to ascertain whether liberalising practises that enable individuals to be assisted to end their lives have negative consequences and to determine whether the safeguards that the state puts in place are sufficient to prevent abuses occurring. Hence, the studies may provide evidence that allows us to determine whether increasingly liberal attitudes towards euthanasia and assisted suicide have negative implications for disabled people. It is important to note that even the most recent papers to report findings from the studies – those published in 2003 – only consider cases up to 2001.[97] As a result, information about the impact of the 2002 legislation on the development of euthanasia and assisted suicide is not yet available.

The first survey took place between 1990 and 1991 and examined medical decisions at the end of life (MDEL) throughout the Netherlands.[98] The survey

94 This decision was reached in the case of Pieter Admiraal, Nederlandse Jurisprudentie 1985, nr. 707.

95 The Dutch Termination of Life on Request and Assisted Suicide (Review Procedures) Act was debated and passed 10 April 2001 and came into force 1 April 2002.

96 *Id.*, Chapter 2, Due Care Criteria, Section 2.

97 Van der Wal, G., Van der Heide, A., Onwuteaka-Philipsen, B.D. and Van der Mass, P.J., *Medische besluitvorming aan het einde van het leven*: de praktijk en de toetsingsprocedure euthanasia, Utrecht, de Tijdstroom, 2003; Onwuteaka-Philipsen, B.D., Van der Heide, A., Koper, D., Keij-Deerenberg, I., Rietjens, J.A.C., Rurup, M.L., Vrakking, A.M., Georges, J.J., Muller, M.T., Van der Wal, G. and Van der Maas, P.J., 'Euthanasia and Other End-of-Life Decisions in the Netherlands in 1990, 1995 and 2001', *The Lancet*, 2003, 362, 395–399.

98 Van der Maas, P.J., Van Delden, J.J., Pijnenborg, L. and Looman, C.W., 'Euthanasia and Other Medical Decisions concerning the end of Life', *The Lancet*, 1991, 338, 8768, 669–674.

estimated that of 128,786 deaths in the Netherlands in 1990, 38 per cent had occurred as a result of medical decision-making.[99] Of this number, 1.8 per cent involved active euthanasia and 0.3 per cent assisted suicide.[100] Non-treatment decisions had hastened the deaths of 17.5 per cent and another 17.5 per cent of deaths had been a consequence of pain relief.[101] In response to concerns that legalising euthanasia could lead to abuses, the report notes that:

> Many physicians who had practised euthanasia mentioned that they would be most reluctant to do so again, thus refuting the 'slippery slope' argument. Only in the face of unbearable suffering and with no alternatives would they be prepared to take such action. Many respondents mentioned that an emotional bond is required for euthanasia and this may be one reason why euthanasia was more common in general practice where the doctor and patient have often known each other for years and the doctor has shared part of the patient's suffering.[102]

This tends to suggest that the doctors' primary concern was the best interests of their patients. However, the report also records that in 0.8 per cent of all deaths, euthanasia had taken place without the explicit and repeated consent of the individual.[103] This failure to gain the consent of patients could be evidence that their interests were overridden during a period of ill-health when they were perhaps particularly vulnerable. However, it is reported that the reason for failing to obtain consent in such cases was often that individuals lacked competence. The authors of the survey explain:

> Sometimes the death of patient was hastened without his or her explicit and persistent request. These patients were close to death and were suffering grievously. In more than half such cases the decision had been discussed with the patient or the patient had previously stated that he would want such a way of proceeding under certain circumstances. Also, when the decision was not discussed with the patients, almost all of them were incompetent.[104]

In cases where a patient is incompetent, the medical team will generally make a decision about continued treatment based on its view of the 'best interests' of the patient. Ideally, this decision should pay specific attention to any previously expressed wishes of the patient, and it will also usually take account of the views

99 *Ibid.*, p. 670.
100 *Id.*
101 *Id.*
102 *Ibid.*, p. 673.
103 *Ibid.*, p. 672.
104 *Ibid.*, p. 673.

of relatives. However, as we have noted, there can be a lack of congruence between what the patient would actually have wanted and what third parties believe is best for them.[105]

We have argued that it is not an ethical requirement to sustain human life in all circumstances; for example, when a life has lost – and will not regain – the capacity for sustaining relationships with others, or when the person is 'alive' but has no biographical 'life'. This is because in such circumstances it is likely that the patient will lack the attributes which we associate with a worthwhile human life. Thus, in a country where active euthanasia is legal, it may be seen as morally acceptable to extend such best-interest judgments to justify actively ending lives which fall into these categories. However, the study by van der Maas *et al.* also acknowledges that in a 'few' cases decisions were 'possibly' made to end a life when patients were competent and not near to death.[106] This is a cause for concern, but more information is required to determine the particulars of each case. Only with such information is it possible to determine whether legalised euthanasia and assisted suicide create an unavoidable risk to disabled people.

Finally, given concerns that the societal acceptance of euthanasia and assisted suicide could lead to disabled people having their lives ended arbitrarily, it is important to note that the majority of people who died in the Netherlands in 1990 by means of euthanasia were cancer patients. Van der Maas *et al.* report that while cancer related deaths made up only 27 per cent of all deaths in 1990, 68 per cent of euthanasia deaths were cancer related, 15 per cent of euthanasia deaths were recorded as due to 'other' illnesses and 9 per cent as due to cardiovascular disease.[107]

Van der Maas *et al.* conducted a second study between 1995 and 1996 on MDELs.[108] A new procedure for reporting cases of euthanasia and assisted suicide had come into operation since the original study. It was thought that this would lead to a large increase in the number of euthanasia and assisted suicide cases that were reported.[109] However, the initial study had also suggested that greater openness about euthanasia and assisted suicide would mean that the incidence of euthanasia without consent would decrease.[110] The second study, like the first, utilised information drawn from interviews with physicians and a study of death certificates.[111]

---

105 For further discussion, see Chapter 5.
106 Van der Maas, P.J., Van der Wal, G., Haverkate, I., de Graaff, C.L., Kester, J.G., Onwuteaka-Philipsen, B.D., Van der Heide, A., Bosma, J.M. and Willems, D.L., 'Euthanasia, Physician-Assisted Suicide, and Other Medical Practices Involving the End of Life in the Netherlands, 1990–1995', *The New England Journal of Medicine*, 1996, 335, 22, p. 672.
107 *Id.*
108 Van der Maas *et al.*, *op. cit.*, pp. 1699–1705.
109 *Id.*, p. 1699.
110 *Id.*, p. 1703; cited earlier, p. 673.
111 Van der Maas *et al.*, *op. cit.*, 1996 at p. 1699f.

The study found that overall the reported rise in euthanasia and assisted suicide since the 1990 study was 9 per cent (135,546 deaths in total).[112] Over the same period the study of death certificates found instances of euthanasia increased from 1.7 per cent to 2.4 per cent and in the interview study from 1.9 per cent to 2.3 per cent.[113] In respect of physician-assisted suicide (PAS), there was only a slight increase in deaths in the interview study (0.3–0.4%).[114] Deaths resulting from decisions not to continue treatment increased from 17.9 per cent (best estimate 17.5%) in 1990 to 20.2 per cent in 1995.[115] The 1995 survey recorded doctors as reporting that euthanasia deaths without the patients' consent took place in 0.7 per cent of cases (a slight decrease from 0.8 per cent in 1990).[116] The authors state:

> Further scrutiny of the case histories in the interview study showed that decisions to end life without the patient's request covered a wide range of situations, with a large group of patients having only a few hours or days to live, whereas a small number had a longer life expectancy but were evidently suffering greatly, with verbal contact no longer possible.[117]

This study also found that compared to all cancer deaths in the Netherlands during this period (27%) cancer patients comprised a large percentage of euthanasia (80%) and assisted suicide (78%) deaths.[118] In relation to the cases of euthanasia that occurred without explicit consent, it is reported that the patients 'tended to be relatively young, and cancer was the predominant diagnosis. In fact 60% of these cases were linked to cancer'.[119]

Information from the first two reports from the Netherlands on euthanasia and assisted suicide does not provide conclusive proof on either the benefits or dangers of legalisation. Van der Maas et al. conclude:

> A major issue in the debate about euthanasia is whether some form of acceptance of euthanasia or assisted suicide when it is explicitly requested by a greatly suffering, terminally ill, competent patient is the first step on a slippery slope that will lead to an unintended and undesirable increase in the number of cases of less careful end-of-life decision making and to the gradual social acceptance of euthanasia performed for morally unacceptable reasons. Obviously, our data provide no conclusive evidence in either direction.... Nevertheless, in our view, these data do not support the idea that physicians in the Netherlands are moving down a slippery slope.[120]

112 *Ibid.*, p. 1700.
113 *Id.*
114 *Id.*
115 *Id.*
116 *Id.*
117 *Ibid.*, p. 1702.
118 *Ibid.*, p. 1703.
119 *Ibid.*, p. 1701.
120 *Ibid.*, p. 1705.

Their position is supported by Griffiths *et al.*, who state that:

> In the end, a reasonable observer would have to conclude, we think, that
> there is no significant evidence that the frequency of termination of life
> without an explicit request is higher in the Netherlands than it used to be;
> and if there has been any increase, it is almost certainly the result of things
> (medical technology; demographic changes) that have nothing to do with
> legalization of euthanasia.[121]

However, in their assessment of the van der Maas *et al.* surveys, Jochemsen and
Keown suggest that the guidelines used to regulate euthanasia in the Netherlands
are insufficient to prevent abuses.[122] There is particular concern over the
instances of euthanasia that were conducted without consent. They argue:

> The survey casts doubt on central assurances which had been given by the
> advocates of voluntary euthanasia: that euthanasia would be performed only
> at the patient's explicit request and that doctors terminating life without
> request would be prosecuted for murder; that euthanasia would be used only
> in cases of 'last resort' and not as an alternative to palliative care . . . [123]

Indeed, physicians conducting euthanasia in the Netherlands without it being
expressly requested to do so can still be prosecuted. As the 2003 Report from
Regional Euthanasia Review Committees notes:

> The notifications rules do not apply to life-terminating procedures that are
> not expressly requested. No separate arrangements have yet been made for
> the latter, and for the time being they are still governed by the 1994
> notification rules, which require the municipal pathologist to refer to the
> public prosecutor all cases in which termination of life was not expressly
> requested.[124]

In 2002 five physicians were reported to the Public Prosecution Service for
acting without due care and a further nine in 2003.[125]

121 Griffiths, J., Heleen, W. and Alex, B., 1998, *Euthanasia and Law in the Netherlands*, Amsterdam, Amsterdam University Press, at p. 301.
122 Jochemsen, H. and Keown, J, 'Voluntary Euthanasia Under Control? Further Empirical Evidence from the Netherlands', *JME*, 25, 1999, 16–21.
123 *Ibid.*, p. 20.
124 Regional Euthanasia Review Committees, *2003 Annual Report*, p. 4.
125 Regional Euthanasia Review Committees, *2002 Annual Report* at p. 11; Regional Euthanasia Review Committees, *2003 Annual Report* at p. 2. Reports for 2004 and 2005 were not available in English translation at the time of going to press.

However, Jochemsen and Keown seem primarily concerned that failures to enforce such legislation stringently reveal that even well-regulated state-sanctioned euthanasia was always likely to slip towards abuse and a decline in standards. A number of points can be made in response to this. First, the 2002 and 2003 reports of the regional euthanasia committees show a slight fall in those requesting euthanasia and assisted suicide: 1,882 (2002) and 1,815 (2003); this continues what has been a downward trend since 2001.[126] Second, the most recent quantitative study available on the performance of assisted suicide and euthanasia in the Netherlands does not sustain claims that a gradual slip (or rapid decline) in standards is occurring. Rather, the data shows a *decrease* in the number of physicians ending lives without consent. As Onwuteaka-Philipsen *et al.* report:

> The proportion of physicians who were even engaged in the ending of life without a patient's explicit request decreased from 27% in 1990 to 23% in 1995, and further to 13% in 2001. Furthermore, physicians' unwillingness to ever do so increased, especially after 1995, from 45% in 1995 to 71% in 2001.[127]

The paper by Onwuteaka-Philipsen *et al.* represents the third in the series of quantitative studies funded by the government in the Netherlands and replicates the methods of its predecessors; surveying death certificates and conducting physician interviews. The study reports that physician interviews found that there was a slight decline in involuntary euthanasia from 1995 (0.7%) and 2001 (0.6%).[128] The studies of death certificates found a similar progression – 0.8 per cent in 1990, 0.7 per cent in 1995 and 0.7 per cent in 2001.[129] These statistics do not support the notion that more lives are steadily being ended without patient consent. That said, the report acknowledges that 'physicians who are still willing to end life without a patient's explicit request may be engaging in the practices frequently.'[130] However, it seems likely such practices would continue regardless of the liberalising of attitudes/legislation in this area, and we know that such cases also arise in countries which have not legalised assisted dying.

The issues raised by involuntary euthanasia highlight the distinction that exists between law and ethics: what is illegal is not necessarily unethical and vice versa. While physicians who fail to secure consent have acted outside the law it may be that adhering to legal requirements in certain circumstances would produce unethical behaviour in needlessly allowing terminal suffering to

126 *Id.*
127 *Ibid.*, p. 397.
128 *Ibid.*, p. 396.
129 *Id.*
130 *Ibid.*, p. 398.

continue. This helps to reveal the difficulty of drafting adequate legislation in this area: identifying and enforcing definitive legal standards neither ensures appropriate ethical conduct nor prevents abuse in cases in which legal standards are adhered to. But not liberalising legislation also fails to provide a safeguard against abuse.

The difficulties that exist are particularly evident when considering the topic of disability. As we have seen in previous chapters any physical or mental condition that leads people to receive poor treatment within society can be counted as a disability. The recent change made to the definition of disability in the United Kingdom, for example, defines cancer patients as 'disabled'. Studies of euthanasia in the Netherlands show significant numbers of people with cancer have requested euthanasia and assisted suicide: 30 per cent in 1990, 29 per cent in 1995 and 29 per cent in 2001.[131] The Annual Reports of Regional Euthanasia Review Committees in the Netherlands record the details of many such cases.[132] Furthermore, we have seen that the 1990 and 1995 studies of end-of-life decisions in the Netherlands also found that instances of euthanasia which took place without patient consent were often intended to end the suffering of individuals with a terminal prognosis.[133] That is, that decisions to end the lives of patients who were likely to be 'disabled' without their consent are often motivated by a desire to end the suffering caused by illness and impairment and not by disdain for disability *per se*.

However, in the context of disability euthanasia procedures that are consented to could conceal the possibility that the individuals whose lives was ended had, perhaps because of lack of resources or counselling, failed to come to terms with their disability. In this respect, it is important to note that large numbers of patients are listed as requesting euthanasia for 'other or unknown' reasons: 40 per cent in 1990, 43 per cent in 1995 and 46 per cent in 2001.[134] These figures allow for the possibility that negative assumptions about disability could have played a part in such decisions. Furthermore, although the yearly reports of the Regional Euthanasia Review Committees in the Netherlands provide useful information, they do not include details of cases in which consent was not gained. This is because the role of such committees is to refer such cases to the public prosecutor.[135] Thus, it is difficult to ascertain exactly what proportion of cases of involuntary euthanasia are well-intentioned (though illegal) instances of ending extremely burdensome lives when death is imminent, what number (if any) involve actions that are clearly to be classed as abusive and whether any of these involved flawed paternalistic assumptions about the value of disabled lives.

---

131 Onwuteaka-Philipsen *et al.*, *op. cit.*, 2003 at p. 397.
132 Regional Euthanasia Review Committees, *2002 Annual Report*; Regional Euthanasia Review Committees, *2003 Annual Report*.
133 Van der Maas *et al.*, *op. cit.*, 1991 at p. 673; Van der Maas, *op. cit.*, 1996 at p. 1702.
134 Onwuteaka-Philipsen *et al.*, *op. cit.*, 2003 at p. 397.
135 Regional Euthanasia Review Committees, *2002 Annual Report* at p. 15.

Hence the impact on disabled people of liberalising euthanasia and assisted suicide in the Netherlands is unclear.

Oregon

Another region from which we can obtain data that allows us to consider the impact of legalising physician assisted-suicide (PAS) is the US State of Oregon. In November 1994 citizens of Oregon voted to legalise PAS, although because of legal challenges the practice was not finally rendered lawful until October 1997.[136] Since that time the Oregon Department of Human Resources has produced annual surveys that outline the demographic development of PAS.[137] The reports are based on information obtained from physicians who are required to report the lethal prescriptions they write, a study of death certificates and interviews with physicians.[138] The reports generate information by comparing the details of individuals who died as a result of PAS with the deaths of all Oregonians who had similar underlying medical conditions, and a control group who had similar underlying conditions but had not participated in the regime established by the Death with Dignity Act.[139] An examination of these reports may further enlighten our evaluation of the implications of legalising practices such as PAS and euthanasia.

The Oregon Death with Dignity Act allows individuals to obtain prescriptions for lethal drugs with which they can end their own lives providing that they are:

- adults (18 years of age or older);
- residents of Oregon;
- capable (defined as able to make and communicate healthcare decisions);
- diagnosed with a terminal illness that will lead to death within 6 months.[140]

---

136 The legislation recently survived a further attempt to defeat it. See http://news. bbc.co.uk/1/hi/world/americas/4621328.stm (accessed on 7 July 2006).

137 Chin, A.E., Hedberg, K., Higginson, G.K. and Fleming, D.W., *Oregon's Death with Dignity Act: The First Year's Experience*, Oregon, Department of Human Resources, 1999; Sullivan, A.D., Hedberg, K. and Fleming, D.W., *Oregon's Death with Dignity Act: The Second Year's Experience*, Oregon, Department of Human Services, 2000; Hedberg, K. et al., *Oregon's Death with Dignity Act. Three Years of Legalised Physician-Assisted Suicide*, Oregon, Department of Human Services, 2001; Hedberg, K. et al., *Fourth Annual Report on Oregon's Death with Dignity Act*, Oregon, Department of Human Services, 2002; Hedberg, K. and Kohn, M. (eds) *Fifth Annual Report on Oregon's Death with Dignity Act*, 2003, Oregon, Department of Health and Human Resources.

138 Chin, A.E. et al., *Oregon's Death with Dignity Act: The First Year's Experience*, Oregon, Oregon Health Division, 1999 at p. 2f.

139 *Ibid.*, p. 3.

140 *Ibid.*, p. 1f.

To be valid, a request for PAS must be made twice verbally over a certain period and once in writing. It is also necessary for physicians to inform a patient who requests PAS of the other treatment options that are available. Before the prescription can be provided, two physicians must judge the patient to be competent. In cases where 'either physician believes the patient's judgement is impaired by a psychiatric or psychological disorder, such as depression, the patient must be referred for counselling'.[141]

The first report on PAS in Oregon found that in 1998 – the first year in which assisted suicide had been legal – 23 patients received prescriptions for lethal drugs from their physicians to allow them to die. Of this number, 15 patients died from taking the prescription, 6 from their underlying illnesses and 2 patients were still alive in January 1999.[142] The average age of those who died was 69 years, all patients were white and 52 per cent were male. Only 4 of the 21 patients who died were regarded as needing a psychological consultation to determine whether they were competent.[143] Of the 15 patients who died by means of PAS, 13 were cancer patients (87%).[144]

When comparing those who chose PAS with others who had died from similar diseases in Oregon the survey found that age, race and sex were not determining factors.[145] The educational levels of those who chose physician-assisted death and those who did not were also similar. One difference between the two groups was that people who were divorced or who had never married were 6.8 times and 23.7 times respectively, more likely to opt for PAS than those who were married.[146]

The reasons individuals chose PAS are particularly important when considering the relationship between the legalisation of assisted death and disability. This is so because it is often suggested that disabled people may be unusually susceptible to pressure to end their lives, or may choose PAS because they are having trouble coming to terms with their disability. The Oregon report broke down the reasons for choosing PAS as follows: 80 per cent of individuals who chose PAS were concerned about losing autonomy as a result of their illness; 53 per cent were concerned about losing bodily functions; 67 per cent were concerned that they would not be able to participate in activities that give value to life; 13 per cent feared that they would be a burden to others; and 7 per cent anticipated that their pain would not be sufficiently controlled.[147] In comparison, the control group appeared less concerned about losing the ability to be self-determining. Of this group, 40 per cent were concerned about losing their autonomy; 19 per cent about losing bodily functions; and 60 per cent

141 Chin, A.E. *et al.*, *Oregon's Death with Dignity Act: The First Year's Experience*, Oregon, Oregon Health Division, 1999 at p. 2.
142 *Ibid.*, p. 4.
143 *Id.*
144 *Ibid.*, p. 13.
145 *Ibid.*, p. 5.
146 *Ibid.*, p. 5.
147 *Ibid.*, p. 16.

about being unable to participate in activities. However, more of the control group (35%) were concerned about being a burden and the same number (35%) about having inadequate pain control.[148] These statistics led to the conclusion that:

> The primary factor distinguishing persons in Oregon selecting physician-assisted suicide is related to the importance of autonomy and personal control. Patients who chose physician-assisted suicide were more likely to be concerned about loss of autonomy and loss of bodily functions than control patients. Autonomy was a prominent patient characteristic in physicians' answers to open-ended questions about their patients' end of life concerns. Many prescribing physicians reported that their decision to request a lethal prescription was consistent with a long-standing philosophy about controlling the manner in which they died.[149]

In addition, the report states:

> The proportion of patients in each group who expressed concerns about being a physical or emotional burden, or about the inability to participate in activities that made life enjoyable, were similar. However, patients who chose physician-assisted suicide were significantly more likely than controls to express concern to their physician about loss of autonomy, and more likely to express concern about loss of control of bodily functions (e.g., incontinence, vomiting) due to their illness. At death, patients who chose physician-assisted suicide were significantly less likely than controls to be completely disabled and bedridden.[150]

The report acknowledges that there are widespread concerns about the impact that legalising PAS could have on socially marginalised groups. Yet the fact that relatively few people chose PAS makes it difficult to identify small differences between the characteristics of those who chose PAS and the control group.[151] However, on the basis of the statistics provided in respect of the first year of assisted suicide in Oregon, no evidence exists that any one group has received discriminatory treatment. It explains:

> Considerable debate has focused on the characteristics of terminally-ill patients who choose physician-assisted suicide. Some feared that patients who were minorities, poor, or uneducated would more likely be coerced into

---

148 *Id.*
149 *Ibid.*, p. 8f.
150 *Ibid.*, p. 6.
151 *Ibid.*, p. 9.

choosing physician-assisted suicide. Others feared that terminally-ill persons would feel pressured, either internally or through external forces (e.g., family members or health care systems), to choose physician-assisted suicide because of the financial impact of their illness. To date, the Oregonians who have chosen physician-assisted suicide have not had these characteristics.[152]

Most recently the *Eighth Annual Report on Oregon's Death with Dignity Act* was published in March 2006.[153] During 2005, 38 deaths from assisted suicide were reported.[154] This comprised 32 of 64 patients who were given lethal prescriptions in this year and 6 patients who had held prescriptions over from 2004.[155] This figure represents a steadying out of the numbers using PAS in Oregon. Between 1999 and 2004 the numbers using PAS have been: 27 in 1999, 27 in 2000, 21 in 2001, 38 in 2002, 42 in 2003 and 37 in 2004.[156]

The majority of patients (84%) using PAS in 2005 had various forms of cancer.[157] This figure is also consistent with the cases of PAS between 1998 and 2004. A summary of figures for these years show that in total 79 per cent of those using PAS were cancer patients.[158] The factors of influence leading individuals to seek PAS between 1998 and 2005 were: fear of loss of autonomy (86%), loss of ability to undertake activities that made life enjoyable (85%), loss of dignity (83%), loss of control of bodily functions (57%), being a burden (37%), inadequate pain control (22%) and the financial costs of treatment (3%).[159]

The Eighth report on the Oregon Act has also failed to identify any tendency for those seeking to use PAS to come from marginalised groups. Between 1998 and 2005, 97 per cent of those using PAS have been white, 41 per cent have had a degree, 21 per cent a college education, 29 per cent a high school education and only 9 per cent did not have a high school education.[160]

One figure which certainly began to raise concerns was that relating to the number of individuals who sought PAS from fear of being a burden. In an initial report published in 1999 this was only 13 per cent of those seeking PAS, although interestingly the number in the control group (who had not sought PAS) was 35 per cent.[161] The figure in the former group, however, increased

---

152 Chin, A.E. *et al.*, *Oregon's Death with Dignity Act: The First Year's Experience*, Oregon, Oregon Health Division, 1999 at p. 8.

153 Lehman, R. (ed), *Eight Annual Report on Oregon's Death with Dignity Act*, Oregon, Oregon Department of Human Services, 2006.

154 *Id.*, p. 4.

155 *Id.*

156 *Id.*

157 *Id.*, p. 19.

158 *Id.*, p. 19.

159 If at p. 23.

160 If at p. 19.

161 Chin *et al.*, *op. cit.*, 1999, p. 16.

steadily and may be relevant to the treatment of disabled people at the end of life, since it could represent increased pressure or a perception of such pressure on people to end their lives. The third report on the Death with Dignity Act stated that:

> Patients have increasingly expressed concern about becoming a burden to family friends or caregivers (2000, 63%; 1999, 26%; 1998, 12%; Cochran-Armitage Trend Test, p < 0.001). All but one patient expressing this concern in 2000 also expressed concern about losing autonomy.[162]

We have seen that for the period 1998 to 2005, 37 per cent of people cited concern over being a burden as one reason for seeking PAS.[163] This does not mean that this is the sole reason, but it does raise concerns about how to ensure that decisions at the end of life are supported by the principle of respect for persons. However, it is worth noting that the control group who did not use the legislation experienced a higher rate of concern about this. Because the details of the PAS cases are unknown it is impossible to ascertain whether pressure 'not to be a burden' is real or perceived; nor is it clear why those who did not seek PAS experienced similar anxieties but chose not to act. While the number citing being a burden among those seeking PAS has levelled off, both the relatively high numbers in the control group in the first report on PAS in Oregon and amongst those seeking PAS appear to support concerns that society has an uncomfortable relationship with the notion of dependence. Crucially, information drawn from control groups representing the attitudes of those not selecting PAS is unavailable in the years following the first report of the functioning of the Act. So it is not possible to extend the comparison of attitudes regarding being a burden amongst those who did and not seek PAS to other years.

Since legalisation in the Netherlands and Oregon, Belgium has also endorsed legalised voluntary euthanasia,[164] and a number of other countries are actively debating legalisation.

Belgium

In 2002, Belgium became the latest European country to legalise voluntary euthanasia (but not assisted suicide). The Act on Euthanasia describes euthanasia as 'intentionally terminating life by someone other than the person concerned at the latter's request'.[165] The Act requires that the patient must be 'in a futile

---

162 Hedberg, K. *et al.*, *op. cit.*, 2001 at p. 12.
163 *Id.*
164 The Belgian Act on Euthanasia was passed on 28 May 2002.
165 s 2.

medical condition of constant and unbearable physical or mental suffering that cannot be alleviated and that the request for euthanasia must be "voluntary, well-considered and repeated." '[166] A second medical opinion must be obtained and at least one month must pass between the patient's written request for euthanasia and the act itself.[167] The recent House of Lords Select Committee reported that:

> The first report of the FCEC [Federal Control and Evaluation Commission], covering the 15-month period from 23 September 2003 to 31 December 2003 recorded 259 cases of euthanasia, and average of 17 cases per month...the 259 cases were reported by 143 different physicians. In 2004, 347 cases of euthanasia were reported, an average of 29 cases per month. The Commission's first report did not report any instances of non-compliance with the law and did not see a need for new legislative initiatives.[168]

One other European country must also be briefly considered, as it takes a much more liberal position than those already discussed.

Switzerland

Article 114 of the Swiss Penal Code makes voluntary euthanasia a criminal offence. However, assisting a suicide in an effort to help someone who is suffering is not a crime.[169] In June 2003 it was reported that '[a]ssisted suicide plays a role in more than half of all deaths in Switzerland.'[170] Interestingly, unlike the situation in the other countries considered, it is not necessary that the person offering the assistance is a doctor. A further difference is that there is no residence requirement, which means that voluntary organisations can offer assistance in dying to people travelling to Switzerland precisely for that purpose. Reports that a growing number of British citizens have travelled to Switzerland for assistance in dying have generated considerable media coverage,[171] and – according to the Select Committee on the Assisted Dying for the Terminally Ill Bill[172] – this has caused some concern in Switzerland itself.

The Swiss situation is particularly liberal in contrast to other jurisdictions in that it does not link the availability of assisted dying to the existence of a

---

166 s 3.
167 s 3.3.2.
168 House of Lords Select Committe, *op. cit.*, pp. 73–4, para 212.
169 Article 115.
170 'Scotland on Sunday', 29 June 2003 at p. 23.
171 See for example, 'Swiss clinic investigated', 26 May 2003; 'No Charges over Assisted Suicide', 9 April 2003; 'Suicide Man's "Dignified" Death', 24 January 2003 – all available from http://www.bbc.co.uk/news (accessed on 14 July 2003).
172 Cited earlier.

terminal condition; the debates in the Netherlands over whether depression or simple dissatisfaction with life should be sufficient to trigger lawful assistance in dying would have no place in Switzerland. Where, however, doctors are involved, the Swiss Academy of Medical Sciences has drawn up a code of ethics, described by the House of Lords Select Committee as follows:

> … while a doctor's primary role is to alleviate symptoms and to support the patient, there may be situations in which the patient asks for help in committing suicide and persists with this wish. In this dilemma, between established medical practice and support for his patient's wishes, the doctor may either refuse to comply with the patient's request or accede to the request provided that he is satisfied that three conditions have been met – that the patient's state of health makes it clear that he or she is nearing the end of life; that alternative possibilities have been discussed and, if desired by the patient, implemented; and that the patient who requests help to end his or her life is capable, free from external pressure and has thought through his or her decision. The Academy recommends also that, in such situations, a third person should verify that the third condition has been met [173]

However, the majority of assisted suicides in Switzerland do not involve doctors,[174] and these criteria are therefore not routinely applied. Given what has been said earlier in this chapter about the possible problems associated with tightening regulation of legalised assisted dying, it is – perhaps paradoxically – possible that this essentially deregulated situation may actually be preferable. On the other hand, deregulation is unlikely to be supported by those who fear that the disability that can be consequent on impairment might drive people to end their lives prematurely and without being aware of alternative opportunities or coping mechanisms.

Conclusion

The evidence from the Netherlands and Oregon is unfortunately inconclusive. Belgium has legislated too recently for any firm conclusions to be drawn from the experience there and the Swiss position is unique. Despite this, many commentators have been prepared to draw conclusions from the experience in these countries, most notably, those who oppose legalisation of assisted suicide or voluntary euthanasia. Indeed, the fear generated by legalisation has been claimed to be so great that 'we may rapidly be reaching the point at which disabled people avoid obtaining medical treatment, for fear of the outcome'.[175]

173 P. 70, para 197.
174 P. 70, para 198.
175 Light, R., *A Real Horror Story: The Abuse of Disabled People's Human Rights: Disability Awareness in Action Human Rights Database*, Disability Awareness in Action, 2002 at p. 21.

Interestingly, the opposite proposition has also been made, namely, that people actually fear being kept alive by medical treatment beyond the point at which they would wish, resulting in increased rates of suicide in certain groups, most particularly the elderly.[176]

Nonetheless, in the United Kingdom, the DRC remains highly suspicious of legalisation, echoing the concerns expressed above, although they do 'not oppose, in principle, legalisation of euthanasia for people who freely choose it'.[177] However, in evidence to the House of Lords Select Committee on the Assisted Dying for the Terminally Ill Bill, the DRC also claimed that:

> ...we believe that in the current climate of discrimination against disabled people, where a lack of access to palliative care and social support means that free choice does not really exist, the threat to the lives of disabled people posed by such legislation is real and significant. We, therefore, cannot currently support legalisation of euthanasia.[178]

We have argued that the ethical assessment of euthanasia and assisted suicide depends in large part on evidence being provided to show that disabled people *are* actually harmed by legalising these practices, that is, it is important specifically to link the legalisation of euthanasia to discrimination against disabled people if the concerns to which we have referred are to be significant in the debate. It is not sufficient merely to assert that there is a link. So far, the surveys from the Netherlands and Oregon do not provide such evidence. Nonetheless, it was reported recently that, '[a] European human rights group rejected a proposal promoting euthanasia and said that doctors should not be encouraged to end the lives of terminally ill or disabled patients.'[179] Further, a debate in the Council of Europe[180] rejected a call to legalise assisted dying primarily 'because it would call on European countries to define procedures for ending treatment of such patients or for discontinuing lifesaving medical treatment when doctors believe there is little hope for survival'.[181]

In reviewing the evidence from countries which have legalised assisted dying, however, a number of points can be made although any conclusions drawn must

---

176 Angell, M., 'Prisoners of Technology: The Case of Nancy Cruzan', 322 *New England Journal of Medicine* 1226 (1990) at p. 1228.

177 Evidence to the House of Lords Select Committee on the Assisted Dying for the Terminally Ill Bill, cited earlier, Volume II, at p. 220, para 1.2.

178 *Ibid.*, p. 220, para 1.3.

179 Ertelt, S., 'European Human Rights Group Condemns Euthanasia of Disabled', Lifenews.com, 27 April 2005, available at http://66.195.16.55/bio940.html (accessed 16 June 2005).

180 Council of Europe Parliamentary Assembly, Wednesday, 27 April 2005, Assistance to Patients at the End of Life, debate, available at http://assembly.coe.int/documents/records/2005–2/e/0504271000e.htm (accessed on 24 June 2005).

181 Ertelt, *loc. cit.*

be tentative. First, inertia about disability issues could be responsible for poorly drafted survey questions that fail to give sufficient attention to how legislation actually impacts on disabled people. The recent House of Lords Select Committee cast doubt on the value of the opinion poll evidence which has been growing over the years about people's attitudes to legalisation. The Committee commissioned Market Research Services (MRS) to review opinion research over the last 10 to 20 years. The MRS report 'found that virtually all the surveys which had been carried out over the period were quantitative rather than qualitative in nature...',[182] and therefore might be seen as somewhat one dimensional. Nonetheless, the review did note unequivocal evidence – within the limitations expressed – that support for legalisation is both strong and growing. Gaining better, or more qualitative, information from those with disabilities and those without would certainly assist in facilitating a robust interrogation of the benefits and drawbacks of legalisation in this area. Equally, it is of considerable importance that sufficient information is available on the details of particular cases. This is because general statistical data provide insufficient grounding for ethical judgements. Although the detailed case studies provided by the DRC and similar organisations act as an excellent resource with which to evaluate concerns about the treatment disabled people receive, or are likely to receive, to support general ethical arguments, more subtle and detailed data are required.

For the moment, a cautious approach is probably indicated, since truly reliable data are not yet available. However, the other side of that same coin is that the evidence available to date does not seem to show a link between legalisation of assisted suicide and discrimination against disabled people, even though the expanded UK definition of disability means that more people who are described as 'disabled' would likely be involved in assisted dying where it is legal. However, it remains perfectly plausible to argue that denying disabled people the right to choose their own assisted death is an additional form of discrimination, rather than a protection. We agree that it is vital that such decisions or 'choices' are indeed real, but this is not an issue confined to any one group. It is just as important for those who are not impaired, although it mandates focusing on the elimination of any additional pressures on disabled people. We have already suggested that nobody acts in a truly free manner; this is widely accepted. However, what must be argued for is that disabled people are able to make such decisions from a 'level playing field'. Only the removal of wider social and legal discrimination will enable this to occur. As the DRC says:

> ... legislation works in a context. There is a body of opinion internationally, that says that it is impossible to safely legislate in the current climate of discrimination, where disabled people do not have access to good palliative care or social support to enable a good quality of life. There are questions

---

182 P. 74, para 217.

over whether, in such a climate, disabled people will be coerced into seeking assistance to die, whether self-regulation by doctors can work, whether decisions by the courts based on advice from the medical profession will be safe, and if not what other kind of regulation can be put in place.[183]

These are indeed important questions, and frankly they seem to us unlikely to be easily resolved. Perhaps this alone would merit rejection of attempts to liberalise the law. If the fears of one or more groups in the community (however large or small) can be shown to have substance, it may well be that others will need either to build a society in which these fears are no longer valid or sacrifice some of their own interests to protect those who are vulnerable. Indeed, the ProLife submission to the recent House of Lords Select Committee argued that '[o]nly a very tiny number of patients could not commit suicide if they wished to do so. Changing the law for their alleged benefit at the expense of frightening many thousands of vulnerable disabled or ill people makes no sense.'[184]

However, this assertion paradoxically ignores the fact that the majority of those who could *not* commit suicide without assistance are those likely to be physically impaired or psychologically incapable of so doing. Rather than respecting these people, the ProLife alliance would prevent them from having access to a chosen death, access that is valued by many others who are not impaired. Nonetheless, this sentiment also pervades much of the literature deriving from the disability rights lobby itself. For example, the National Council on Disability (US) argues that:

> Current evidence indicates clearly that the interests of the few people who would benefit from legalizing physician-assisted suicide are heavily out-weighed by the probability that any law, procedures, and standards that can be imposed to regulate physician-assisted suicide will be misapplied to unnecessarily end the lives of people with disabilities and entail an intolerable degree of intervention by legal and medical officials in such decisions.[185]

It is not clear precisely what this 'evidence' is. However, it is also undoubtedly the case that no one would wish to see a society in which we were casual about respecting others or deliberately and knowingly put them at risk. Whether that would be the result of legalising assisted dying is unclear.

It must also remain moot whether or not the expressed wishes of the majority of the population (at least anecdotally) – including apparently substantial

---

183 P. 9, para 1.18.
184 ProLife submission to Select Committee, 22 February 2005, available at http://www. prolife.org.uk (accessed 22 February 2005).
185 National Council on Disability (US), Assisted Suicide: A Disability Perspective, available at http://www.ncd.gov/newsroom/publications/1997/suicide.htm (accessed on 16 June 2005 at p. 3).

numbers of disabled people – should be ignored because of the hypothesised, but unproven, additional threat to some disabled or impaired people. In the absence of evidence, we must conclude by being either precautionary or radical. This will require an intricate balancing of the interests of different individuals and groups within the community.

Finally, it is important to note that currently euthanasia and assisted suicide are illegal in the United Kingdom, yet there is evidence that they take place.[186] It is a plausible hypothesis that the scope for abuse is greater in an unregulated than in a regulated situation. Not only are healthcare professionals breaking the law, but a recent National Opinion Poll (NOP) survey (commissioned by the Voluntary Euthanasia Society) of 790 people indicated that '47% would help terminally ill loved ones die if they were suffering', and that '50% of all Britons would consider going abroad to receive medical assistance to die if they were suffering from a terminal illness.'[187] Additionally, as was said in evidence to the recent Select Committee, 'Lord Joffe's Bill would offer to those seeking assistance...[in dying] many more safeguards than are currently available for those who at present can lawfully choose to die.'[188]

We have highlighted the fact that discriminatory analyses and practices often seem to inform the way in which disabled people are treated in the healthcare setting. While this means that efforts to reveal, critique and prevent such discrimination should be redoubled, it is difficult to show that there is a direct causal link between the legalisation of assisted dying and the treatment disabled people receive.

It seems, in conclusion, that it is unlikely – if not impossible – to find evidence that will ever satisfy the opponents of legalisation of assisted suicide and euthanasia, unless a global agreement is reached on the relevant and important questions to be asked when legal frameworks are interrogated. Given the history of discrimination against people with disability or impairment, it would seem that we are unlikely to uncover sufficiently stringent evidence to satisfy disabled people, or at least some disabled people. Of course, it cannot be said that *all* disabled people oppose legalisation of assisted suicide or voluntary euthanasia, and the dilemma remains as to how their equally strongly held views can be accommodated. We considered earlier the extent to which the opinions of one group should be allowed to dominate those of others, a seemingly intractable dilemma, at least for those representing the wide range and mixture of opinion from disabled people who are, after all, no less diverse than those who are non-disabled. Perhaps this dilemma can only be adequately addressed when it is accepted that *no* system is infallible, and even perhaps that to demand a perfect

186 See, for example, McLean, S.A.M. and Britton, A., *Sometimes a Small Victory*, Glasgow, Institute of Law and Ethics in Medicine, 1996.
187 'Half Would Help Loved Ones Die', http://www.news.bbc.co.uk (accessed on 09 May 2005).
188 HL Paper 86-II, p. 14.

system is to deny the content and significance of the debate itself. In the final analysis, we may be forced to conclude on the side of the solution that generates the least harm, rather than seeking to achieve the (improbable) absolute absence of harm. If we are to respect people with impairment, as we propose, we should strive to avoid stereotypes on either side.

Disability does not prevent people from making free choices, even for death. Nor does it deserve prejudice and discrimination. However, there is a danger that those who speak vehemently in favour of the models of disability we discussed in Chapter 2, are side-stepping the real issue, that is, respecting people's own wishes. Neither model directly confronts this: rather, they assume either that people's experiences and interests can be reduced to a description of their physical or mental state, or that only society's manifest failures are significant when they make decisions. The principle of respect for persons on the other hand avoids this trap by forcing us to address the *quality* of the decision itself. It can, therefore, be called into play both to argue for greater social support for people with disability and to respect the competent and informed choices of those who wish assistance in dying.

Chapter 7

Countering discrimination against the 'disabled'

What good are ethics and law?

Introduction

In this concluding chapter the primary aim is to delineate the impact of ethico-legal analysis as a method for identifying and defeating the discrimination that people regarded as 'disabled' encounter at the beginning and end of their lives. The focus of this book has been to identify and address the discrimination that many people – impaired and unimpaired – perceive disabled people to experience. We have focussed on the discrimination that occurs within specific contexts, but there are of course many other situations in which people's impairment or disability may have a negative effect. Arguably however, it is at the beginning and end of life that discriminatory decision-making has the most profound impact. The very real fear that people will be prevented from coming into being, or that lives will be casually ended because their quality of life (QoL) is mistakenly presumed to be poor or untenable, understandably permeates much of the disability lobby's commentary on healthcare issues and is increasingly being reflected in wider academic literature.

Models of disability reconsidered

So concerned has the disability community been about the pervasive nature of discrimination against people with impairments that it cultivated an understanding of disability (the social model) that directly associates the discrimination that disabled people experience with the limitations imposed by social circumstances. This understanding of disability contrasts sharply with the medical approach to disability that preceded it and which still has significance in the medical and legal assessments of disability (the medical model).

We have perceived and found throughout our examinations that both the medical and social models of disability can contribute to efforts to confront the discrimination about disability that is so problematic at the beginning and end of 'disabled' human life. That is, the medical view of disability focuses on mental and physical causes of disability (impairments) that will justly, if they are sufficiently severe, be at the heart of life-and-death decisions. On the other hand, exponents of the social model warn us that it is often prejudicial attitudes towards impairment (disability) rather than clinical status and prognosis that are the final arbiter in decision making. This view also has value.

However, we have also argued that neither the medical nor the social model provides *in itself* a sufficient basis from which to consider the problems we have identified. From our perspective, the medical model lacks the critical resources to consider whether its judgements are discriminatory, and exponents of the social model do not focus on issues directly related to impairment, issues that often are appropriate to life-and-death decisions.

The impression created by the ongoing disputes between competing ideas of disability is one of incommensurability. That is, the social and medical theses of these opposed camps seem so different that it is not possible to measure them using the same yardstick. This, as Alasdair MacIntyre has suggested in the context of the state of contemporary moral theory, means that debates go on *ad infinitum* because they can find no resolution.[1] Given the urgent life-and-death issues with which we are concerned, this theoretical limitation has serious implications for efforts to confront the discrimination experienced by people with impairments at the beginning and end of their lives.

Fortunately, the work of some disability theorists suggested this impasse could be no more than a theoretical illusion. In Chapter 2, for example, we noted that some members of the disability community have expressed their dissatisfaction with efforts to conceptualise disability as an exclusively social phenomenon. Their concerns focus on the failure of the social model to give any importance to the negative experiences that *can* come from impairments. This acknowledgement helps to forge common ground with the medical understanding of disability. Yet it does this without abandoning the idea that people with impairments *also* experience limitations as a direct result of social failures to accommodate their mental and physical differences. This suggests that the central insights of the medical and social understandings of disability are not mutually exclusive.

The ripples of discontent raised within the disability community over the failure of the social model to include experience are arguably yet to make an impact on decision-making at the beginning and end of life. Indeed, the concession to the medical model – the acknowledgment that impairments can disable – could be seen by those who support the interests of disabled people as surrendering much hard-won ground. From our perspective as (we hope) independent observers, however, it marks a significant advance that has important implications for debates at the beginning and end of life. This is because it allows us to conceive of disability and impairment in a more inclusive way and so incorporate all the issues that actually influence decision-making at the beginning and end of life.

---

1 MacIntyre, A., *After Virtue: A Study in Moral Theory* (2nd Ed), London, Duckwork, 1985.

We have contended that one of the most important issues to emerge from the claims of some disability theorists regarding the importance of experiences that are associated with impairment is the need to distinguish carefully between unjust discrimination and justified differentiation. This is because their insights have helped to clarify the degree to which differential treatment is sometimes necessary and ethically acceptable. Juxtaposing the medical and social spurs to disability, allowing that both have a place in decision-making, intensifies the need to determine when impairment is legitimately cited as a reason for preventing or ending a life and when it is little more than a façade for social prejudice (discrimination). In light of these concerns we commenced our primary task of investigating the benefits and disbenefits of ethico-legal work for elevating discrimination against disabled people in decision-making at the beginning and end of life.

The contribution of ethics reconsidered

In Chapter 3, a number of principles that are widely considered to be foundational within bioethical debate – human dignity, the sanctity of life and respect for persons – were examined to determine whether they could give further specificity to the values that should be shared by those involved in protecting and advancing the interests of disabled people. It was hoped that one way they might do this was by helping to formulate a more precise idea of the boundary between justly differential treatment and unjust discrimination.

We argued that two of the principles – human dignity and sanctity of life – lacked sufficient clarity or content. Thus, while they may be useful in other contexts, they were insufficiently robust for our requirements. That is, it is possible to argue that both preventing and allowing the birth of an impaired infant respect the sanctity of life, and that sustaining or ending a severely impaired life, respect human dignity. It is also clear that the sanctity-of-life argument cannot be applied to non-persons. Hence utilising these malleable principles to help formulate definitive standards for when impairment ethically permits differential treatment – to prevent or end a life – and when it does not, gets us nowhere. For similar reasons, human dignity and the sanctity-of-life principles do not really advance our efforts to forge common ground between the various stakeholders in disability debates. This is because, without drawing on other more precise ethical principles, neither the principle of sanctity of life nor human dignity provides a sufficiently clear account of the values that *should* be shared by all involved in these debates. Indeed we discovered that much needed detail is often provided to the sanctity of life and human dignity principles by drawing on other principles like respect for persons and self-determination. Thus we then turned to examine whether respect for persons was better equipped to help inform life-and-death decision-making in the context of disability and impairment.

The principle of respect for persons was argued to hold more promise for our efforts to unify debates and to determine just when differential treatment turns to discrimination. Two different expressions of Kant's categorical imperative were examined. The first determined the worth of actions by assessing whether they are universalisable – could everyone act in this way without contradiction, and the second stated the necessity of treating people as an end in themselves. Both requirements support the ethical imperative to respect persons. The principle of universalisability does this by demanding equal treatment for all people; thus, differential treatment can only be provided if there are criteria that justify its provision. In the absence of such criteria, differential treatment becomes an instance of discrimination. The requirement not to treat individuals solely as a means to another's end adds substance to the need to respect persons by requiring that individuals should – wherever possible – be able to choose how to lead their lives, rather than have choices imposed on them by others.

The clear substantive content to this principle points to the common ground that should unite all stakeholders in debates concerning disability at the beginning and end of life. Namely, we act ethically when we respect persons by allowing them, and when necessary enabling them, to make choices about how to live and – possibly – when to end their lives. However, as we have seen there is an important proviso: we must be able to allow *all* people who are in a similar predicament to make the same choices without contradiction. Thus, the universalisation criterion essentially functions as a device to help distinguish between judgements that differentiate fairly and those that discriminate unjustly. In this way, it can impose limitations on individual choice and so prevent our ethical world from being a subjective free-for-all. When respect for persons receives support from principles and concepts such as autonomy, consent and rights its benefits are reinforced. Nonetheless, it does not follow that the use of this principle will always foster agreement on particular issues, nor that its benefits extend to all areas of life-and-death decision-making.

Arguably, one of the greatest problems facing efforts to better manage debates in the context of disability at the beginning and end of life by appealing to principles and concepts that are central to the liberal tradition – respect for persons, autonomy, consent and rights – is that they are not well suited to cases involving dependency, incompetence and the doubtful nature of personhood. This is perhaps best illustrated by referring briefly to how such broadly liberal commitments are realised in legal analyses involving the incompetent or the unborn.

The contribution of law reconsidered

It is particularly important that the legal approach is informed by appropriate ethical principles, since we are dealing with particularly vulnerable stages of life. The law has a special obligation here to be fair, consistent and robust. However, as we have seen, the temptation has often been to resort – in our view unnecessarily – to the use of legal devices such as 'best interests' or 'quality of life', which are vague, subjective and possibly, therefore, open to discriminatory interpretation. This is because agent-centred concepts such as autonomy and their procedural equivalents – consent and rights – cannot be easily applied to individuals who cannot actively choose for themselves. This situation is exacerbated for embryos, which are not taken to have the status of persons. It is at this point in analysis that room for differential treatment may still remain, but whether it is plausible to describe this as discrimination is, we have suggested, doubtful.

The concern is that concepts such as best interests and QoL feign a degree of objectivity that they do not in fact possess and hence can easily allow for discriminatory decisions to be smuggled into discussions. Against this, however, must also be set the converse; that is, that we should not *assume* that judgements that are made are inevitably discriminatory merely because they involve consideration of impairment or disability. Hence, it remains necessary to distinguish between differential treatment and unjust discrimination.

In this respect, the importance of rejecting decisions that cannot be universalised remains an essential tool. When applied to third party decision makers it essentially requires that they provide criteria that explain decisions to prevent or end a life. Arguably, in cases involving impairment explanations to justify such decisions can be provided just as readily as can criticisms of these choices after the event. In the final analysis, given the universal nature of impairment and dependency we are all dependent on healthcare providers to make decisions that legitimately protect out interests. It is hoped that ethical principles like respect for persons and those that facilitate its attainment – autonomy, consent and rights – will help to inform medical and legal decision-makers how to make the best possible decisions.

At the beginning of life we have argued that some decisions about who should be born – while they do in fact arise specifically in the case of certain kinds of condition (primarily impairment) – are not *in se* unreasonable or unintelligible. Nor, arguably, are they discriminatory since there is no person present against whom discrimination could be shown. Despite this, however, it must be conceded that some existing people may feel that the ability or right to make pre-implantation or prenatal choices leads inevitably to discrimination against those who currently live with the condition being screened out. For example, Saxton says:

> Disability rights activists have begun to articulate a critical view of the practice of prenatal diagnosis with the intent to abort if the fetus appears to be destined to become a disabled person. Some people with disabilities, particularly those who are members of the disability rights community, perceive that selective abortion may be based on the assumption that any child with a disability would necessarily be a

burden to the family and to society, and therefore would be better off not being born.[2]

We have already suggested that the voices of people with impairment or disability have not necessarily been given sufficient weight, and this might seem like an excellent situation in which to heed them. If, for example, screening out certain impairments at the pre-implantation or prenatal stage does *in fact* mean that people with disabilities are seen as a burden on others, might it not be argued that we should prevent such decisions from being made in order to raise awareness of the underlying mind-set that influences them?

The problem, however, is that we do not know *for a fact* either that this is the basis for the decisions taken by intending parents or that permitting them to make such decisions has a detrimental or discriminatory impact on people living with the same conditions, although some – for example, the Department of Health – have to an extent taken on board the notion that they may. Although prenatal testing, for example, may produce 'welcome consequences for the health of children', so too, it is argued, it may challenge 'beliefs in the equal worth of all human beings regardless of genetic (or other) disability.'[3] More controversially, even if we did know for a fact that this would be the effect, it remains questionable whether or not that would justify limiting the respect which we would otherwise accord to the procreative decisions of competent, adult persons. It would arguably be unacceptable to interfere with the reproductive choices of potential parents in order, speculatively or as a matter of fact, to avoid the possible discrimination associated with deeming certain conditions to be undesirable. A more fruitful way forward, we have suggested, would be to re-state, firmly and without equivocation, the respect for persons to which everyone is entitled, and put in place operationally the mechanisms which support this. This may involve paying close attention to the arguments contained in the social model of disability, but it also must include to an extent those of the medical model, while transcending the inherent limitations of each.

Moreover, in the neonatal period, decisions that the lives of some babies would be intolerable might also be permissible, assuming that they are based on sound clinical diagnosis and prognosis and that they have taken account of the respect which is due to it as a person. As Taylor, LJ said in the case of *Re J (a minor) (wardship: medical treatment)*[4]:

> Despite the court's inability to compare a life afflicted by the most severe disability with death, the unknown, I am of the view that there must be

2 Saxton, M., 'Why Members of the Disability Community Oppose Prenatal Diagnosis and Selective Abortion', in Parens, E. and Asch, A. (eds), *Prenatal Testing and Disability Rights*, Washington, DC, Georgetown University Press, 2000, 147–164 at p. 147.

3 *Our Inheritance, Our Future: Realising the Potential of Genetics in the NHS*, London, Department of Health, June 2003, Cm 5791–II at p. 43.

4 (1990) 6 BMLR 25 (CA).

extreme cases in which the court is entitled to say: 'The life which this treatment would prolong would be so cruel as to be intolerable.[5]

Like many others, Taylor here is referring to the use of the 'best interests' test as a decision-making tool. However, we have seen that best-interests decisions risk being made not from the perspective of the impaired infant but from that of a third party – usually an able-bodied adult – who may all-too-readily assume that all disabled experience is bad experience. In the case of *Re Wyatt (a child) (medical treatment: parents' consent)*,[6] Hedley J said:

> Whilst the sanctity of her life and her right to dignity are to be respected, she can exercise no choice of her own. In those circumstances someone must choose for her... That choice must be exercised on the basis of what is in her best interests.[7]

Yet the same judge noted the difficulties associated with this test, which, as we have seen, plays a vital role in decision-making for children with severe impairments. He referred, with approval, to the statement of Lord Donaldson in *Re J (a minor) (wardship: medical treatment)*,[8] when he said:

> We know that the instinct and desire for survival is very strong. We all believe in and assert the sanctity of human life... even very severely handicapped people find a quality of life rewarding which to the unhandicapped may seem manifestly intolerable. People have an amazing adaptability. But in the end there will be cases in which the answer must be that it is not in the interests of the child to subject it to treatment which will cause increased suffering and produce no commensurate benefit, giving the fullest possible weight to the child's, and mankind's, desire to survive.[9]

In refusing to modify the original order that Charlotte Wyatt should not be treated aggressively, Hedley said:

> In reaching... [my] view I have of course been informed by the medical evidence as to the prospects and cost to her of aggressive treatment. I hope, however, that I have looked much wider than that and seen not just a physical being but a body, mind and spirit expressed in a human personality of unique worth who is profoundly precious to her parents.[10]

---

5 At p. 42.
6 (2004) 84 BMLR 206.
7 At p. 211.
8 (1990) 6 BMLR 25.
9 At p 35.
10 At p. 217.

On appeal, the court restated the need to treat Charlotte in accordance with what were her best interests,[11] and upheld the earlier judgement, even in the face of the parents' wish that she should be treated. However difficult it is to be entirely comfortable with decisions which result in the death of a vulnerable child, it arguably cannot be said that this decision, and others like it, amount to discrimination. To be sure, it is her physical condition that necessitates such decisions being considered, but – as we have asserted earlier – the *fact* of impairment is not always irrelevant. In cases like this, failure to take account of the impact of impairment could be more rather than less respectful of the child. Charlotte, has of course confounded the medical experts, and the order made in respect of her treatment has, as we saw earlier, been modified.

However, it may be that other, extraneous, influences will bear on the decision. For example, in the case of *Re J (a Minor) (wardship: medical treatment)*[12] it was said that, '[i]n an imperfect world resources will always be limited and on occasion agonising choices will have to be made in allocating those resources to particular patients.'[13] It seems reasonable to conclude therefore that, where there is already suspicion about the quality of life likely to be experienced by people with impairments, and in the face of competition for resources, actual discrimination may arise. It is on this, therefore, that efforts to resist untenable assumptions should be focussed, and it is here that we can also first identify the lack of subtlety or nuance that characterises efforts to slot decision-making about impairment and disability into one or other of the models discussed in Chapter 2. Because of this, we contend that attention to the foundational principle of respect for persons outlined in Chapter 3 would provide a more effective and appropriate basis from which to evaluate our decisions.

With this concern in mind we have suggested that QoL decisions should be based on criteria that appreciate and respect the value of even the most basic characteristic human experiences. Thus, providing that the benefits of relational interaction are not outweighed by burdens such as pain, the potential value of such lives should not be ignored.

Two broad classes of decisions at the end of life were identified in Chapters 5 and 6. First, is the situation where (usually) third parties make a preemptive decision that – in the event of an adverse and life-threatening event – no

---

11 *Wyatt v Portsmouth NHS Trust & Anor* [2005] EWHC 693 (Fam), available at http://www.bailii. org/ew/cases/EWHC/Fam/2005/693.html (accessed on 2 September 2005). Mr Justice Hedley said: 'a society is measured by the way it treats its most disabled members. The law's answer in relation to those who lack capacity to decide for themselves is that they are treated in accordance with their best interests, those being usually established by agreement between those who have the responsibility for that person's care or where, as here, no such agreement can be found, by decision of the court.'

12 (1990) 6 BMLR 25 (C A).

13 At p. 30.

cardiopulmonary resuscitation (CPR) should be attempted: the so-called Do Not Resuscitate order (DNR). As we have seen, CPR is notoriously unsuccessful and very often decisions not to offer it will be based firmly on scientifically validated criteria. However, there are two causes for concern. First, and this applies generally, there is concern that patients are not themselves sufficiently involved in these critical decisions. As has been said:

> Unfortunately, even when discussions about DNR orders do occur between physicians and patients or their proxies, they usually occur late in the patient's illness, often after extensive and painful medical interventions have occurred. In many cases, patients may no longer be competent and may be unable to participate in these discussions themselves. In one study, 86% of families but only 22% of patients had participated in discussions about DNR orders.[14]

Second, there is a perception that where the life under consideration is one whose quality is presumed to be low or inadequate, as might be the case particularly for those with impairments or disabilities in addition to their current clinical problems, attempts to prolong life by resuscitation might be regarded as less appropriate because of the discrimination or prejudice that we have identified. Thus, there is reason for concern that DNR orders may be made on the basis of the erroneous or unfounded perceptions of third parties as to the quality of life experienced by the individuals themselves. Equally, decisions to withhold or withdraw treatment may hinge on the perceived dependence/disability of the individuals concerned, leading to unjustified discrimination against them. It was reported, for example, on 25 July 2006, as one example of a sad reality, that the family of a 91 year-old woman who had suffered a stroke are claiming that she was denied access to basic nutrition, hydration and antibiotics by a hospital, despite there being a court order in place, because the hospital believed that her QoL was poor.[15] It is suspected that such decisions are being made often in the healthcare sector; close attention to the principle of respect for persons would, we argue, provide the most robust defence of the rights of individuals in this situation.

The second class of decisions concerns those where, on the contrary, the person him or herself wants to choose death over life. Again, there are two subsets in this area. First, there are those who wish to die passively – that is by requiring the removal or withholding of certain treatments. In the case of Ms B,[16] for example, at issue was her request that life-saving ventilation should be removed, thereby allowing her to die. She had become seriously physically

---

14 Ebell, M.H., Doukas, D.J. and Smith, M.A., 'The Do-Not-Resuscitate Order: A Comparison of Physician and Patient Preferences and Decision-Making', *The American Journal of Medicine*, 91, 1991, 255–260 at pp. 255–256.

15 '*The Times*', 25 July 2006, p. 20.

16 *Ms B v An NHS Hospital Trust* (2002) 65 BMLR 149.

impaired and chose not to live in that condition, even although an alternative regime was offered to her. The fact of her impairment, and its concomitant disability, was judged *by her* to mean that the quality of her life *on her own calculation* was unacceptable. Dame Elizabeth Butler-Sloss, although acceding to her decision, nonetheless clearly regretted it and declared herself sure that she would have had a contribution to make to her society.[17] However, for Ms B, that was not enough and she was permitted to choose death. Again, respect for persons, with its facilitating principles of autonomy and consent, found a way to resolve the question *to the satisfaction of the woman herself.*

In the second sub-set are those who also wish to die but need active assistance in achieving their aim. Into this group fall people like Diane Pretty whose battle to have assistance in dying gripped the public and exercised the courts both in the United Kingdom and Europe.[18] The refusal to allow Mrs Pretty to realise her choice was, at every level, in part informed by concerns about the message that this would send to people with impairments or disabilities, or simply those who are old.[19] It was also based on the distinction drawn by the courts between acts and omissions: a distinction about whose validity we have expressed considerable doubt in such situations. We are not alone in this. Lord Mustill, in the case of *Airedale NHS Trust v Bland*,[20] expressed his concerns about this distinction, describing it as 'morally and intellectually dubious'.[21]

Whatever the reason for denying Diane Pretty the right to make the choice for assisted death, the response of some in the disability rights lobby – in this case the DRC – is not concerned with legal niceties. Rather, they believe that 'disabled people will be open to direct coercion to seek assistance to die from others who have an interest in their death.'[22] Given that the DRC prefers the social model of disability to the medical one, it reiterates its concern that:

> ... many disabled people are living intolerable lives, not because of their impairment, but due to lack of choice, control and autonomy brought about by the lack of basic amenities and support services including inaccessible and inadequate housing, insufficient help with personal care, and lack of essential equipment.[23]

Although expressing these concerns forcefully the 'DRC is committed to the principle of autonomy for disabled people' and concludes that it 'does not

17 At p. 172.
18 *Pretty v United Kingdom* (2002) 66 BMLR 147.
19 See, for example at p. 169.
20 (1993) 12 BMLR 64.
21 At p. 142.
22 Disability Rights Commission, Policy statement on voluntary euthanasia and assisted suicide, available at http://www.disability.gov.uk/drc, p. 13, para 3.6 (accessed on 12 October 2004).
23 P. 11, para 3.1.

oppose, in principle, legalisation [of assisted dying] for competent adults who freely chose it'.[24]

Given the DRC's concerns, it is unsurprising that its view on legalisation can be described as somewhat lukewarm. In other words, although it would wish to see people with disability given the same rights as others, its fear that the debate will actually be resolved from the perspective of the 'abled' is intelligible. What good would come from merely situating disabled people on an apparent par with their non-disabled peers if the equivalence of their positions is a fiction? On the other hand, would merely satisfying the social needs of people in situations like that of Mrs Pretty (were that actually possible) *in fact* have stopped her or others like her from wanting to choose assisted dying? Yet again, it is necessary to critique the absolute commitment to the social model. Any presumption that it is only social circumstances that motivate a choice for death ignores the physical or emotional reality of the impact of the impairment itself, which may be separable from the circumstances within which it is experienced, and may disrespect the values of those who wish to make such decisions. As Harris, for example, points out:

If the harm of ending a life is principally a harm to the individual whose life it is and if this harm must in turn be understood principally as the harm of depriving that individual of something that they value and want, then voluntary euthanasia will not be wrong on this account.'[25]

Thus, where people find that they no longer want something – in this case, life – that others would want, it would be wrong to frustrate a competent decision. In a comment particularly relevant to our discussion, Harris also says:

The real problem of euthanasia is the tragedy of the premature and unwanted deaths of the thousands of people in every society who die for want of medical and other resources or who are allowed to die or are killed because others believe their lives are not worth sustaining. It is, I believe, an idle and perverse arrogance to frustrate the wishes of those who want to die or preserve indefinitely the lives of those who have irrevocably lost personhood when the wishes of people who do not want to die are consistently and callously disregarded.[26] (emphasis added)

Disregarding competently expressed wishes would, for Dworkin, amount to 'a devastating, odious form of tyranny'.[27] We believe, therefore, that although prima facie the DRC and others are correct to be cautious, their concern may be

---

24 At p. 34.
25 Harris, J., 'Euthanasia and the Value of Life', in Keown, J. (ed), *Euthanasia Examined: Ethical, Clinical and Legal Perspectives*, Cambridge: Cambridge University Press, 1995, 6 at p. 10.
26 *Loc. cit.*, p. 20.
27 Dworkin, R., *Life's Dominion*, London, Harper Collins, 1993 at p. 217.

overstated in the presence of a competently expressed statement from an individual about the quality of his or her own life, and its tolerability. In those countries where assisted dying has been legalised, the evidence as to abuse is at worst ambivalent and at best absent. Although there has been intense debate about whether or not the Dutch experience shows that legal rules can be discounted or ignored,[28] experience in the State of Oregon suggests that the rules are facilitating competent choice. As Rothschild, for example, says:

> The figures provided by the Oregon Department of Human Services annual reports are not assumptions; neither are they assumptions or rhetoric, as arguments fearing the 'slippery slope' are. They provide evidence that the safeguards and regulations provided by the Act are working and only those for whom the Act was intended are making use of it.[29]

Equally, we have highlighted the fact that in those countries where assisted dying is outlawed it nonetheless occurs, sometimes in greater numbers than where it is lawful.[30] It is not legalisation, arguably, that is to be feared, but rather the opportunity for improper behaviour of those charged with the responsibility for care. The GMC is clear on this:

> Doctors have a duty to give priority to patients on the basis of clinical need, while seeking to make the best use of resources using up to date evidence about the clinical efficacy of treatments. Doctors must not allow their views about, for example, a patient's age, disability, race, colour, culture, beliefs, sexuality, gender, lifestyle, social or economic status to prejudice the choices of treatment offered or the general standard of care provided.[31]

Whether this occurs in practice or not may be moot, but it is to ensuring that it is in fact the norm that attention should be turned, rather than denying those who competently wish to die the right to make that choice. Of course, law reform would be necessary to achieve this in the United Kingdom, but arguably competently and precisely drafted legislation – based on respect for *all* persons – will minimise the opportunity for discrimination.

Conclusion

From what has gone before, we can see that a variety of tests are applied in making decisions about who should live and who should not, and a number of

---

28 See Chapter 6.
29 Rothschild, A., 'Oregon: Does Physician Assisted Suicide Work?', *Journal of Law and Medicine*, 12, 2004, 217–225 at p. 219.
30 For discussion, see Chapter 6.
31 *Withholding and Withdrawing Life-prolonging Treatments: Good Practice in Decision-making*, London, GMC, 2002, 25.

perspectives exist on how such decisions should be evaluated. Although we have proposed that there are certain non-derogable principles that should generally be applied, superimposed on them are other concepts which, we argue, may only serve to muddy the waters. Perhaps most particularly these revolves around tests applied in law such as 'quality of life' and 'best interests' but also involve ethical principles such as the sanctity of life. This is because such principles arguably provide an uncertain basis on which to make such decisions, and equally each is susceptible of a variety of interpretations.

As to quality-of-life judgements, these are unhelpful because as Goering, says:

> We view certain physical states as diseases because of our judgments about what is dysfunctional, and those judgments depend on our values and social norms, resources, and standard medical practices. These may differ across societies and across time periods, as well as within societies and time periods.[32]

In terms of quality of life, Lord Hoffman has said:

> Our belief in the sanctity of life explains why we think it is almost always wrong to cause the death of another human being, even one who is terminally ill. *It will also, however, depend on the extent to which we as a society are willing and able to celebrate difference, whatever its nature.*[33]
>
> (emphasis added)

As for the 'best interests' test, we have shown just how difficult this is to pin down. Courts have articulated it in different ways, but it is now generally accepted that 'best interests' are more than just 'best medical interests'. As Dame Elizabeth Butler-Sloss put it:

> When considering the best interests of a patient it is...the duty of the court to assess the advantages and disadvantages of the various treatments and management options, the viability of each such option and the likely effect each would have on the patient's best interests and, I would add, his enjoyment of life.[34]

This last clause is of particular importance. For one thing, it seems to recognise that where ascertainable an individual's *own* enjoyment of life is critically important. Of course, enjoyment of life might be enhanced by making the societal

---

32 Goering, S., 'Gene Therapies and the Pursuit of a Better Human', *Cambridge Quarterly of Healthcare Ethics*, 9, 3, 2000, 330 at pp. 334–335.
33 *Airedale NHS Trust v Bland* (1993) 12 BMLR 64 at p. 96.
34 *An NHS Trust v S and others* (2003) 71 BMLR 188 at p. 203.

changes that the social model of disability requires. On the other hand – where the impairment *itself* causes people not to experience 'enjoyment of life' – this should not be taken to be irrelevant.

Given the vagueness of these tests, it is particularly important that we re-evaluate the way in which we address the difficult choices at the beginning and end of life that are often made in respect of people with impairment or disability. In this book we have maintained that exercising choice is of considerable importance for *all* human persons who have this capacity. We supported this view by drawing on a number of traditional ethics principles: respect for persons, autonomy, consent and rights. By invoking these principles we have found that often ethics does not provide theoretical tools to help us definitively in disputes that arise at the beginning and end of life in a manner that all will find satisfactory. This is because the ethical principles we have utilised actually help to foster a plurality of opinions rather than to forge a homogenous account of appropriate behaviour. However, we have also contended that it is possible to cultivate minimal ethical standards to help us assess the legitimacy of such decisions and help us to differentiate discriminatory from acceptable treatment.

We concede that this is problematic in the case of those not yet born, as respect for persons mandates respect for those already in existence. There are no autonomy or rights-based arguments which can be applied to those not yet implanted or born (unless, of course, we believe in the sanctity of all life from the moment of conception or implantation). This may, of course, lead to the conclusion – which for many may be untenable – that it is always and in any circumstance mandatory to respect parental choice, no matter its nature. For example, it may allow potential parents to make decisions about which children to have on the basis of the sex or abilities of their child. However, this is only a logical conclusion if we do not accept – as we generally do – a gradualist approach to the embryo of the human species: an approach which accords it increasing respect as it matures.[35] Thus, for example, the gradualist approach might be able to take account of the argument that late pregnancy termination on the basis of serious disability in the foetus is discriminatory as it targets only one group – those with impairments. In other words, the concern that *only* impaired foetuses (except where the woman's life is at risk) can be destroyed after viability is a clear discrimination against them. The gradualist approach permits the conclusion that well-developed foetuses are worthy of some respect and might argue against the law which currently permits such selective terminations.

Although our preferred foundational principle is not directly applicable to people in a hopeless condition – such as in a permanent vegetative state PVS – it is not entirely irrelevant. The manner in which we bring about their inevitable demise is important and should reflect the respect for persons, which we have

---

35 This is the approach taken by the Committee of Inquiry into Human Fertilisation and Embryology (Warnock report) Cmnd 9314/1984.

identified as a core value. Thus, we might have to reach a different conclusion about *how* these people die. For example, the death by dehydration that will be their fate under the current legal regime, and the sophistry which we have argued attends such decisions, disrespects the person. If the desired outcome is death – as it unequivocally is – then respect for persons surely argues for an active intervention. As Lord Browne-Wilkinson said in the case of *Airedale NHS Trust v Bland*, 'the whole purpose of stopping artificial feeding is to bring about the death of Anthony Bland.'[36] He further asks:

> How can it be lawful to allow a patient to die slowly, though painlessly, over a period of weeks from lack of food but unlawful to produce his immediate death by a lethal injection, thereby saving his family from yet another ordeal to add to the tragedy that has already struck them? I find it difficult to find a moral answer to that question. But it is undoubtedly the law...[37]

It is arguably not morally required that such lives be sustained indefinitely, because principles such as autonomy and consent only make sense, or have any value, when they form part of a life which is able, or will retain the ability, to reap their benefits. Equally it is not always legally required that people in such tragic circumstances have their existence continued with aggressive or intrusive treatment. However – and this is of vital importance – the appropriate way to reach such conclusions is not by using vague and occasionally disingenuous tests such as 'quality of life' or 'best interests'; rather, we argue, respect for persons provides the cornerstone for decision-making. One benefit of this, in addition to the removal of the subjectivity that permeates quality-of-life or best-interests tests, is that it demands that all life is *prima facie* given equivalent value. Decisions about when or whether it should end become the right of the individual, him or herself, and when this is not possible, third parties must develop robust criteria, based in respect and founded in fact not speculation.

We have argued that some disabilities or impairments are of such significance to the people concerned that they will be directly relevant to life-and-death choices, and should therefore be deemed relevant and treated with respect. In some cases, the adverse consequences of impairment or disability can be ameliorated or removed by making social and practical changes. Considerable concern exists over cases in which social attitudes or assumptions about disability – and not proper evaluation of the impairments themselves – determine the treatment that is or is not provided in certain cases.

In some cases, on the other hand, it will be the fact of the impairment itself that is important, and medical treatment to ameliorate the associated problems

---

36 Bland, cited earlier, p. 127.
37 At p. 131.

will be welcomed. In such circumstances, clinical and legal judgements on life-and-death situations may appropriately be dominated by the medical model, whose currency in contemporary debate is low. Its application in such cases is largely to be welcomed because the issues which *should* be at the centre of treatment decisions are medical ones which involve accurate diagnosis, prognosis and provision of an appropriate treatment regime. That is, some decisions can be appropriately made by viewing disability solely from a perspective which investigates whether medical treatment can help to make impairment just one more characteristic of a valuable human life. This may seem to make the social model redundant. However, what the work of social modellists reveals is that to assume that a neutral, purely clinical assessment of an impaired life is possible is at best naïve and at worst poses a considerable threat to individuals with impairments. Thus the critical resources provided by the social model highlight the importance of adopting a position which is self-critical and allows us to interrogate our own assumptions and prejudices as well as to critique the positions of others.

However, even this position still finds it difficult to distinguish between acceptable and unacceptable (legitimately differential and discriminatory) treatment at the beginning and end of life. We have suggested that one reason for this is that the ethical principles which should influence clinical decisions themselves foster diversity and, therefore, disagreement. The prominence of individual freedom within the western tradition of liberal rights that dominates bioethical and legal decisions at the beginning and end of life allows for considerable diversity. That is, the tradition is able to support decisions both to end and to sustain a life when the clinical aspects of the case are the same.

It has been suggested that in law:

> In the last three decades perceptions of disability have begun to undergo a fundamental transformation. In particular, the decision in...[one particularly important case] reflects a shift away from a purely medical model of disability.[38]

It has also, however, been asserted that:

> Notwithstanding...developments, there is ample evidence internationally of continued acceptance of the individual model of disability in policy circles. Thus, the 'functional limitations' approach is widely incorporated within anti-discrimination legislation (as in the USA and Britain)....[39]

38 *Cockburn v Chief Adjudication Officer, and Secretary of State for Social Security v Fairey (also known as Halliday)* [1997] 1, WLR 799 referred to in Wikely, N., 'Benefits, Bodily Functions and Living with Disability', *MLR* Vol. 61, No 4, 1998, 551–560 at p. 560.
39 Barnes, C. and Mercer, G., *Disability*, Oxford, Polity Press, 2003 at p. 15.

What seems clear to us – bearing in mind that we are not disability theorists – is that an alternative approach, such as that articulated here, might be better suited to addressing the potentiality or actuality of discriminatory influences, practices or decisions. Holding our foundational and supporting ethical principles firmly in mind requires that decisions about 'quality of life' or 'best interests' must be resisted when it is possible to use respect for persons as the guiding principle. Accepting the value of autonomy, consent and human rights requires individuals' involvement in decisions about their lives to be the dominant paradigm; not a matter of medical or other choice. Where this is not possible, proxy decision-makers must also hold to the value of respect, rather than making an attempt to second-guess the quality of another's life. We do not, of course, minimise the significance of the contribution of models such as the social model. We do, however, seek to expose its limitations, as well as those of the medical model, not least because each fosters the separation from the rest of the community of those with impairments. Our preferred model unites the 'abled' and the 'dis-abled' within the constructs of respect for persons, and – where possible – respect for autonomy. Ensuring that the law also accepts and endorses these principles would, we believe, significantly improve decision-making and add an important layer of protection to those who fear discrimination because of their impairment or disability.

Index

Printed in the United Kingdom
by Lightning Source UK Ltd.
121202UK00004B/44